The Irish
Bed & Breakfast
Book

The Irish
Bed & Breakfast
Book

Elsie Dillard and Susan Causin

A GINIGER BOOK

PELICAN PUBLISHING COMPANY
GRETNA 2008

The word "Pelican" and the depiction of a pelican
are trademarks of Pelican Publishing Company, Inc.,
and are registered in the U.S. Patent and Trademark Office.

Library of Congress Cataloging-in-Publication Data

Dillard, Elsie.
  The Irish bed & breakfast book / by Elsie Dillard and Susan Causin.
    p. cm.
  "A Giniger book."
  Includes index.
  ISBN 978-1-58980-559-0 (pbk. : alk. paper) 1. Bed and breakfast accommo-
dations–Ireland–Guidebooks. 2. Ireland–Guidebooks. I. Causin, Susan. II.
Title. III. Title: Irish bed and breakfast book.
  TX907.5.I73D58 2008
  914.15'064–dc22
                                        2008006023

 PELICAN B&B Guide Series
Registered U.S. Patent and Trademark Office

Printed in the United States of America

Published in association with The K.S. Giniger Company, Inc.
1045 Park Avenue, New York, New York 10028

Published by Pelican Publishing Company, Inc.
1000 Burmaster Street, Gretna, Louisiana 70053

Contents

Introduction

The Irish people themselves would be reason enough to visit, with their exceptional warmth and hospitality, but add the beauty of the countryside and Ireland becomes the perfect holiday choice.

We have researched over the four seasons and highly recommend a visit to Ireland in the off-season, when it is easy to get around and there is still plenty to interest the visitor. We have personally visited each property listed in this guide, and there are no charges for inclusion. Our criteria for entry are based upon the warmth of the welcome and cleanliness of the property, with many other facts being taken into consideration. We have covered every county, including areas not normally considered as tourist regions to accommodate business travelers, visits to friends, and family gatherings.

The Republic has restrictions on smoking in public buildings, including restaurants, hotels, and bars. Most bed and breakfast establishments are completely non-smoking, and if permitted, there are usually restrictions; it is best to confirm these details when booking.

Children are normally welcome. Sometimes the location or style of a house makes it unsuitable for children; however, houses that provide facilities are noted. Off-street parking is usually available. It is best to check if a property is located in a city.

When booking, it is advisable to verify specifics, such as child reductions, single supplement, access for disabled guests, special off-season or long stay rates, opening times, and meals and dietary requirements. Most establishments have facilities in the bedrooms, which could include tea and coffee making facilities, hair dryer, telephone, TV, trouser press, Internet access, safes, and air conditioning. If this is important, please check ahead of time to find out what is available. Obtaining clear driving directions is also recommended. At the time of publication prices were correct, but please be aware of seasonal variations.

Entries include the owner's name, but it is possible that a change in ownership may have occurred, which could lead to significant changes in the standard of accommodation.

At the time of publication, and to the best of our knowledge, the details in this book were correct. However, changes do occur for which we cannot be responsible. We would like to thank Bord Failte and the Northern Ireland Tourist Board for their help in making this book possible.

We welcome any comments you have on your personal experiences about properties in this book. We would be delighted to receive your recommendations for consideration for future inclusions. Please send your comments and recommendations to Elsie Dillard and Susan Causin, PO Box 54107, Redondo, WA 98054.

Important Note:

All bed and breakfast prices are per person sharing, unless otherwise stated. A "single supplement" refers to the practice of charging a single visitor an additional amount for occupying a double, twin, or family room.

It is advisable to confirm the rates when booking as well as the method of payment. Some establishments may not accept credit cards. The prices listed for accommodation in the Republic of Ireland are given in euros (€); whilst in Northern Ireland, they are given in pounds sterling (£).

The Irish
Bed & Breakfast Book

DUBLIN AND THE EAST

COUNTY DUBLIN

From above Killakee on the northern slopes of the Dublin Mountains is a wonderful view of both city and county. You can see to the northeast the majestic sweep of Dublin Bay, the beautiful peninsula of Howth Head, and to the south of the bay, South Killiney Head. The city stretches across the plain, divided by the River Liffey. The large green patch in the northwest, some 116 hectares, is Phoenix Park, one of Europe's finest city parks.

The country north of Howth has long sandy beaches and fishing villages, which, in spite of their proximity to the city, retain their character and charm, as well as a wealth of archeological sites. Howth's castle dates from 1464 but has been altered over the centuries. The gardens, open to the public, are famous for their rhododendrons and eighteenth-century formal garden. Malahide Castle belonged to the Talbot family from 1195 to 1976 when the property was sold to the Dublin County Council. It now houses a large part of the National Portrait Collection.

To the south of the Liffey, Blackrock and Dalkey retain their village identity, and the popular Victorian holiday resort of Dun Laoghaire is one of the main sea-gateways to Ireland.

The city of Dublin is beautifully situated, and the people have a friendliness and wit that captivates most visitors. Relatively speaking, it is a small and compact city. The city center, stretching between Parnell Square and St. Stephen's Green north to south, and Dublin Bay and Phoenix Park east to west, can be covered easily by foot. Most points of interest in the city lie between these boundaries. Like most European capitals, there is so much to see in the city that it would take weeks to do it full justice, taking in not only the principal sites of churches, museums, and galleries, but also taking the time to browse and absorb the atmosphere, people, shops, theatres, and pubs as well. Amongst the sights at the top of the list to visit are the National Museum, the National Gallery, and the Municipal Gallery. St. Patrick's Cathedral, dating from 1190; Christchurch Cathedral, restored in the nineteenth century; St. Michan's, where intact bodies still lie in vaults; the fine eighteenth-century church of St. Anne's;

and St. Werburgh's Church are among the most noteworthy churches to visit.

Dublin Castle, with its beautifully decorated State Apartments, was used by the British for state functions, and since 1938, it has been the scene of the inauguration of the Presidents of Ireland. The General Post Office on O'Connell Street is where the Free Republic was proclaimed in 1916. The Custom House is one of the most impressive buildings in Dublin. Parliament House, now the Bank of Ireland, was built in 1785 by James Gandon, Dublin's most famous architect. The Book of Kells is kept in the Library of Trinity College, a restful spot away from the bustle of the city.

DUBLIN

Aberdeen Lodge
Pat Halpin
53 Park Avenue, Ballsbridge, Dublin 4, Co. Dublin
Tel: 01 283 8155 Fax: 01 283 7877
E-mail: aberdeen@iol.ie
Web site: www.halpinsprivatehotels.com

Aberdeen Lodge is a substantial, brick-built Edwardian house in an elegant residential area, easily accessible both to the center of Dublin and Dun Laoghaire. Considerable renovation work has been done here over the years and a lot of the original features have been saved, such as the ceiling work and fireplaces. The décor is elegant and tasteful, and it is nicely furnished. The drawing room and dining room are comfortable, pleasant rooms, and a "drawing room" menu is available offering light snacks and wines to residents in the afternoons and evenings. Other amenities include air conditioning and Internet access. The house has a large peaceful garden, beyond which is the cricket ground. Central Dublin can be reached in a few minutes on the DART railway.

OPEN: all year
ROOMS: 7 double, 6 twin, 3 triple, 2 family; all en suite
TERMS: from €69; single supplement; child reduction
MEALS: drawing room menu from €10

Adare
Catherine Foy
20 Pembroke Park, Ballsbridge, Dublin 4, Co. Dublin

Tel: 01 668 3075
E-mail: catherinefoy@eircom.net
Web site: www.adarehouse.com

This charming red brick Victorian house is the recipient of the Royal Dublin Society Award, situated in one of Dublin's most prestigious areas, and is close to universities and the Lansdowne Road rugby stadium.

It is a beautifully maintained immaculate property, with several original features, including wood floors and stained glass doors. The luxurious accommodations are spacious and have en suite facilities. There are three rooms, one of which is a family room equipped with a double and two single beds.

The house is traditionally furnished, in keeping with its character, and has a pleasant, informal ambience. Guests are well taken care of and will enjoy a tasty breakfast served on fine china, with a selection of starters, followed by a choice of continental or cooked food.

Catherine Foy is a very congenial lady, happy to advise guests on what to see and do in the area and offers suggestions of local restaurants for evening meals. Herbert Park is nearby, which has an array of unusual plants and public tennis courts. Private parking.

OPEN: all year
ROOMS: 3 double/family/twin; all en suite
TERMS: from €40; single supplement; child reduction

Almara Bed & Breakfast
Alan and Maria Fanning
226 Collins Avenue West, Dublin 9, Co. Dublin
Tel: 01 851 0512
E-mail: info@almarabb.com
Web site: www.almarabb.com

Almara is a family run, award winning bed and breakfast. It stands on a corner lot in a quiet area of Dublin, halfway between the airport and Dublin City. The bus stop is a few feet away.

This is an elegant, beautifully maintained property, offering a high standard of accommodation. Guests will appreciate the warm welcome extended by the inviting owners, Alan and Maria Fanning.

The bedrooms have crisp cotton sheets, quality bed covers, and comfortable beds. Five are en suite, the standard rooms share three bathrooms, and all have quality fittings and toiletries. A twin/double is on the ground floor. There are two well-furnished lounges with a TV, where guests can help themselves to tea and filtered water.

Maria and Alan were former 5-star hotel managers and brought their expertise to Almara. Their aim is to make certain guests are well taken care of and have everything necessary to ensure a comfortable and relaxing stay.

A freshly prepared tasty breakfast, which includes a choice of starters, is served in the bright dining room overlooking the garden. Safe and secure parking.

OPEN: closed for Christmas
ROOMS: 11 rooms; 7 en suite
TERMS: from €48; single supplement; child reduction

Annagh House
John and Delia Devlin
301 Clontarf Road, Dublin 3, Co. Dublin
Tel: 01 833 8841
E-mail: info@annaghhouse.ie
Web site: www.amnnaghhouse.ie

Annagh House is a traditional Victorian house, with views of the bay and colorful flowering window boxes in summer. Refurbished to a high standard, it has all the modern comforts but retains the ambience of a bygone era. There are some interesting features, including stained glass, a beautiful marble fireplace with an inlaid tulip design, and an eighteen-century photo found in the attic of H. Hubert, a music hall writer.

John and Delia Devlin enjoy chatting to guests and extend a true Irish welcome. Delia is interested in genealogy and is happy to assist guests interested in tracing their family tree. Guests who like to walk and enjoy outside activities will be happy with the close proximity of the beach and Dollymount Park.

Off-season breaks are on offer and there are discounts for long stays. Annagh House is 5 kilometers from Dublin city and frequent buses stop by the front door. It is within easy driving distance of the airport, Point Depot, Ferry Port, golf, pubs, and restaurants.

OPEN: January 1-December 23

ROOMS: 3 double/twin/triple; all en suite
TERMS: from €36; single supplement; child reduction

Egan's House
Patrick and Monica Fina
7-9 Iona Park, Glasnevin, Dublin 9, Co. Dublin
Tel: 01 830 3611 Fax: 01 830 3612
E-mail: info@eganshouse.com
Web site: www.eganshouse.com

Egan's House is an attractive, red brick, turn of the century house, which started out as two separate houses, tastefully converted to provide comfortable accommodation. Extensive renovations have been undertaken, and the house is in excellent decorative order, well furnished, and comfortable.

The elegant dining room has original cornices and a marble fireplace. Drinks can be obtained from reception. The bedrooms have good-sized modern bathrooms, quality furnishings, and are individually decorated in soft shades and rich colors of blue, grey green, and wine.

There are twelve ground floor bedrooms and all are well appointed. There are over 100 videos for guests to select. Two lounges provide comfortable areas in which to relax, are furnished in keeping with the character of the house, and have rich green velvet curtains. The house is situated on a quiet residential street 1.6 kilometers from the city center, and the bus stop is a few minutes walk away. Guests who have a car would be well advised to leave it behind and take the bus.

OPEN: all year
ROOMS: 32 double/twin/family; all en suite
TERMS: from €29; seasonal rates apply

Glenogra Guesthouse
Peter Donohoe
64 Merrion Road, Ballsbridge, Dublin 4, Co. Dublin
Tel: 01 668 3661 Fax: 01 668 3698
E-mail: info@glenogra.com
Web site: www.glenogra.com

Glenogra is a beautifully appointed Georgian residence in an excellent location, close to the city center, DART, and all amenities. The

house has been furnished to a high standard of comfort in pleasing fabrics and colors. The bedrooms are a good size, and the dining room, where breakfast is served, is quite ornate with pillars, a decorative ceiling, and a fireplace. Peter Donohoe offers all the facilities of a hotel, combined with the warmth and personal service of a private residence. Glenogra is opposite the Four Seasons Hotel in Ballsbridge. There is off-street parking.

OPEN: January 10-December 22
ROOMS: 8 double, 1 single, 1 family; all en suite
TERMS: from €59.50; single supplement; child reduction

Glenveagh

Joe and Bernadette Cunningham
31 Northumberland Road, Ballsbridge, Dublin 4, Co. Dublin
Tel: 01 668 4612 Fax: 01 668 4559
E-mail: glenveagh@eircom.net
Web site: www.glenveagh.com

Glenveagh is an impressive Victorian house in one of Dublin's most prestigious areas. It retains many original features such as beautiful cornices and a ceiling rose. There are antique furnishings, including a grandfather clock in the hallway. The elegant bedrooms are well appointed, decorated, and furnished to a high standard, providing all the comforts of a first-class hotel in an inviting atmosphere.

Glenveagh is spacious, beautifully maintained, and extremely comfortable, retaining the friendliness of a private home. Little wonder the Cunninghams are recipients of so many awards.

Joe and Bernadette are a gracious couple who enjoy welcoming people to Dublin and are happy to offer advice on what to see and do.

Freshly prepared breakfasts are presented on fine china in the charming dining room. The lounge has soft furnishings and a fireplace. Children are welcome, baby-sitting can be arranged, and laundry facilities are available on request.

There is an excellent bus service to town, and the house is minutes from the DART station. There are several venues within walking distance for evening meals. Private parking.

OPEN: all year
ROOMS: 11 double/twin/family; all en suite
TERMS: from €55; single supplement; child reduction

Griffith House
Gene and Ou Maguire
125 Griffith Avenue, Drumcondra, Dublin 9, Co. Dublin
Tel: 01 837 5030
E-mail: grigghse@indigo.ie
Web site: www.griffithhouse.com

Griffith House, a red brick, turn of the century house, stands on the corner of one of Europe's most beautiful and longest tree-lined drives. Gene and Ou Maguire have been in business since 1992 and work hard as a team to maintain their high standards. The good-sized bedrooms are charmingly decorated with soft pastels and rich colors.

Ou, a bright and cheerful lady, is from Thailand, and there are many items from her country that can be seen around the house. There is an elegant lounge, which has a fireplace and beautiful drapes of swags and tails, made by a friend. Breakfasts are served on white linen tablecloths in the tastefully furnished dining room. This is a warm and welcoming place to stay and a popular choice too. Early reservations are recommended. Private parking gives guests the opportunity to take the bus to town, which runs every seven minutes.

OPEN: all year
ROOMS: 4 double/twin/single; 2 en suite
TERMS: from €35; single supplement; child reduction

Harrington Hall
McGill Family
70 Harcourt Street, Dublin 2, Co. Dublin
Tel: 01 478 3677
E-mail: harringtonhall@eircom.net
Web site: www.harringtonhall.com

A family owned and run establishment, Harrington Hall has been magnificently restored and renovated. The splendors of the Georgian architecture and details have been saved, and it offers guests a comfortable, peaceful retreat with every modern amenity in the heart of Dublin. Facilities include private parking, a full bar service, elevator, and access to the Internet.

St. Stephen's Green is just round the corner, and most of Dublin's famous sites are nearby.

OPEN: all year
ROOMS: 28 double/twin/family; all en suite
TERMS: from €93.75

Iona House
Jack and Karen Shouldice
5 Iona Road, Dublin 9, Co. Dublin
Tel: 01 830 6217
E-mail: conrad.shouldice1@btinternet.com

This attractive red brick residence, built at the turn of the nineteenth century, is situated in one of Dublin's Victorian quarters. Jack and Karen Shouldice bought the property in 1963 and offer comfortable accommodation. Décor and furnishings are rich and tasteful, and several original features remain, such as attractive covings, a ceiling rose, and marble fireplace. Fine prints adorn the walls, and the spacious lounge, decorated predominantly in green, is available to guests as is a patio.

Bathrooms are of a good size and well appointed. Breakfast is served in the dining room, which has booth-style tables. There are several venues for evening meals within walking distance. The house is well located for the airport and convenient for the city center.

OPEN: all year
ROOMS: 4 double, 4 twin, 2 single; all en suite
TERMS: from €45; single supplement; child reduction

Joyville
Roma and John Gibbons
24 St. Alphonsus Road, Drumcondra, Dublin 9, Co. Dublin
Tel: 01 830 3221

Roma Gibbons is a delightful, kindly lady who extends a warm welcome to her immaculate red brick Victorian home, situated opposite St. Alphonsus Convent and Church.

The bedrooms are average in size with orthopedic beds. There are no en-suite rooms, but there are two shower rooms, two toilets, and the bedrooms have washbasins. The lounge has a TV and an original marble fireplace, which guests are welcome to share with Roma and John. Roma enjoys meeting people and is happy to recommend restaurants for evening meals. Joyville is a popular B&B and good value accommodation. Advance reservations are recommended. Limited street parking. There is a good bus service and guests would be well advised to take the bus to the center to avoid parking problems.

OPEN: February 1-November 30
ROOMS: 4 double/twin
TERMS: from €34; single supplement; child reduction

Kincora Lodge
Caroline and Paul Connolly
54 Kincora Court, Clontarf, Dublin 3, Co. Dublin
Tel: 01 833 0220 Fax: 01 833 0007
E-mail: info@kincoralodge.com
Web site: www.kincoralodge.com

Caroline and Paul Connolly extend a warm welcome to their immaculate red brick townhouse close to the city, airport, and ferry. The spacious rooms have new modern furnishings, comfortable beds and colorful bed covers, and coordinated fabrics.

Although convenient to most amenities, this is a quiet location, and guests will be comfortable and well taken care of. Excellent breakfasts are served, and there are several venues for evening meals close by. Golf courses and the beach are within walking distance. Guests arriving by car would be advised to leave their car at the house and take the bus to the city center.

OPEN: all year
ROOMS: 3 double/twin/family; all en suite
TERMS: from €37.50; single supplement; child reduction

Merrion Hall
Pat Halpin
54 Merrion Road, Ballsbridge, Dublin 4, Co. Dublin
Tel: 01 668 1426 Fax: 01 668 4280
E-mail: merrionhall@iol.ie
Web site: www.halpinsprivatehotels.com

This substantial Victorian brick-built house is set back off the main road, opposite the Royal Dublin Showground (RDS) in the heart of Ballsbridge, an elegant Dublin suburb. Expansion into the adjoining building and further renovation work has turned this establishment into one offering top quality, comfortable accommodation. The building has been elegantly furnished and amenities include air conditioning, an elevator, and Internet access. A light drawing room menu is offered throughout the day and evening as well as a selection of wines. Off-street parking is available.

The center of Dublin is easily reached by DART railway or the regular bus service.

OPEN: all year
ROOMS: 14 double, 8 twin, 4 triple, 4 family; all en suite
TERMS: from €79; single supplement; child reduction

Trinity Lodge
Peter Murphy
12 South Frederick Street, Dublin 2, Co. Dublin
Tel: 01 617 0900 Fax: 01 617 0999
E-mail: trinitylodge@eircom.net
Web site: www.trinitylodge.com

Trinity Lodge is probably one of the most centrally located guesthouses in Dublin, almost next door to Trinity College and surrounded by shops, restaurants, cafés, and pubs. A Georgian townhouse, it has been interestingly renovated and decorated in the original strong, bright, old Irish colors  to match the colors of the paintings by the artist Knuttel (who lives close by). The walls are lined with prints of his work. The house is elegantly furnished and beautifully equipped. The bedrooms have safes and air conditioning. Some rooms are located across the street. Recently opened is Trinity Lodge's bistro—George's Wine Bar, which is open for lunch and dinner Monday to Saturday. Although the establishment does not have its own parking, the staff will make sure parking is available.

OPEN: closed for Christmas
ROOMS: 8 double, 6 twin, 2 single; all en suite
TERMS: from €90; child reduction

Waterloo House
Evelyn Corcoran
8-10 Waterloo Road, Ballsbridge, Dublin 4, Co. Dublin
Tel: 01 660 1888 Fax: 01 667 1955
E-mail: waterloohouse@eircom.net
Web site: www.waterloohouse.ie

Waterloo House is situated on a tree-lined avenue. It combines two refurbished Georgian houses in the prestigious Ballsbridge district. It is tastefully furnished in keeping with the character of the house and decorated to a very high standard. An elegant lounge and conservatory overlook the garden. The bedrooms are large, comfortable, and well-appointed, and some are equipped with bath and shower. There is an extensive breakfast menu served in the dining room overlooking the conservatory and gardens. Evelyn Corcoran is very welcoming and helpful, and the house is immaculately kept. An added bonus is the lift, and there is safe parking.

OPEN: closed for Christmas
ROOMS: 14 double, 3 twin, 2 single, 2 family; all en suite
TERMS: from €49; single supplement; child reduction

Willow House
Bernadette Flynn
130 Upper Drumcondra Road, Dublin 9, Co. Dublin
Tel: 01 837 5733
E-mail: willowhouse@hotmail.com
Web site: www.willowhousedublin.com

This pleasant turn of the century house is well located for the airport, city center, and most amenities. The rooms are bright and cheery, with a soft pastel décor, and have comfortable beds. Recently refurbished to a high standard, Willow House offers quality accommodation. A well-furnished sitting room is available for guests, and there is private parking. A substantial breakfast is served with brown and soda bread. There is an interesting plate collection in the kitchen.
  It is advisable to take the bus into the center.

OPEN: January 15-December 20
ROOMS: 4 double/twin/family; all en suite
TERMS: from €33; single supplement; child reduction

DUBLIN 17

Belcamp Hutchinson
Doreen Gleeson and Karl Waldburg
Carrs Lane, Malahide Road, Balgrippin, Dublin 17, Co. Dublin
Tel: 01 846 0843 Fax: 01 848 5703
E-mail: belcamphutchinson@eircom.net
Web site: www.belcamphutchinson.com

This superb, ivy-clad Georgian house, hidden away down a narrow lane off the main Malahide road, is named after Francis Hely-Hutchinson, third Earl of Dunoughmore. Renovated with the utmost care, the house has preserved its features and elegance, whilst introducing the best of modern comforts. It stands in seven hectares of fields and gardens, including a walled garden and maze.

The house is superbly furnished and extremely comfortable and has an easygoing, relaxed atmosphere. Presided over by Doreen Gleeson, a welcoming and helpful host, she makes sure her guests are well taken care of. Each spacious bedroom has been decorated with a different color scheme. Copious breakfasts are served at the enormous table in the elegant dining room, and the large, long drawing room has an honesty bar. The attractive, little seaside village of Malahide is close by, Dublin can easily be reached by bus, and it is only a few minutes' drive to the airport.

Belcamp Hutchinson is a peaceful and relaxing place to stay, on arrival or departure from Ireland or as a base for visiting Dublin.

OPEN: February 1-December 20
ROOMS: 8 double, 3 twin, 1 single; all en suite
TERMS: €75

DUN LOIGHAIRE

Lynden Town House
Steve and Maria Gavin
2 Mulgrave Terrace, Dun Laoghaire, Co. Dublin
Tel: 01 280 6404 Fax: 01 230 2258

E-mail: lynden@iol.ie
Web site: www.lyndenbandb.com

You feel welcome the minute you step through the door of this 160-year-old terraced house on a quiet residential street very close to the center of town. Maria Gavin is a bubbly, cheerful host who has owned and run, together with husband Stephen, this B&B for the last 27 years.

The bedrooms are simple and comfortable, and there is a lounge and breakfast room. Early breakfasts can be arranged, and there is off-street parking in the garden. Both the DART station and ferry port are a few minutes walk away.

OPEN: all year
ROOMS: 3 double/twin en suite; 1 twin and 1 single with shared bath-room
TERMS: from €35; single supplement; child reduction

HOWTH

King Sitric
Aidan and Joan MacManus
East Pier, Howth, Co. Dublin
Tel: 01 832 5235 & 01 832 6729 Fax: 01 839 2442
E-mail: info@kingsitric.ie
Web site: www.kingsitric.ie

At the extreme eastern end of Howth stands the King Sitric Restaurant, a gaily painted, modest building with nothing to obstruct 90-degree views from its windows to the harbor, the southern cliffs, and out across the Irish Sea. Originally, the old Harbor Master's house, the MacManuses have owned King Sitric since 1971 and built up a reputation as a first-class fish restaurant. Nine years ago, they virtually rebuilt the whole premises, creating eight very comfortable bedrooms. Each one has a sea view and are named after lighthouses. The cleverly designed first-floor restaurant ensures that every table can enjoy the view, and an atmospheric bar on the ground floor incorporates the cellar, which is stocked with a superb selection of wines of which Aidan and Joan are justifiably proud.

Apart from its proximity to the center of Dublin and the airport, Howth is a delightful place to visit, with its fishing harbor, marina, cliff walks, and golf courses.

OPEN: closed for Christmas
ROOMS: 8 double/twin; all en suite
TERMS: from €75; single supplement; child reduction
MEALS: dinner à la carte

KILLINEY

Druid Lodge
Ken and Cynthia McClenaghan
Killiney Hill Road, Killiney, Co. Dublin
Tel: 01 285 1632 Fax: 01 284 8504
E-mail: dlodge@indigo.ie
Web site: www.druidlodge.com

Built in 1832, this delightful family home stands in an old-fashioned garden, complete with a "folly" tower, and has beautiful views over Killiney Bay. The main rooms have lovely carved pine door surrounds, painstakingly stripped by the owners, as was the staircase. The McClenaghans have lived here for 28 years and brought up six children. The two front bedrooms are enormous, with two or three beds apiece, and they have cleverly hidden, small en suite bathrooms, which in no way detract from the original shape of the rooms. Smaller rooms on the ground floor do not have sea views but are comfortable. Guests eat breakfast at one large table in the dining room, and there is a lovely, comfortable drawing room. It is a ten-minute walk from the DART station, with trains running every 15 minutes into central Dublin.

DIRECTIONS: Killiney Hill Road is above the center of Killiney and Druid Lodge is located between Druid's Chair Pub and Killiney Avenue.

OPEN: closed for Christmas
ROOMS: 2 double, 2 family; all en suite
TERMS: from €45

PORTMARNOCK

South Lodge B&B
Pat and Colin Burton
Strand Road, Portmarnock, Co. Dublin

Tel/Fax: 01 846 1356
E-mail: southlodgebb@eircom.net
Web site: www.southlodgebb.com

This very attractive, compact brick building stands just inside an impressive gateway right next to the golf course, beyond which is the sea. It has been the family home of Pat and Colin Burton for the last 30 years or so, and just eight years ago they started a bed and breakfast business. To offer the best accommodation possible they cleverly redesigned the house, creating a small wing for themselves and rebuilding the first floor, which now provides four charming bedrooms. They are spacious, furnished, and decorated with simplicity and have beamed pitched, atticlike ceilings, and some overlook the golf course. There is a sitting area in the breakfast room, which has views of the golf course beyond the small attractive garden. The patio in front of the house is a nice place to enjoy fine weather. South Lodge, built in 1873, was a gate lodge to the James family home, of distiller fame, now the Portmarnock Links Hotel. This fabulous location for the golf lover has great access to Dublin (bus stop just outside) and the airport, and the lovely sandy beach of Portmarnock is a few minutes away.

OPEN: closed for Christmas
ROOMS: 1 double, 2 family; all en suite; 1 double with private bathroom
TERMS: €40; child reduction

COUNTIES LOUTH AND MEATH

The Boyne Valley cuts right through the center of this area, one of the most historic and evocative places in Irish history and for thousands of years the center of political power. Innumerable remains from every century lie scattered across this fertile, green valley. Dominating the town of Trim are the ruins of King John's Castle, the largest Anglo-Norman castle in Ireland, dating from 1172. The Duke of Wellington's family came from here, as did the family of Bernardo O'Higgins, a prominent figure in Chilean history.

Apart from a few earthworks, there is not much left to see at the Hill of Tara, seat of Ireland's kings since prehistoric times. Imagination is needed to conjure up the sight of great buildings and a mass of warriors and nobles who inhabited this place in days gone by.

At the attractive village of Slane, the old castle overlooks the river, and a little farther along the valley is Brugh na Boinne (the Palace of the Boyne), an enormous cemetery with graves dating back to the Neolithic era, the main sites of which are at Newgrange, Knowth, and Dowth.

The pretty village of Kells in the Blackwater Valley was the site of the settlement of the Columban monks who moved here from Iona in 807. St. Columba's house still stands, and the church holds a copy of the famous Book of Kells.

Monasterboice and Mellifont are the sites of the two ancient ecclesiastical centers, and at Drogheda, in the Church of St. Peter, one can see the preserved head of St. Oliver Plunkett, former Archbishop of Armagh. The Cooley Peninsula is an attractive and unspoiled area with lovely views, and the old town of Carlingford has lots of historical sites, including King John's Castle.

COUNTY LOUTH

DROGHEDA

Highfield House
Kitty McEvoy
Termonfeckin, Drogheda, Co. Louth
Tel: 041 9822172

Highfield House can be found in the middle of the village of Termonfeckin by its signs for meats and delis (as well as the Bord Failte sign). The main house, built in 1725, stands just off the road and behind are attractive whitewashed farm buildings, where Kitty McEvoy's son has his butcher's shop and deli. He rears his own pigs, hens, and beef to supply the shop. Kitty herself is a chatty, friendly lady. The bedrooms are very spacious and comfortably furnished, and the large dining room has a decorative bar in one corner. Guests also have use of a sitting room. A new restaurant and coffee shop will be opening in the farm courtyard in 2008. The sea is only 5 minutes away and there are a couple of golf courses nearby.

DIRECTIONS: Take the R166 from Drogheda town

OPEN: March 1-October 31
ROOMS: 2 double en suite; 1 double with private bathroom
TERMS: €35; single supplement

COUNTY MEATH

ATHLUMLEY

Athlumley Manor
Pat and Pauline Boylan
Athlumley, Navan, Co. Meath
Tel: 046 9071388
E-mail: stay@athlumleymanor.com
Web site: www.athlumleymanor.com/location.htm

Architecturally designed, Athlumley Manor is a very appealing spacious house. The Boylans have been in the hospitality business for three generations, and they are very knowledgeable about the area. All the well-appointed bedrooms are on the ground floor, five of which have views of the floodlit castle, and the family room can accommodate five people in two linking bedrooms. The bright sitting room is on the upper floor and has a pleasant aspect overlooking the well-landscaped garden. Pat and Pauline are happy to arrange individual tours starting from the house. The megalithic tombs at Newgrange, Knowth, and Dowth are a short distance from Navan, and the recently opened Interpretive Centre, Battle of the Boyne is a new attraction.

DIRECTIONS: From the N3 in Navan, Athlumley is 2 kilometers on the R153

OPEN: closed for Christmas
ROOMS: 7 en suite
TERMS: from €35; single supplement; child reduction

DOWTH

Glebe House
Elizabeth Addison
Dowth, nr. Drogheda, Co. Meath
Tel: 041 9836101 Fax: 041 9843469
E-mail: elizabeth-glebe@hotmail.com

This attractive, whitewashed, small country house is covered in wisteria, clematis, and roses. Set in a pretty garden, and with lovely views over the tennis court to distant hills, Glebe House is at the heart of the Boyne valley, between Newgrange and Drogheda.

Mrs. Addison is a delightful welcoming person, who apart from her bed and breakfast business specializes in small functions and private dinner parties. The reception rooms are welcoming and warm, with fireplaces in both the large formal drawing room and the small, cozy study/sitting room, and mauve carpets cover the entire ground floor. The bedrooms are pretty and comfortable. Cream teas are served to the public. For those who wish to improve their art skills, there are art workshops.

DIRECTIONS: Glebe House is signposted at Dowth.

OPEN: closed for Christmas
ROOMS: 2 double, 2 twin; all en suite
TERMS: from €60

DULEEK

Annesbrook
Kate Sweetman
Duleek, Co. Meath
Tel/Fax: 041 9823293
E-mail: sweetman@annesbrook.com
Web site: www.annesbrook.com

An impressive gate and a long wooded drive lead to the interesting house of Annesbrook, the core of which is seventeenth century with additions of different periods. The pedimented portico of the house and the ballroom were added on to impress George IV who visited in 1821, and the front entrance hall is beautifully proportioned with a lovely winding staircase. Another distinguished visitor was William Thackeray. A relaxed and welcoming family atmosphere has replaced the formal hospitality of those days. All of the bedrooms are comfortable, with folders detailing events of local interest and suggested walks and drives to local attractions.

The reception rooms have big log fires. The décor of the purple and gold dining room is a little unusual, with the ceiling almost matching the carpet.

DIRECTIONS: The house can be found south of Duleek on the R152.

OPEN: April 1-September 30
ROOMS: 5 double/twin/family; all en suite
TERMS: from €56; single supplement; child reduction

NAVAN

Village B&B
Teresa and Gerard Brennan
Kilmessan Village, Navan, Co. Meath
E-mail: info@meathvillagebandb.com
Web site: www.meathvillagebandb.com

Right in the center of the village,
this brightly colored, neatly kept,
old house is easy to find. The wing
that accommodates guests was originally a shop. Teresa and Gerard
Brennan rebuilt the interior to provide six rooms, two of which are suitable for disabled guests. There are
wooden floors throughout, pine furniture, and simple, clean décor.
The cozy breakfast room is in the original part of the house.
    DIRECTIONS: In center of village

OPEN: all year
ROOMS: 2 double, 3 double/twin; all en suite
TERMS: from €40; single supplement; child reduction

OLDCASTLE

Knockbrack
Kitty Bevan
Oldcastle, Co. Meath
Tel: 049 8541771
E-mail: kittybevan@eircom.net

Set in 60 acres of park and farmland, Knockbrack is in a delightful,
peaceful position. Dating from 1821, it has an attractive garden and
views to the Loughcrew Hills and to Mullaghmeen Forest. There are
spacious, comfortable public rooms for guests' use. An enormous
drawing room is part of a later addition including a large bedroom
with an enormously long bathroom.

Kitty Bevan is a welcoming, chatty host and an innovative cook, using vegetables and herbs from the garden and local produce. Loughcrew Cairns and Loughcrew Gardens are close by.

OPEN: May 1-September 30
ROOMS: 2 double with private bathroom; 1 double en suite
TERMS: from €75; single supplement
MEALS: dinner €35

Loughcrew House
Charles and Emily Naper
Oldcastle, Co. Meath
Tel: 049 8541356 Fax: 049 8541921
E-mail: info@loughcrew.com
Web site: www.loughcrew.com

The Loughcrew estate has been in the Naper family for over 400 years, and Charles and Emily's home is a conversion of what used to be an elegant conservatory designed by Cockrell. It stands next to part of the ruins of the old house, and the estate comprises a lake, tennis court, the family church of St. Oliver Plunkett, and Loughcrew Gardens, which are open to the public.

Emily Naper is an amazing woman; a friendly person with boundless energy, she is one of Ireland's leading gilders and has a studio adjoining the house where she restores gilded furniture and frames and designs hand-finished decorative furniture. She also runs a school for gilding and specialist paint finishes, providing courses in botanical water-color painting and ceramic sculpture. This is all in addition to running the house and garden and tending to the needs of her children. Charles is the cook, producing fine meals from local produce and homegrown herbs.

Loughcrew is a lived in family home, an eccentric and unusual place, with whimsical décor, some frescoes and interesting pieces. Guests have use of a long room for breakfast combined with a sitting room, as well as a small cozy sitting room with wood burning stove. Visitors here enjoy the atmosphere and countryside.

DIRECTIONS: Off the N3, 13 miles northwest of Kells

OPEN: January 5-December 18
ROOMS: 1 double; 2 twin with private bathrooms
TERMS: €75; single supplement; child reduction

SLANE

Rosnaree House
Aisling Law
Slane, Co. Meath
Tel: 041 9820975 Fax: 041 9824162
E-mail: rosnaree@eircom.net

The Laws moved back to Ireland after spending several years in Africa seven years ago to take over their family home. Set in 200 acres of garden, woodlands, and farmland, the property stretches down to and along the Boyne. From the house, built in 1700, there are views of the River Boyne and to Newgrange. It was from here that the High Kings from Tara would wait before crossing to Newgrange.

Rosnaree House is a splendid old house with a distinctly family home atmosphere, and much of it has been renovated since the Laws took over. The furniture and furnishings are an interesting mixture of old family pieces, furniture and artifacts from Africa, and sculptures and artwork created by Aisling and her side of the family. The bedrooms vary in shape, size, and décor—one has an all encompassing mural partly painted by Asiling. The old library is used as a film club, is where Aisling sometimes teaches yoga, and is a comfortable place to relax. Dinner is available for four or more people if booked in advance, and there is fishing on the Boyne. Weddings and private functions can also be booked. Child friendly.

DIRECTIONS: From the N2, turn east at the brown sign for Newgrange south of Slane. The driveway is through white gates on a sharp bend on the left of the road.

OPEN: closed for Christmas
ROOMS: 3 double, 1 twin; all en suite or with private bathroom
TERMS: from €80; single supplement; child reduction
MEALS: dinner €45

TRIM

Crannmor
Anne O'Regan
Dunderry Road, Trim, Co. Meath
Tel: 046 9431635 Fax: 046 9438087
E-mail: crannmor@eircom.net
Web site: www.crannmor.com

This old country house is in a peaceful setting surrounded by pleasant gardens and 2.5 hectares of fields. The O'Regans took over the house at the beginning of 2000 and have done a lot of refurbishment. Three of the bright, cheerful guest rooms are on the ground level in what was once the stable block, and one is particularly suited for disabled guests. The fourth room is on the first floor in the main part of the house. The breakfast/sitting room is very charming with antique furniture and an open fire. Anne O'Regan is a cheerful, capable woman, who has been in the guesthouse business for many years, and Crannmor is a friendly and comfortable place to stay.

Historic Trim, which boasts the largest Norman castle in Ireland, is only 1 kilometer away. One of Trim's attractions is the annual Trim Fair; "The Power and the Glory" is a multimedia exhibition explaining the background of Trim's medieval ruins.

DIRECTIONS: From Trim, leave Super Valu on the right, take the next right, stay right at next junction, and the house is 400 yards on the right.

OPEN: March 1-November 30
ROOMS: 1 double, 1 twin, 3 family; all en suite
TERMS: from €40; single supplement; child reduction

COUNTY WICKLOW

Lying just to the south of Dublin, this county is an area of hills and mountains, lakes and streams—a pleasant, peaceful place of escape after the bustle of the city. From Dublin, one comes first to Bray, a large seaside resort, and then to Enniskerry. Here one can visit the gardens of Powerscourt Estate. The house, which had been one of the most beautiful in Ireland, was destroyed in the 1950s, leaving only the shell still standing. Glendalough is a beautiful, scenic place in the mountains, set between two small lakes near the ruins of St. Kevin's Kitchen; St. Kevin founded the church and the cathedral in 520. Just beyond is the small twelfth-century priory of St. Saviour. The county town, Wicklow, is on the coast, and farther south is Arklow, a popular resort and fishing center. At Blessington is Russborough House, a beautiful Palladian-style house containing a marvelous art collection, and the Poulaphouca Reservoir, which was formed by damming the River Liffey.

ARKLOW

Ballykilty House
Oliver Nuzum
Coolgreany, Arklow, Co. Wicklow
Tel: 0402 37111 Fax: 0402 37272
E-mail: ballykiltyfarmhouse@eircom.net

This 200-year-old house stands in a lovely garden with a tennis court in the peaceful countryside. It is part of an 80-hectare dairy farm with 100 milking cows. The house has a warm and welcoming atmosphere and is now run by Annie Nuzum's son, Oliver. There are two cozy sitting rooms with open fires on each side of the front door, and one has a TV. The dining room was the original kitchen and still has the old beams and cooking pots and a big open fireplace.

This is a good base for exploring Powerscourt and Mount Usher

Gardens, Avondale House and Forest Park, Russborough House, Castleruddery Transport Museum, and the Vale of Avoca.

DIRECTIONS: Ballykilty is on the road between Coolgreany and Arklow, 5 kilometers from Arklow.

OPEN: May-October 31
ROOMS: 2 double, 2 twin, 1 triple; all en suite
TERMS: from €38; single supplement; child reduction

Fairy Lawn
Rita Kelly
Wexford Road, Arklow, Co. Wicklow
Tel: 0402 32790
E-mail: fairy-lawn@hotmail.com

Fairy Lawn is a brick and plaster house set back off the main road. The comfortable bedrooms are regularly redecorated and are simply furnished. There is a comfortable guest lounge with TV, and breakfast is served in the dining room. Mr. Kelly is a keen gardener, maintaining the well-landscaped gardens and colorful window boxes.

DIRECTIONS: 1 kilometer from Arklow on the road to Gorey

OPEN: May 1-October 1
ROOMS: 1 double en suite; 2 twin en suite; 1 double with private bathroom
TERMS: €35; child reduction

Moneylands Farm
Michael and Lillie Byrne
Arklow, Co. Wicklow
Tel: 0402 32259 Fax: 0402 32438
E-mail: mland@eircom.net
Web site: www.moneylandsfarm.com

This neat, small, whitewashed farmhouse is located down a quiet country lane on the outskirts of Arklow and has pleasant views. The ground-floor family room has a small sitting area and French doors that open onto the garden. The comfortable lounge leads through to the large conservatory, where breakfast is served and tea and coffee are available. Mr. and Mrs. Byrne, who are a kindly couple, have made many additions to the farm. They include an indoor heated swimming pool, gym, sauna, and tennis court, which are available both to bed and breakfast guests, as well as to those staying in the self-catering court-yard of renovated stone-built coach houses.

DIRECTIONS: 1 kilometer south of Arklow off the N11

OPEN: May 1-October 31
ROOMS: 3 double/twin, 1 family; all en suite
TERMS: from €40; single supplement; child reduction

Plattenstown House
Margaret McDowell
Coolgreaney Road, Arklow, Co. Wicklow
Tel/Fax: 0402 37822
E-mail: mcdpr@indigo.ie
Web site: www.plattenstownhouse.com

This old farmhouse was built in 1853 for Lady Jane O'Grady. It is set in 20 hectares of farmland, supporting cows and goats, and has a lovely, peaceful, mature garden with water features. The attractive whitewashed farm buildings are at the back of the house. There is a comfortable draw-ing room and a small TV sitting room with fireplace. Dinner is served, if booked in advance, and a light lunch or sandwiches can also be pro-vided. Guests have use of bicycles and can play croquet and table ten-nis. Beaches can be found within 5 to 7 kilometers, and there are pleasant forest walks.

DIRECTIONS: 5 kilometers from Arklow on the Coolgreaney road

OPEN: closed for Christmas
ROOMS: 3 double en suite; 1 twin with private bathroom
TERMS: from €42; single supplement; child reduction
MEALS: dinner €30

AUGHRIM

Clone House
Carla Watson
Aughrim, Co. Wicklow
Tel: 0402 36121 Fax: 0402 36029
E-mail: stay@clonehouse.com
Web site: www.clonehouse.com

A historically interesting house dating back to the 1600s, it was burned to the ground in 1798, rebuilt in 1805, and has a priest's hiding place and an underground passage extending some 500 meters. Old features still intact include the fine molding in the drawing room, which dates pre-1840. For the past 50 years of its life, it has been a guesthouse, acquired by the Watsons a few years ago when they moved to Ireland from the United States. They have done wonders to the house and grounds, including a major refurbishment of the house and the creation of a lovely garden. Every bedroom is a different shape and size, and each one is individually decorated. Gourmet five-course dinners are served in the formal dining room, and for less formal occasions, the small dining room is used. The music room is a cozy place with a roaring fire, two pianos, and a flagstone floor.

Carla (Uruguayan-Italian) is a gregarious, conservatively flamboyant lady and a passionate cook. She uses all natural foods, including produce from the kitchen garden, and Jeff (American) is an avid gardener, who is responsible for the landscaping project.

Clone House is set in the heart of the countryside with views of the Wicklow Mountains.

DIRECTIONS: Plenty of signs from Aughrim and Woodenbridge

OPEN: all year
ROOMS: 7 double/twin; all en suite
TERMS: from €70; single supplement
MEALS: dinner from €55

AVOCA

Keppel's Farmhouse
Joy and Charles Keppel
Ballanagh, Avoca, Co. Wicklow
Tel: 0402 35168
E-mail: keppelsfarmhouse@eircom.net
Web site: www.keppelsfarmhouse.com

Built around 1880, Keppel's Farmhouse is set in quiet countryside with beautiful views over the Vale of Avoca. A more recent wing contains a large dining room (where breakfast, including homemade bread and preserves, is served), a lounge, and two first-floor bedrooms. The bedrooms are clean, bright, and full of fresh country air.

Guests are welcome to walk around the farm, watch the cows being milked, and enjoy the large garden. A woodland park gives visitors the option of taking a pleasant 20-minute stroll to Avoca, where the famous Avoca handweavers can be seen.

DIRECTIONS: Turn right in front of Fitzgerald's Bar, having crossed the bridge into the village. There are signs from the village.

OPEN: April-October
ROOMS: 3 double, 1 twin, 1 triple; all en suite
TERMS: from €40; single supplement; not suitable for children

The Old Coach House
Michael and Barbara Robinson
Meeting of the Waters, Avoca, Co. Wicklow
Tel/Fax: 0402 35408
E-mail: avocacoachhouse@eircom.net
Web site: www.avoca-coachhouse.com

Built in 1840, it was originally a stop for stagecoaches on the Dublin to Wexford road. It has a peaceful setting on the river with lovely views of the Avoca Valley and is only 400 yards from the Meeting of the Waters, immortalized by the poet Thomas Moore.

Michael and Barbara Robinson love what they do, are hospitable, and maintain a very high standard. There are polished wood floors, tiles in the entryway, and a warming fire on chilly days in the original fireplace in the elegant lounge. The bedrooms are large and very well equipped, catering to the travelers' every need.

Evening meals are available by arrangement and special diets catered for.

DIRECTIONS: Between Avoca and Rathdrum

OPEN: all year
ROOMS: 4 double, 1 triple, 2 family; all en suite
TERMS: from €37.40

Sheepwalk House
Jim and Regina McCabe
Avoca, Co. Wicklow
Tel: 0402 35189 Fax: 0402 35789
E-mail: sheepwalk@eircom.net
Web site: www.sheepwalk.com

Built for the Earl of Wicklow in 1727, Sheepwalk House commands a magnificent view of the sea. Daniel Murray, who later became Archbishop of Dublin, was born here in 1768. Today the house has been restored to provide accommodation of a high standard, whilst retaining many of its original features, such as the cast iron fireplaces and its elegant staircase.

Jim and Regina McCabe are friendly, outgoing, and golf lovers. There is a spacious sitting room with open fireplace and TV, and guests comment on the "five-star breakfast," which is served in the conservatory. The bedrooms are very well equipped, two of which have sea views.

DIRECTIONS: 2 miles from Avoca

OPEN: March-October
ROOMS: 6 double/twin/triple; all en suite
TERMS: €45; child reduction

DUNLAVIN

Rathsallagh House
The O'Flynn Family
Dunlavin, Co. Wicklow
Tel: 045 403112 Fax: 045 403343
E-mail: info@rathsallagh.com
Web site: www.rathsallagh.com

Set in 214 hectares of beautiful, mature parkland, the house is reached up a majestic, long, sweeping driveway across the Rathsallagh Championship Golf Course, which, were it not for the odd sign to stop and watch for golfers, one would hardly be aware of. The original house was built in the early 1700s and was burned down in the rebellion of 1798. Unable to afford to rebuild the house, the family moved into the Queen Anne stables, which now form Rathsallagh House. Its long rooms and comparatively lower ceilings give it a relaxed, country house feel, in comparison to the more formal, high-ceilinged, ornate Georgian houses. Built around a courtyard, the bedrooms are arranged off one side of the long narrow corridors. Some rooms are very spacious with lovely parkland outlooks and are comfortably and unfussily furnished with every amenity included.

The food at Rathsallagh is an experience: beautifully presented dishes are served in the light-paneled dining room, and there is an extensive breakfast buffet and excellent menus in the evening, using organically produced food, fresh fish, and game when in season. Light lunches are available for residents only.

There are a number of activities within the estate for guests to enjoy, including golf, tennis, croquet, snooker, sauna, and massage. Arrangements can be made for riding, shooting, deer stalking, and archery.

DIRECTIONS: Rathsallagh is signposted in Dunlavin village.

OPEN: March-December
ROOMS: 29 double; all en suite
TERMS: from €135; single supplement; not suitable for children

Tynte House
John and Caroline Lawler
Dunlavin, Co. Wicklow
Tel: 045 401451 Fax: 045 401586
E-mail: info@tyntehouse.com
Web site: www.tyntehouse.com

Built in the early 1800s, Tynte House is a tall, whitewashed building standing right in the middle of town. In its later days, it was a pub until 1930. John Lawler's father bought the house, and there was still a lot of work to be done when John and Caroline took it over. It has been furnished and decorated appealingly in keeping with its style and age. The bedrooms, some of which are on the second floor, are unfussily furnished and decorated. There is a cozy snug room, and the dining room is in two different areas—separate tables in a darker, inner room, and one big table in a large, bright room with a sitting area at one end. Caroline is friendly and welcoming and also offers eight self-catering mews cottages in the courtyard, which were originally stables and lofts. There is a games room, a hard tennis court, a children's playground, and golf courses and riding nearby.

DIRECTIONS: In the middle of town

OPEN: closed for Christmas
ROOMS: 3 twin, 6 family; all en suite
TERMS: from €35; single supplement; child reduction

ENNISKERRY

Ferndale
Noel and Josie Corcoran
Enniskerry, Co. Wicklow

Tel/Fax: 01 2863518
E-mail: info@ferndalehouse.com
Web site: www.ferndalehouse.com

This attractive, 160-year-old house stands right in the center of Enniskerry and has been in Noel Corcoran's family for a good part of its life. He and his wife, Josie, took it over a few years ago and did up the whole house, almost to the extent of rebuilding it. There is a relaxing drawing room and elegant bedrooms with brass and old iron beds. The dining room, with one large table covered with a white linen tablecloth, is in the basement and leads into the conservatory, which in turn has doors out to the beautifully terraced rear garden with a gazebo, which eventually ends in the car park. Ferndale is close to Powerscourt.

DIRECTIONS: In the center of town

OPEN: April 1-October 31
ROOMS: 2 double, 2 twin; all en suite
TERMS: from €45; child reduction

GLENDALOUGH

Carmel's Bed & Breakfast
Carmel Hawkins
Annamoe, Glendalough, Co. Wicklow
Tel/Fax: 0404 45297
E-mail: carmelsbandb@eircom.net

The house was built by the Hawkins in 1970 and has been added onto a few times, most recently to enlarge the lounge/dining room area and bedrooms. Carmel's is a warm and welcoming house, set back off the main road in a large immaculately kept garden, where everyone is treated as a family friend and plied with cups of tea or coffee on arrival. All of the bedrooms are on the ground floor.

Carmel and her husband are local people, willing to assist with sightseeing and local events. Glendalough Fun Park is close by and hiking and walking can also be enjoyed.

DIRECTIONS: Carmel's is on the R755 from Glendalough to Dublin.

OPEN: March-October
ROOMS: 1 double, 1 twin, 2 family; all en suite
TERMS: from €35

Doire Coille House
Mary Byrne
Glendalough, Cullentragh, Rathdrum, Co. Wicklow
Tel: 0404 45131
E-mail: marybyrne@esatclear.ie
Web site: www.doirecoillefarmhouse.com

Just off the R755 road in the Avonmore Valley, Doire Coille is a pleasant farmhouse surrounded by a large, colorful garden, with nice views of the wooded valley. Behind the house are the farm buildings and land used for sheep rearing, stretching up the hill. Mary Byrne is a welcoming, down-to-earth lady, who runs a clean and efficient house. The rooms are small, simply furnished in pine, and have good firm beds. A large ground-floor room, which has doors out to the garden, doubles as a breakfast room and sitting area.
    DIRECTIONS: On the R755

OPEN: May-October
ROOMS: 7 double/twin; all en suite
TERMS: from €35; single supplement; child reduction

GLENEALY

Ballyknocken House & Cookery School
Catherine Fulvio
Glenealy, Ashford, Co. Wicklow
Tel: 0404 44627 Fax: 0404 44696
E-mail: cfulvio@ballyknocken.com
Web site: www.ballyknocken.com; www.thecookeryschool.ie

Ballyknocken House, built in the 1850s, is set in a wooded valley below Carrick Mountain. The Byrne family acquired the house in the 1940s, and today Catherine Byrne Fulvio is the third generation of the family to own Ballyknocken. She and her Italian husband, Claudio, have carried out renovation work,  including transforming the old kitchen with its original inglenook fireplace into an additional dining room and decorating and finishing the bedrooms in keeping with the period of the house. The rooms are fresh and bright and some have brass beds, and the bathrooms have claw foot baths. However, the main feature of Ballyknocken is the warmth of an unhurried welcome and its casual informality. Catherine exudes an infectious special warmth and enthusiasm and makes her guests feel immediately at home. She and Claudio are experts in food and wine, and guests enjoy wonderful culinary experiences at dinner and breakfast.

Ballyknocken Cookery School opened recently and offers a selection of courses, including an introduction to Irish bread and baking. Guests are welcome to use the tennis court, wander around the gardens, admire the herb garden, and walk in the adjoining forest.

DIRECTIONS: In Ashford, turn at the Texaco filling station toward Glenealy. Ballyknocken is 3 miles on the right.

OPEN: closed December and January
ROOMS: 10 double/twin/single/family; all en suite
TERMS: from €67; single supplement; child reduction
MEALS: dinner from €30

KILTEGAN

Barraderry House
Olive and John Hobson
Kiltegan, Co. Wicklow
Tel/Fax: 059 6473209
E-mail: jo.hobson@oceanfree.net
Web site: www.barraderrycountryhouse.com

On the western edge of the Wicklow Mountains, Barraderry is an attractive Georgian house in a peaceful setting, approached up a long driveway through a parklike setting and surrounded by its own farmland with lovely mountain views. It has been the Hobson family home since 1950 and was farmed by John until recently. Now, one of their daughters has a few sheep and horses, and the rest of the land is leased.

With the children gone, Olive started a B&B business some 10 years ago. She offers a warm and friendly welcome. The four large bedrooms are comfortable and guests have use of a sizeable drawing room. Breakfast is served in the dining room. A feature of the grounds is an unusual 250-year-old twin grafted beech tree.

Golf and racing are well catered for, with six golf courses within 30

minutes. Punchestown, Naas, and The Curragh racecourses are nearby.
   DIRECTIONS: Off the Baltinglass to Kiltegan road

OPEN: mid January-mid December
ROOMS: 2 double, 1 twin, 1 single; all en suite
TERMS: from €50; single supplement; child reduction

RATHNEW

Hunter's Hotel
The Gelletlie Family
Newrath Bridge, Rathnew, Co. Wicklow
Tel: 0404 40106 Fax: 0404 40338
E-mail: reception@hunters.ie
Web site: www.hunters.ie

This attractive, long, low
building, covered with
climbing plants, was
originally an old coach-
ing inn. Built in 1720,
Hunter's Hotel stands
on what used to be the
main road, though now
it is 1 kilometer off the
new Dublin road, 5 kilo-
meters outside Wicklow.

   Owned and run by the Gelletlie family, it has been in the same
ownership since 1840. It is comfortable and old fashioned, combining a lot of Old World charm with modern comforts. Several rooms
overlook the beautiful, colorful garden, and others on the ground
floor are suitable for disabled guests. Tables and chairs are dotted
around the garden, which lies along the banks of the River Vartry,
a delightful place for afternoon tea or a prelunch or dinner
drink.The garden room is available for small conferences or private parties.
   DIRECTIONS: On the R761 just of the N11 near Rathnew

OPEN: closed for Christmas
ROOMS: 16 double/twin; all en suite
TERMS: from €95, child reduction
MEALS: lunch from €23.50, tea €10, dinner €42.50

REDCROSS

Kilpatrick House
The Kingston Family
Redcross, Co. Wicklow
Tel: 0404 47137 Fax: 0404 47866
E-mail: info@kilpatrickhouse.com
Web site: www.kilpatrickhouse.com

Kilpatrick House is a most attractive Georgian country house set in nicely landscaped gardens, enjoying pleasant farmland views, and is part of a beef-rearing farm. The bedrooms are spacious and guests have use of a formal sitting room with widescreen TV. The extensive gardens include a grass tennis court.

DIRECTIONS: The house is signposted off the N11 at Jack White's Cross.

OPEN: May-October
ROOMS: 2 double en suite; 1 double with private bathroom
TERMS: from €45 euros; single supplement; child reduction

Saraville
Henry and Sarah Fleming
Redcross, Co. Wicklow
Tel/Fax: 0404 41745

Right in the middle of the little village of Redcross, Saraville is a small, modernized house with some farm buildings at the back. The Flemings farm in a small way and keep horses. The house is immaculately clean, the cooking fresh and wholesome, with freshly squeezed orange juice for breakfast, and homemade food using local produce is available by request for dinner and lunch. There is a living room with TV. Sarah is charming, the atmosphere is friendly and relaxing, and children are very welcome.

DIRECTIONS: In the middle of the village

OPEN: May 1-September 30
ROOMS: 2 double en suite; 1 double with private bathroom

TERMS: from €35; single supplement; child reduction
MEALS: dinner €22.50; packed lunch; light tea

SHILLELAGH

Park Lodge
Bridie Osborne
Clonegal, Shillelagh, Co. Wicklow
Tel: 05394 29140
E-mail: parklodgebb@hotmail.com

This charming, whitewashed Georgian farmhouse is in a peaceful, rural setting, enjoying lovely views of the Wicklow Mountains. It is surrounded by its 200-acre mixed farm, and sheep, geese, and guinea fowl roam close to the house. Guests here enjoy genuine Irish farmhouse hospitality with home baking, fresh farm produce, and a cheerful, friendly atmosphere. The house offers old-fashioned comfort with large rooms and pretty, quilted bedcovers. Local amenities include horse riding, fishing, golf, and walking.

DIRECTIONS: Park Lodge stands just above the very minor road from Shillelagh to Clonegal.

OPEN: Easter-end October
ROOMS: 3 double/twin, all en suite
TERMS: from €40 euros, single supplement

WICKLOW

Lissadell House
Patricia Klaue
Ashtown Lane, Wicklow, Co. Wicklow
Tel: 0404 67458
E-mail: lissadellhse@eircom.net
Web site: www.geocities.com/lissadellhse

Built in the Georgian style, Lissadell is a modern house surrounded by its own grounds on the outskirts of Wicklow and is part of a mixed farm. The Klaues, who built the house themselves, are a most friendly couple, and the house has a welcoming atmosphere. The rooms are plainly decorated and furnished, and there is a pleasant sitting room and dining room. Both rooms have French windows that open onto the lawn and garden.

DIRECTIONS: Turn off the N11 Wicklow to Wexford road at the Beehive Pub onto the R751. Signposted at the first turning to the left.

OPEN: April-October
ROOMS: 1 twin, 1 family, both en suite; 2 twin; 2 public bathrooms
TERMS: from €35; child reduction

Silver Sands
Lyla Doyle
Dunbur Road, Wicklow, Co. Wicklow
Tel: 0404 68243
E-mail: lyladoyle@eircom.net

This modern, friendly bungalow is on the coast road just outside the town center. It has a reputation for its warm welcome and has lovely sea views. The bedrooms, three of which are on the ground floor, are on the small side, immaculately clean, and simply furnished. Guests share the family lounge, and breakfast is served in the bright dining room overlooking the sea. Lyla Doyle is down to earth, friendly, and always willing to help plan outings to local events and places of interest.
    DIRECTIONS: Just outside the town center

OPEN: closed for Christmas
ROOMS: 2 double, 2 twin, 1 family; all en suite except 1 private bathroom
TERMS: from €35

THE SOUTH AND SOUTHWEST

COUNTY CORK

Ireland's largest county has a spectacular coastline that alternates between long, sandy beaches and wild, rugged cliffs; high, rocky mountains; corn-covered farmland; and subtropical gardens. Cork city is a bustling cosmopolitan, friendly place founded by St. Finbar in the sixth century on some dry land in the Great Marsh of Munster—Cork meaning "a marsh." The appearance of much of the city is nineteenth century, with elegant, wide streets.

The famous Blarney stone—kissing it gives you the gift of the gab—is at the castle, one of the largest and finest tower houses in Ireland. Nineteenth-century Cobh, with its Gothic cathedral is Cork's harbor, some 24 kilometers from the city. Beyond, westward along the coast, is Kinsale, an attractive old town that is popular with yachtsmen and packed with people enjoying its many restaurants and old buildings. There are marvelous cliffs at the Old Head of Kinsale and the remains of a fifteenth century castle, plus a lovely sandy beach at Garretstown.

Youghal is a most attractive seaside town, with many interesting things to see, including the Clock Gate and St. Mary's Collegiate Church. Sir Walter Raleigh is said to have planted the first potato in his garden during the time he was mayor of the town. Nearby is Shanagarry with its pottery, where William Penn lived, and Ballycotton, a small fishing village.

The coastal scenery west of Skibbereen is particularly beautiful, and the view from Gabriel Mountain, which can be easily climbed, is spectacular. Garnish Island has a wonderful garden, which can be visited most days. Bantry House is a most interesting house with a superb view. Castle Hyde, a Georgian house close to Fermoy and former home of Douglas Hyde, first president of the Irish Republic, is one of the most beautiful houses in Ireland. Macroon is set in glorious countryside—the road across the pass of Keimaneigh and through the forest of Gougance Barra is particularly beautiful.

BALLYLICKEY

Ballylickey Manor House
Paco Graves
Ballylickey, Co. Cork
Tel: 027 50071 Fax: 027 56725
E-mail: ballymh@eircom.net
Web site: www.ballylickeymanorhouse.com

On the boundary of Cork and Kerry, amidst sheltered lawns, flower gardens, and parkland and bordered by sea, river, and mountains, stands Ballylickey House. Commanding a magnificent view over Bantry Bay, Ballylickey was built some 300 years ago by Lord Kenmare as a shooting lodge. It has been the home of the Graves family for over four generations. Robert Graves, the poet, was a great uncle of the present owner. The house was burned down in recent years, but was rebuilt, incorporating the best of the old features with a new standard of comfort. This elegant residence is exquisitely decorated with many pieces of antique furniture. The bedrooms are luxurious, and the suites include bedroom, sitting room, and bathroom. Some of the rooms are in the manor house, and others are delightful garden cottages around the swimming pool and gardens. The 4 hectares of grounds include a croquet lawn. There are two golf courses nearby, miles of mountainous coastline, fishing, and two of the finest botanical gardens to visit.

DIRECTIONS: Between Bantry and Glengarriff on the N71

OPEN: April-November
ROOMS: 3 suites, 5 double/twin; all en suite
TERMS: from €50

BANDON

Glebe Country House
Gill Good
Ballinadee, Bandon, Co. Cork
Tel: 021 4778294 Fax: 021 4778456
E-mail: glebehse@indigo.ie
Web site: www.glebecountryhouse.com

Set next to the church in the center of Ballinadee, Glebe Country House is a very pretty Georgian rectory, which was carefully renovated and subsequently redecorated after extensive damage during the 1997 Christmas storm. The bedrooms are spacious, attractively decorated, and furnished, and some have views of the river. Guests have the run of the house, which includes a large drawing room with television and open fire, and the dining room, where good home-cooked dinners are served, features organically homegrown salads and herbs. Guests should bring their own wine. Gill Good is a bright, cheerful person, and the atmosphere is friendly and informal. The attractive garden contains a croquet lawn, and there is a swimming pool under construction. There are several nearby golf courses, and river fishing and sea angling can be arranged. Three self-catering units are available.

DIRECTIONS: Coming from Cork, turn left at Innishannon Bridge from the N71. At open space cross roads, continue through. Glebe House is in the village of Ballinadee.

OPEN: closed for Christmas and New Year
ROOMS: 2 double, 2 twin; all en suite
TERMS: from €45; single supplement; child reduction

Kilbrogan House
Catherine FitzMaurice
Kilbrogan Hill, Bandon, Co. Cork
Tel/Fax: 023 44935
E-mail: kilbroganhouse@gmail.com
Web site: www.kilbrogan.com

Kilbrogan House is a real labor of love for Catherine FitzMaurice—it was a twelve-year undertaking to restore this lovely Georgian townhouse, which Catherine did while still working in London. Doors, ornate ceilings, and wooden and tile floors have all been meticulously preserved, as has the old conservatory, which is halfway up  the stairs between the ground and first floors and overlooks the extensive, nicely landscaped back garden. The gracious reception rooms encompass a dining room, downstairs sitting room, computer room, and original first floor drawing room. Bedrooms are comfortable, spacious, and all have bathrooms with bath and shower. Kilbrogan

House is an ideal base for exploring south and west Cork.
   DIRECTIONS: In Bandon

OPEN: March 1-October 31
ROOMS: 4 double, 1 twin; all en suite
TERMS: from €45; single supplement

St. Anne's
Anne Buckley
Clonakilty Road, Bandon, Co. Cork
Tel: 023 44239
E-mail: stannesbandon@eircom.net

This attractive Georgian house was in need of work when Anne Buckley
bought it. She did a great job renovating it, and now the house offers
bright and attractively furnished bedrooms. Both the dining room,
where breakfast is served, and the sitting room have their original
fireplaces, and guests can enjoy the pretty garden at the back of the
property. Anne is a former schoolteacher, very charming, and attentive to the needs of her guests.
   DIRECTIONS: 1 kilometer from Bandon on the N71 to Clonakilty

OPEN: closed for Christmas
ROOMS: 1 twin, 3 family; all en suite
TERMS: from €35; single supplement; child reduction

BANTRY

Bantry House & Garden
Mr. Egerton Shelswell-White
Bantry, Co. Cork
Tel: 027 50047 Fax: 027 50795
E-mail: info@bantryhouse.com
Web site: www.bantryhouse.com

Bantry House, overlooking Bantry Bay, is one of the finest stately man-
sions in Ireland. Purchased by the White family in 1739, it is furnished
with the most wonderful collection of pictures, furniture, and works of
art. The White family were also responsible for laying out the formal
gardens. Both the east and west wings of Bantry House provide newly
refurbished en-suite accommodation. Residents have use of a sitting
room, bar, library, billiard room, and a balcony TV room overlooking

the Italian garden with its fountain, parterres, and "stairway to the sky." There is a wine license, and guests are welcome to help themselves to drinks from the honesty bar.

Bantry House is open to the public and overnight guests are admitted at no extra charge. There is a tennis court, with rackets and balls provided, and a helicopter landing. The tearoom is open for snacks, light lunches, and tea, and there are self-catering units.

DIRECTIONS: On the edge of Bantry

OPEN: all year. House and Garden, March 17-October 31
ROOMS: 5 double, 2 twin, 1 family; all en suite
TERMS: from €100; single supplement; child reduction

Hillcrest House
Agnes Hegarty
Ahakista, Bantry, Co. Cork
Tel: 027 67045
agneshegarty@oceanfree.net
www.ahakista.com

Hillcrest is an attractive, old-stone dairy farm that was renovated a few years ago and stands in a lovely position on top of a hill overlooking Dunmanus Bay on the "Sheep's Head" peninsula. An extension was built onto the house, linking it with the old barn that now houses the games room, where guests can play table tennis and darts. There are flagstone floors, peat fires, and simply furnished and decorated bedrooms. Fresh farm produce and home baking is used for breakfast. Hillcrest is a 5-minute walk to a sandy beach. There is good sea fishing and mountain walking behind the house, and the Sheep's Head Way walking path runs by the property.

DIRECTIONS: The house is signposted from Durrus.

OPEN: all year
ROOMS: 2 double, 2 twin, 2 family; all en suite
TERMS: from €35; single supplement; child reduction

The Mill
Tosca Kramer
New Town, Glengarriff Road, Bantry, Co. Cork
Phone 027 50278
E-mail: bbthemill@eircom.net
Web site: www.the-mill.net

Tosca and Kees Kramer fell in love with Bantry while on an Irish holiday from their native Holland, so they stayed and made Ireland their home. The Mill is a chalet-style house, set back from the road in colorful gardens. Most of the bedrooms are on the ground floor. Kees Kramer is not only a craftsman, making all the wardrobes, cabinets, and dining room tables, but also an artist. A selection of his work can be found around the house.

A conservatory in front is furnished with cane pieces and is a warm, sunny spot for visitors to sit and relax. The Mill offers a laundry service, there is a kitchen area for guests to make drinks, and there are bicycles for hire. The town center is only a 5-minute walk away. There are plenty of excellent pubs and restaurants in the area, and close by are possibilities for golf, fishing, and horseback riding.

DIRECTIONS: On the outskirts of Bantry

OPEN: Easter-October
ROOMS: 4 double, 1 twin, 1 family; all en suite
TERMS: from €37.50; single supplement; child reduction

BLARNEY

Ashlee Lodge
John and Anne O'Leary
Tower, Blarney, Co. Cork
Tel: 021 4385346 Fax: 021 4385726
E-mail: info@ashleelodge.com
Web site: www.ashleelodge.com

Ashlee Lodge is a modern, whitewashed bungalow with a porticoed front porch standing in the village of Tower, 3 kilometers from Blarney. John and Anne, who used to be in the hotel business, constantly strive to offer their guests top-quality accommodation. The latest refurbishment has resulted in spacious rooms equipped with every possible need, including air conditioning, whirlpool baths, wide-screen TV, hi-fi unit, safe, and Internet access. One room is suitable for the disabled. Ashlee Lodge is professionally run and immaculately clean and has a pleasant open plan sitting/dining room/bar with cathedral ceilings and fireplace. There is an outdoor hot tub, sauna, Internet room, and a pet friendly bedroom. Dinner is available with several choices.

DIRECTIONS: On the R617 Blarney to Killarney road

OPEN: January 20-December 20
ROOMS: 10 doubles/twins; all en suite
TERMS: from €55; single supplement; child reduction
MEALS: dinner à la carte

Traveller's Joy B&B
Gertie O'Shea
Tower, Blarney, Co. Cork
Tel: 021 4385541
E-mail: travellersjoybandb@hotmail.com

Traveller's Joy is an unassuming little bungalow set in a pretty garden, but what makes it special is the friendly welcome from warm-hearted Gertie O'Shea and the atmosphere of a home away from home. The rooms are simple and spotlessly clean, and there is a cozy guest lounge with TV, off which is the small breakfast room where breakfasts "to last you the day" are served. A recent extension to the front of the house has enlarged the lounge area and one of the bedrooms.

The O'Sheas are happy to offer advice on local sightseeing and where to find the best traditional entertainment.

DIRECTIONS: 4 kilometers from Blarney just off the main road to Killarney

OPEN: February 1-December 20
ROOMS: 1 twin, 2 family; all en suite
TERMS: from €35; child reduction

CASTLELYONS

Ballyvolane House
Justin Green
Castlelyons, nr. Fermoy, Co. Cork

Tel: 025 36349 Fax: 025 36781
E-mail: info@ballyvolanehouse.ie
Web site: www.ballyvolanehouse.ie

In a magnificent parkland setting, Ballyvolane is a gracious, beautifully restored country house. It is surrounded by its own farmland, wooded grounds (quite spectacular in bluebell time), formal terraced gardens, and three restored lakes stocked with trout. It was built in 1728 on the site of an older house and later altered to the Italianate style. Guests experience here a blend of elegance, informality, and charming hosts. Justin and Jenny Green took over the house from Justin's parents, Merrie and Jeremy—so the tradition of great hospitality continues.

The Greens have done a superb job, gradually furnishing and restoring the house, which offers very comfortable and spacious bedrooms—one en suite bathroom has a wonderful old bathtub encased in wood and raised on two steps. Five newly opened one-bedroom suites in the old walled garden are very popular. The lovely pillared hall has a baby grand piano and plenty of comfortable chairs in front of the open fire. Beautifully presented, delicious food is served in the elegant dining room at the long dining room table; the open fire is lit both in the evening and at breakfast time. Recently the huge kitchen has been changed back to the drawing room it once was, which is a comfortable spot to enjoy predinner drinks and meet fellow guests. Salmon fishing is available by arrangement on Ballyvolane's own stretch of the River Blackwater; there is trout fishing in the lakes and a croquet lawn

DIRECTIONS: There are signs for the house on the N8 at River Bride and the R628 just before Rathcormac, coming from Cork

OPEN: closed for Christmas
ROOMS: 6 double/twin, 5 suites; all en suite
TERMS: from €95; single supplement; child reduction
MEALS: dinner €60

CLONAKILTY

An Garran Coir
Michael and Jo Calnan
Castlefreke, Clonakilty, Co. Cork
Tel/Fax: 023 48236
E-mail: angarrancoir@eircom.net
Web site: www.angarrancoir.com

The original family farmhouse is close to the old farm buildings, some 200 meters up the lane. An Garran Coir was built by the Calnans and then extended to accommodate bed and breakfast guests. It offers clean and comfortable rooms, which have recently been upgraded. The reception area has an Irish coffee bar, the dining room has a piano, and there are plush red chairs in the smartly decorated lounge. Evening meals, using fruit and herbs from the herb garden, are available by arrangement, and you can pick your own free-range eggs for breakfast. Children are well catered for with their own play area, and adults can use the tennis court, hire bicycles, or take a lovely walk to the award winning village of Rathbarry.

DIRECTIONS: Signposted at the Maxol Gas Station on the N71 Clonakilty-Skibbereen road

OPEN: all year
ROOMS: 5 double, 2 twin, 1 family; all en suite
TERMS: from €40; single supplement; child reduction
MEALS: dinner à la carte

Ard Na Greine Farmhouse
Norma Walsh
Ballinascarthy, Clonakilty, Co. Cork
Tel: 023 39104
E-mail: info@ardnagreine.com
Web site: www.ardnagreine.com

Ard Na Greine is a working dairy farm set in pleasant farming countryside and enjoying lovely views. The atmosphere is friendly and informal, and guests immediately feel at home, many returning year after year. Norma Walsh is hospitable, warm-hearted, and offers simple farmhouse comfort, as well as copious amounts of good home-cooked food. The bedrooms are comfortable, and there is a cozy TV lounge and dining room with separate tables. Guests are welcome to bring their own wine. Ard Na Greine is well placed for Kinsale and visiting the attractive south and west Cork coastlines, and some guests like to watch the cows being milked.

DIRECTIONS: Signposted on the N71 between Bandon and Clonakilty

OPEN: March 1-November 1
ROOMS: 1 double, 2 twin, 2 family, 1 single; all en suite
TERMS: from €45
MEALS: dinner €35

Duvane Farm
Noreen and Rensei McCarthy
Clonakilty, Co. Cork
Tel: 023 33129
E-mail: duvanefarm@eircom.net
Web site: www.duvanehouse.com

This Georgian farmhouse was built around 1870 and has been in the McCarthy family for quite a while; before that, it belonged to a bishop. It is beautifully furnished and has some brass and half tester beds. The farm supports cattle, with the attractive farm buildings lying behind the house. There is  woodland, a lovely garden where guests can sit and relax, and bicycles for the more energetic. Breakfast includes honey from the farm's own bees; evening meals and high teas are available if arranged in advance.

DIRECTIONS: On the N71, 2 kilometers west of Clonakilty

OPEN: March 20-November 20
ROOMS: 2 double, 2 twin, 1 family; all en suite
TERMS: from €45
MEALS: evening meals; high tea

CORK

Garnish House
Mr. and Mrs. Conor Lucey
Western Road, Cork, Co. Cork
Tel: 021 4275111 Fax: 021 4273872
E-mail: garnish@iol.ie
Web site: www.garnish.ie

Conveniently located on the western edge of town opposite University

College Cork, Garnish House is a double-fronted Victorian townhouse, set back from the main road by its parking area. It is a comfortable house, efficiently run in a businesslike fashion by pleasant, helpful staff, and offering such facilities as a night porter and a 24-hour service for arrivals and departures. The bedrooms vary in size, some being quite spacious, and quite a few have Jacuzzi baths, and they are equipped with every amenity including special pillow top

mattresses, fresh fruit, and flowers. Guests have use of a small TV lounge, and the highly acclaimed breakfast with its extensive menu is served in the dining room from 6:00 until 11:00 A.M. or midday. Disabled guests are catered for as well as those with special diets.

DIRECTIONS: 5 minutes from city center

OPEN: all year
ROOMS: 14 double, 11 twin, 3 single, 4 family; all en suite
TERMS: from €50; child reduction

DONERAILE

Creagh House
Michael O'Sullivan and Laura O'Mahony
Main Street, Doneraile, Co. Cork
Tel: 022 24433 Fax: 022 24715
Email: info@creaghhouse.ie
Web site: www.creaghhouse.ie

Michael O'Sullivan and Laura O'Mahony, both environmental engineers, were looking for a small house in County Cork. They ended up with 10,000 square feet of Creagh House—room for themselves and guests! Renovation was a mammoth task, but the results are quite spectacular. Built in the early 1800s, Creagh House is considered to be one of

the finest and largest Georgian townhouses outside Dublin. The magnificent ceiling cornices have been painstakingly restored, and the sheer size of the rooms is almost overpowering. The hallway, broken into two halves by double doors, the drawing, and dining room are each 600 square feet in size. The house has many literary associations, including Thackeray (whose wife was a Creagh), Elizabeth Bowen, Canon Sheehan, and Daniel O'Connell. For anyone with an interest in history or literature Michael is an enthusiastic expert. Supper must be booked by noon and is served from 8:00 to 10:00 P.M. Creagh House is adjacent to the Golf Club and Doneraile Court.

DIRECTIONS: In the center of Doneraile

OPEN: April-September
ROOMS: 3 double; all en suite
TERMS: from €100
MEALS: supper €30

GOLEEN

Fortview House
Violet Connell
Gurtyowen, Toormore, Goleen, Co. Cork
Tel: 028 35324
E-mail: fortviewhousegoleen@eircom.net
Web site: www.fortviewhousegoleen.com

Although it was built only a few years ago by the Connells, Fortview House has an air of rustic charm. A small, stone-built farmhouse on a working dairy farm, it is an excellent location for exploring the Mizen Head, Sheep's Head, and the Beara Peninsula. The interior of the house is very attractive, fresh, and bright and simply but comfortably furnished with pine floors, antique country-pine furniture, and brass and iron beds. Drinks are available by donation in the sitting room. The dining room has a tiled floor and wood-burning stove; excellent breakfasts are served, which include freshly squeezed orange juice and pancakes. There is also a self-catering cottage.

DIRECTIONS: 10 kilometers from both Schull and Goleen on the R591, signposted at Toormore

OPEN: March 1-October 31
ROOMS: 1 double, 2 twin, 1 single, 1 family; all en suite
TERMS: €50; single supplement

The Heron's Cove
Sue Hill

The Harbour, Goleen, Co. Cork
Tel: 028 35225 Fax: 028 35422
E-mail: suehill@eircom.net
Web site: www.heronscove.ie

Situated on the edge of the water, The Heron's Cove is in an idyllic spot overlooking a small picturesque cove on the edge of the little village of Goleen. Four of the five bedrooms have this view, which is better still from their balconies. Downstairs a large room with wooden floors, simple pine furniture, and the same lovely outlook serves as bar, cozy sitting area, and restaurant. A small outside patio is a wonderful place on a sunny day. The restaurant is known for its organic fare and fresh fish, but duck, lamb, and vegetarian choices are also on the menu. Goleen is 10 kilometers from Mizen Head, Ireland's spectacular most southwesterly point, with the Fastnet Rock Lighthouse. The Heron's Cove is a great place for beaches and hill walking along majestic cliffs.

DIRECTIONS: In Goleen

OPEN: closed for Christmas and New Year's
ROOMS: 3 double; 1 twin, 1 family; all en suite
TERMS: from €35; single supplement
MEALS: dinner à la carte

KANTURK

Glenlohane
Desmond and Melanie Sharp Bolster
Kanturk, Co. Cork
Tel: 029 50014
E-mail: glenlohane@iol.ie
Web site: www.glenlohane.com

Glenlohane is a superb Georgian country house set in beautiful parkland grounds with some wonderful old trees and views to the distant mountains. The present owners are direct descendants of the family who built it in 1741. Desmond lived and worked in the United States and Melanie is American, and between them, they have combined the very best of modern comforts with the character and atmosphere of the past. Glenlohane is an informal house with log fires to relax in front of. The large, comfortable drawing room features a square bay window, a superb full-length mirror, baby grand piano, grey marble fireplace, and

interesting pictures and furniture.
There is also a small study filled with
books and a dining room. A traditional
stable yard is attached to the house.
There are plenty of animals around,
and the farm includes sheep and cattle. Guests are welcome to watch the
daily farm activities, play croquet, or

just relax in the old walled gardens. Fishing is available only 1 kilometer away on the River Blackwater, and there are a variety of golf courses
and lovely walks nearby.

DIRECTIONS: From Kanturk, take the R576 towards Mallow, bear
left on the R580 towards Buttevant, then take the first right towards
Ballyclough. Look for the first residential entrance on the left after
2.2 kilometers—there is no sign.

OPEN: all year
ROOMS: 1 double, 2 twin, 1 single; all en suite
TERMS: €100

KILBRITTAIN

The Glen Country House
Diana and Guy Scott
Kilbrittain, Co. Cork
Tel/Fax: 023 49862
E-mail: info@glencountryhouse.com
Web site: www.glencountryhouse.com

This Victorian farmhouse set
in 300 acres of its own farmland with views of Courtmac-
sherry Bay offers guests a
wonderfully relaxing stay.
The tenth generation of the
family to have lived on the
property, Guy and Diana
Scott completely renovated
the house in 2003 both for

their own family, and with guests in mind. The bedrooms are spacious and beautifully furnished, some having views of the bay, and
the family suite's two rooms has a bathroom in between, which is

ideal for families. Produce from the walled kitchen garden, free-range eggs, and local organic food provide the breakfast ingredients. Guests can enjoy the large garden and play croquet. Kinsale, with its many restaurants, is a 20-minute drive away, and within 10 minutes are many other restaurants from which to choose. There are beautiful sandy beaches, golf courses, sea and river fishing, riding, and endless walking opportunities nearby.

DIRECTIONS: From Kinsale, follow signs for Clonakilty, stay on the R600 until you see the signs. The Glen is 12 miles from Kinsale.

OPEN: April 1-October 31
ROOMS: 4 double/twin, 1 family; all en suite
TERMS: €70

KILLEAGH

Ballymakeigh House
Margaret Browne
Killeagh, Co. Cork
Tel: 024 95184 Fax: 024 95523
E-mail: ballymakeigh@eircom.net
Web site: www.ballymakeighhouse.com

The friendliest of welcomes, superb food, and comfortable rooms make Ballymakeigh House a delightful place to stay. The 250-year-old farmhouse is located in the rich farmlands of east Cork, and guests are welcome to walk around the intensive dairy farm and watch the cows being milked. For the energetic, there are bicycles available, a full-sized hard tennis court, and horseback riding. The conservatory offers lots of sunny sitting space, and the bedrooms are constantly being upgraded. Margaret Browne has won countless awards over the years and has written a book containing some of her favorite recipes— *Through My Kitchen Window*. Copies are available for sale at the house. Margaret is a superb cook, and a stay at Ballymakeigh would not be complete without having dinner. This is a marvelous spot in peaceful and tranquil surroundings and convenient to beaches, Fota Wildlife Park, Trabolgan Leisure Centre, and Blarney Castle.

DIRECTIONS: Ballymakeigh is signposted at the Old Thatch pub in the village of Killeagh on the N25.

OPEN: March-November
ROOMS: 3 double, 2 twin, 1 single; all en suite

TERMS: €65
MEALS: dinner €45

KINSALE

Chart House
The O'Connor Family
6 Denis Quay, Kinsale, Co. Cork
Tel: 021 4774568 Fax: 021 4777907
E-mail: charthouse@eircom.net
Web site: www.charthouse-kinsale.com

Down a side street off the harbor, Chart House is a delightful Georgian townhouse, which has been completely renovated by Bill and Mary O'Connor. It has a calm and peaceful atmosphere and has been beautifully furnished with antiques. The bedrooms, save the single, are spacious, and some have big bathrooms. Each room has its own color theme, and they all have antique beds (but the best quality mattresses!). Afternoon tea or coffee is offered on arrival in the attractive reception/sitting area. A good menu is available for breakfast, which is served at the William IV table in the dining room. All of Kinsale's amenities are within easy walking distance.
   DIRECTIONS: In Kinsale

OPEN: closed for Christmas
ROOMS: 2 double/twin, 1 double, 1 single; all en suite
TERMS: from €55; single supplement

Old Bank House
Cioron Fitzgerald
11 Pearse Street, Kinsale, Co. Cork
Tel: 021 4774075 Fax: 021 4774296
E-mail: info@oldbankhousekinsale.com
Web site: www.oldbankhousekinsale.com

As its name implies, Old Bank House was originally a bank, dating back some 250 years. The whole building was virtually gutted and transformed into a luxury place to stay with plenty of charm and character. The bedrooms are beautifully furnished and equipped and a little on the small side, each one having the ability of being either a double or twin, and each bathroom has both bath and shower. Breakfast is served in the atmospheric, long dining room with the original exposed brickwork. The elevator is a big asset to those with bedrooms on the third floor. The Old Bank House is in the very middle of Kinsale, with its harbor, marina, wine bars, pubs, and restaurants.

DIRECTIONS: In Kinsale

OPEN: closed for Christmas
ROOMS: 17 double/twin
TERMS: from €60; child reduction

Perryville House
Laura Corcoran
Kinsale, Co. Cork
Tel: 021 4772731 Fax: 021 4772298
E-mail: sales@perryville.iol.ie
Web site: www.perryvillehouse.com

This spectacular house stands right in the center of Kinsale on the quay overlooking the marina and the colorful streets of the medieval fishing port. Laura Corcoran, who previously owned Albany House in Dublin, bought Perryville House in a very rundown state and transformed it into a

place of elegance and comfort, opening for business in 1997. The house is run with a quiet air of friendly professionalism. It has lovely furniture and tasteful décor; the Hessian covered floors offset the colorful rugs.

The bedrooms, which are luxuriously appointed, vary in shape and size, some overlooking the harbor, some in a new wing, but even the smallest room is a good size. Most en suite bathrooms have separate baths and showers.

The drawing room, where morning coffee and afternoon tea are served daily, is comfortable and elegant, and the large, open reception area is another place to sit and relax. Substantial buffet-style breakfasts are available in the dining room, including home-baked breads and preserves, local cheeses, and fresh fruit.

DIRECTIONS: In Kinsale

OPEN: April 8-October 31
ROOMS: 22 double/twin, 4 junior suites; all en suite
TERMS: from €100

Raheen House
Maria Sweetnam
Kilgobbin, Ballinspittle, Kinsale, Co. Cork
Tel/Fax: 021 4778173
E-mail: raheenhouse@eircom.net
Web site: www.raheenhouse.com

Raheen House belonged to Maria Sweetnam's grandparents. Maria, a bright, cheerful mother of teenage children, and her builder husband have added to and improved the house over the years. Guests now enjoy very comfortable accommodation, with three en suite rooms upstairs and a perfect family suite of two bedrooms and bathroom on the ground floor. There is a sitting room and dining room, both facing the sweeping views over rolling farmland to the sea and Old Head of Kinsale. Breakfast includes home baking, and there is a conveniently placed restaurant at Ballinspittle for evening meals. The land surrounding the house is used for keeping and breeding show horses, which is an activity the Sweetnams are involved in. Horseriding, fishing, sailing, and golf are available locally, as are lovely beaches, historic forts, and museums.

DIRECTIONS: Raheen House is signposted between Ballinspittle and Ballinadee and is approximately 10 kilometres from Kinsale.

OPEN: May 1-September 15
ROOMS: 2 double, 1 twin, 1 family; all en suite
TERMS: €40; single supplement; child reduction

MALLOW

Dromagh Castle Farm
Robert and Anne Marie O'Leary
Mallow, Co. Cork
Tel: 029 78013
E-mail: dromaghcastle@eircom.net

The property's name is an apt description—a 1930s farmhouse beside a ruined late sixteenth-century castle. Robert's father bought the farm, which included the castle, in the 1920s. At that time, he lived in a house in the castle courtyard, later building the present day farmhouse. The castle is an impressive square ruin with four towers. The enormous courtyard was used in later years as the farmyard. The house is clean, bright, and pleasantly furnished and has a subdued atmosphere. Of the two double front-facing rooms, one is known as the "twin's room." Here, in the 1930s, twins were born weighing only $1^1/_2$ pounds each, and, miraculously, both survived. The twin-bedded room is popular as it has views of the castle. Some of the pictures have interesting connections to the history of the property, and there is a floor-to-ceiling press on the upstairs landing, which was built at the same time as the house. Dromagh Castle is reached up a long driveway through farmland.

DIRECTIONS: About halfway between Mallow and Killarney on the N72

OPEN: February–December
ROOMS: 1 twin, 1 double, 1 family; all en suite
TERMS: €35; child reduction

Longueville House Hotel
The O'Callaghan Family
Mallow, Co. Cork
Tel: 022 47156 Fax: 022 47459
E-mail: info@longuevillehouse.ie
Web site: www.longuevillehouse.ie

This impressive, listed Georgian manor house is set in beautiful park-like grounds with lovely views overlooking the Blackwater River valley, surrounded by 200 hectares of woods, farmland, a vineyard, and gardens, which include 1.2 hectares of kitchen gardens. Visitors flock to Longueville House primarily for its food, which mostly comes from the river, garden, and farm and is under the direction of William O'Callaghan. The lovely peaceful setting, the salmon fishing on the Blackwater, which runs through the estate, and its position as a good touring base for exploring both the south and southwest coasts also contribute to its popularity.

The bedrooms are supremely comfortable, ranging in shape and size, and seven have mini suites, which include sitting areas and luxury bathrooms. In spite of the grandeur, the atmosphere is warm and welcoming; guests have use of the drawing room and games room with a full-sized billiard table. The old conservatory has been restored and is now used as part of the dining room. As well as breakfast and dinner, lunch and bar snacks are available all week. Other amenities include bicycle hire, fishing, and shooting.

DIRECTIONS: On the N72 to Killarney, 5 kilometers west of Mallow

OPEN: March 14-January 6
ROOMS: 9 double, 3 twin, 3 family, 2 single; all en suite
TERMS: from €117.50
MEALS: dinner €60; bar menu

MIDLETON

Barnabrow Country House
Geraldine Kidd
Barnabrow, Midleton, Co. Cork
Tel/Fax: 021 4652534
E-mail: barnabrow@eircom.net
Web site: www.barnabrowhouse.ie

The cathedral at Cloyne was the seat of George Berkeley, the well-known philosopher after whom the Californian university was named. Built in 1639, with two wings added later, Barnabrow—meaning a fairy fort—stands on a hill surrounded by its own 14 hectares and enjoys pleasant country views. The house was gutted and has been most interestingly restored with the four large second-floor bedrooms having high-raftered ceilings. Apart from one bedroom on the first floor, the remainder are in two ranges of converted farm buildings at the back of the house, one of which also houses the bar and restaurant above it. The house has been unusually decorated and plainly and simply furnished with a mixture of old and new. Strong, vibrant, and bright colors are used on the walls, reflecting the colors of Guatemala. A lot of the interestingly shaped furniture and the flooring are made from imported teak from Botswana. Organically grown vegetables from the walled garden

are a part of the delicious food on offer, and the outside terrace is used for barbecuing. There is now an African furniture and crafts shop open daily, and the enlarged restaurant can cater for weddings, conferences, and large parties. Sunday lunch and dinner on Fridays, Saturdays, and Sundays is available. There are also nine self-catering cottages.

DIRECTIONS: Barnabrow is 1¹/₂ miles from Cloyne on the Ballycotton road.

OPEN: closed for Christmas
ROOMS: 16 double, 5 twin; all en suite
TERMS: from €65; single supplement; child reduction
MEALS: lunch €27; dinner €50

MILLSTREET

Ballinatona Farm
Jytte Storm
Ballinatona, Millstreet, Co. Cork
Tel: 029 70213 Fax: 029 70940

Not your typical farm, Ballinatona Farm is a most unusual and wonderful place. Set in beautiful countryside, it has outstanding views of mountains, moors, and farmland. What makes this farm such a special place is cheerful, welcoming Jytte Storm, who immediately makes her guests feel at home. Jytte's Danish origins have a big influence on the décor and the house, which she and her husband originally built some 25 years ago, and then added on to. Ballinatona was meant to be for their retirement, which is a pretty active one, what with running a 40-hectare dairy farm and a six-bedroom guesthouse.

It seems every room in the house was built to take advantage of the best views. The sitting room, conservatory, and dining room are all bright with large windows, as is the honeymoon suite reached via a very narrow spiral staircase. Décor and furnishings are simple, clean cut, and very bright.

Ballinatona Farm is a walker's dream—from the doorstep, there are wonderful hikes, including this most remote and beautiful part of the Blackwater Way, which is part of the coast-to-coast walk and runs on the other side of Clara Mountain, one of the viewpoints from the house.

DIRECTIONS: 3 kilometers from Millstreet on the R582

OPEN: January 4-December 15
ROOMS: 3 double, 2 twin, 1 family; all en suite
TERMS: from €35; single supplement

SCHULL

Rock Cottage
Barbara Klotzer
Barnatonicane, Schull, Co. Cork
Tel/Fax: 028 35538
E-mail: rockcottage@eircom.net
Web site: www.rockcottage.ie

Barbara Klotzer (from Germany) was formerly head chef at Blairs Cove Restaurant, just a few miles away. She bought Rock Cottage (named for a small rock outcrop at the back of the house) and opened for business fifteen years ago. Decidedly a Georgian house, it is by the 1800s standards a cottage and was in fact built as a hunting lodge. It offers delightful, simple, bright accommodation—pine has been used quite extensively. There is an attractive sitting room, and superb meals are served at separate tables in the dining room. Apart from three bedrooms in the house, there are self-catering units on the grounds, built from renovated attractive stone farm buildings. The house is beautifully positioned, on the Mizen Head peninsula, within a short distance of the sea on either side and stands in lovely parklike grounds, with sheep, horses, donkeys, geese, and a pet pig. Dinner should be booked the previous day.

DIRECTIONS: On the R591 between Durrus and Toormore

OPEN: all year
ROOMS: 1 double, 2 double/twin/triple; all en suite

TERMS: €65; single supplement; not suitable for children
MEALS: dinner €45

Stanley House

Nancy Brosnan
Colla Road, Schull, Co. Cork
Tel: 029 28425 Fax: 028 27887
E-mail: stanleyhouse@eircom.net
Web site: www.stanley-house.net

Although it has a modern look, Stanley House is actually a renovated old farmhouse. The house, surrounded by 3 hectares of fields with deer and colorful gardens, is in a wonderful position overlooking Schull Harbour, Roaring Water Bay with its many islands, and Mount Gabriel. Nancy Brosnan has been doing bed and breakfasts for more than 20 years and has a far-flung circle of guests who return again and again to this home away from home. Maeve Binchy, among her regular visitors, wrote, "This is my fifth visit to the gleaming place where all the guests stare in wonder at the sparkling surfaces and shining windows and wonder do folk from another world come and do the housework at night".

The small dining room where breakfast is served has separate tables, and the comfortable TV lounge has a sun porch beyond which is the terrace—a great place to sit and take in the views.

The Brosnans have quite a presence in Schull; Nancy's husband runs the Spar supermarket, and her son manages the restaurant and bar. They also have a self-catering unit.

It is a lovely walk into the village; there are ferries to the islands two or three times a day during the summer; bicycles can be hired, or the energetic can climb to the top of 412-meter Mount Gabriel—well worth it for the wonderful views.

DIRECTIONS: At the top of Main Street, follow the signs for Stanley House

OPEN: March 1-October 31

ROOMS: 3 double, 1 twin, 1 single, 1 family; all en suite
TERMS: €35; single supplement

SHANAGARRY

Ballymaloe House
Myrtle Allen
Shanagarry, Co. Cork
Tel: 021 4652531 Fax: 021 4652021
E-mail: res@ballymaloe.ie
Web site: www.ballymaloe.ie

Famous as one of Ireland's top restaurants and training ground (at Ballymaloe Cookery School) for many of Ireland's best chefs, Ballymaloe's food undoubtedly lures many visitors to this lovely, old family home. Set in 160 hectares of its own farmland, Ballymaloe is built around an old Geraldine castle, the fourteenth-century keep still intact.

The bedrooms, which vary in size and character, are in the main house; around the old coachyard, with four on the ground floor designed to take wheelchairs; and in the gatehouse, where there are five newer rooms. Three small dining rooms open off the main room, with an interesting collection of modern Irish paintings, including works by Jack B. Yeats, brother of poet William Butler Yeats.

In addition to Ballymaloe House, Cookery School, and farm, the Allens run a craft shop on the premises and Crawford Art Gallery restaurant in Cork. Estate facilities include a heated outdoor swimming pool (summer), tennis court, small golf course, and children's play equipment.

DIRECTIONS: 3 kilometers outside Cloyne on the Ballycotton road

OPEN: closed for Christmas
ROOMS: 16 double, 15 twin, 3 single; all en suite
TERMS: from €115
MEALS: lunch €40; dinner €70; children's menu

SKIBBEREEN

Bunalun House
T. Crowley

Skibbereen, Co. Cork
Tel/Fax: 028 21502
E-mail: info@bunalunfarm.com
Web site: www.banalunfarm.com

Mrs. Crowley offers the best of Irish farmhouse hospitality and welcome at Bunalun, a pristinely kept, attractive 200-year-old house. Colorful flowers surround the front of the building, which lies in pleasant farmland, supporting dairy cows and beef cattle. The entrance hall has the original tiled floor, and there are wooden floors in the attractive, small sitting room and dining room where breakfast is served at separate tables.

DIRECTIONS: Off the main Skibbereen to Bantry road

OPEN: May 1-November 1
ROOMS: 2 double, 1 family; all en suite; 1 twin with private bathroom
TERMS: from €36; single supplement; child reduction

Grove House
Anna and Peter Warburton
Skibbereen, Co. Cork
Tel: 028 22957 Fax: 028 22958
E-mail: relax@grovehouse.net
Web site: www.grovehouse.net

Grove House stands in two acres of wild gardens and fields. The Warburtons bought the house in the early 1990s, spending a couple of years on renovation before opening for business. There is a pretty drawing room, where guests can enjoy aperitifs from the "honesty bar," and a dining room, where delicious home-cooked candlelit dinners are served. Bedrooms in the house, which vary in size, are simply furnished. Behind the house, the pretty, old stables and barn building provide three very attractive, cleverly converted bedrooms. Three-course dinners including wine are available if booked in advance. Guests have use of bicycles.

DIRECTIONS: 1 kilometer off N71 on R593 in Bantry direction

OPEN: all year
ROOMS: 4 double, 1 family; all en suite
TERMS: €59; single supplement; child reduction
MEALS: dinner €27 including wine

UNION HALL

Lis-Ardagh Lodge
Jim and Carol Kearney
Union Hall, Co. Cork
Tel: 028 34951
E-mail: info@lis-ardaghlodge.com
Web site: www.lis-ardaghlodge.com

Lis-Ardagh is a striking stone-built house, constructed by the Kearneys seven years ago, and has nice views over farmland. Jim Kearney, a landscape gardener, created the beautiful gardens surrounding the house, and beyond it are fields with sheep. The interior of the house has wooden floors and pine furniture, and the rooms are spacious, clean, and bright. Guests have use of a large sitting room, hot tub, sauna, and mini gym. Breakfast is served at separate tables in the pleasant dining room. There are also two self-catering units.

DIRECTIONS: There is a sign for the house on the N71.

OPEN: all year
ROOMS: 2 family, 1 double; all en suite
TERMS: from €30; single supplement; child reduction

YOUGHAL

Aherne's
The Fitzgibbon Family
163 North Main Street, Youghal, Co. Cork
Tel: 024 92424 Fax: 024 93633
E-mail: ahernes@eircom.net
Web site: www.ahernes.net

The Fitzgibbon family has owned Aherne's for three generations. The inn started life as the family's pub and small grocery store that made sandwiches. It is the present generation of the family who made the transformation from sandwiches to a restaurant, and later built on an entire wing for accommodation.

At the heart of the historic walled port of Youghal, Aherne's is a renowned seafood restaurant serving freshly caught local seafood, including lobster, prawns, crab, salmon, oysters, and sole. Decorated in warm, glowing colors, there are two small, cozy bars with prints and pictures. The exceptionally large bedrooms are restfully deco-rated with very big beds. There are two studios with separate entrances and mini kitchens, one of which is suitable for the disabled. The drawing room has an open fireplace, books, and antique furniture. Residents are served breakfast in the new wing's bright dining room. There is a small conference room, which is a recent addition. River and deep sea fishing, horseback riding, hill walking, and visiting magnificent beaches are activities that can easily by undertaken from Youghal, not to mention the seven nearby golf courses. The restaurant is open from 6:30 to 9:30 P.M. daily, and bar food is available at lunchtime.

DIRECTIONS: In Youghal

OPEN: closed for Christmas
ROOMS: 12 double/twin/suites
TERMS: €110
MEALS: dinner; bar food

Avonmore House
Eileen Gaine
South Abbey, Youghal, Co. Cork
Tel: 024 92617
E-mail: avonmoreyoughal@eircom.net
Web site: www.avonmorehouse.com

Set back from the road in a well-landscaped garden, Avonmore is a handsome restored Georgian house easily accessible to the beach and town center. The atmosphere is peaceful, and Eileen Gaine is a bright, cheerful, welcoming host who maintains a high standard of comfort. The lounge has comfortable leather furniture, and the bedrooms are well equipped.

DIRECTIONS: On the edge of town

OPEN: March-end October
ROOMS: 7 double/twin/triple; all en suite
TERMS: from €35; single supplement; child reduction

Roseville
Phyllis Foley
New Catherine Street, Youghal, Co. Cork
Tel: 024 92571
E-mail: rosevillebandb@eircom.net
Web site: www.rosevillebb.com

In the center of town, this 200-year-old restored townhouse offers a peaceful, quiet setting with its walled garden and bedrooms located around the courtyard. Phyllis Foley is a wonderful host who takes excellent care of her guests and provides excellent breakfasts with homemade breads and preserves. The house is beautifully maintained, and the bedrooms are well equipped.

DIRECTIONS: In town

OPEN: January 20-December 20
ROOMS: 5 double/twin/family; all en suite
TERMS: from €35

COUNTY KERRY

Every tourist wants to visit Kerry to see the beauty of the landscape. There is an inconsistency in the weather—wind and rain from the Atlantic, misty drizzle, or bright light and sunshine—making each day or part of a day different from the next and projecting a constantly changing pattern over the mountains, lakes, and streams. Each type of weather system brings its own peculiar beauty to the landscape.

Killarney town caters to large numbers of tourists and is full of hotels, yet the lakes, mountains, and woods of the surrounding countryside remain unspoiled. Close by is the ruined fourteenth-century Ross Castle. From here, one can hire a boat to Inisfallen Island and visit the ruins of the twelfth-century Augustinian Inisfallen Abbey. Muckross House is now a folk museum and has the most beautiful garden. From the Gap of Dunloe, there is a marvelous view of the Black Valley where huge torrents of water poured through the Gap at the end of the Ice Age.

The Ring of Kerry is a famous scenic drive around the Iveragh Peninsula. Killorglin is known for its annual horse and cattle fair. Puck Fair, held for two days in August, is a great event with pagan origins where a wild mountain goat is captured and enthroned in the center of the town. Waterville is the principal resort on the Ring of Kerry, and at Cahirsiveen, one can see the magnificent police barracks, which were supposed to be built in the northwest frontier of India, but the plans were mixed up. At Ballinskelligs, which is an Irish-speaking area, there are the ruins of a monastery and a fine beach with wonderful views. The Skelligs are rocky islands off the Ring of Kerry, which can be visited to see wild birds, notably kittiwakes, guillemots, petrel, shear-water, and fulmar. One can also see the ruins of the old monastery that stands 183 meters above the landing place and is approached by long flights of stone steps. There are also beehive huts, stone crosses, the Holy Well, oratories, and cemeteries. This is a beautiful, peaceful spot in fine weather, but terrifying in a storm.

The Dingle Peninsula is made up of beautiful mountains, cliffs, glacial valleys, lakes, and beaches. Some 2,000 prehistoric and early

Christian remains have been discovered, and a little of old Gaelic culture can be observed at the tip of the peninsula. The little village of Ventry was the scene of a legendary battle. At Fahan lies the greatest collection of antiquities in Ireland: stone beehive huts, cave dwellings, standing and inscribed stones and crosses, souterrains, forts, cahers, and a church. The spectacular views around Slea Head formed the backdrop for the film *Ryan's Daughter*. Beyond Ballferriter is Gallarus, the most perfect example of early Irish building and dry rubble masonry. The principal town of Kerry is Tralee, a trading and industrial center. At Ardfert, the cathedral that was built in 1250 and has the ruins of its Franciscan Friary is the most striking building.

ANASCAUL

Four Winds
Kathleen and P.J. O'Connor
Anascaul, Co. Kerry
Tel: 066 9135174

Anascaul is the birthplace of the Antarctic explorer Tom Cream and the well-known sculptor Jerome Connor and is home to the Four Winds. Kathleen O'Connor has been running her B&B for about 20 years; she enjoys meeting people, sharing her house, and is an accommodating host. There are wonderful views of the Anascaul Mountains, Dingle Bay, and Ross Bay from the house. The immaculate rooms are fresh and bright. There is a unique chaise lounge in the hallway.

Tasty, freshly prepared breakfasts are served in the conservatory overlooking the view, and there is also a comfortable TV lounge. There are plenty of activities for the visitor, including walks, fishing, sandy beaches, mountain climbing, and archaeological sites. The house is situated on the Dingle/Tralee Way walk. Drying facilities are provided. There is private parking, and a self-catering unit is available.

DIRECTIONS: Situated on the Dingle/Tralee Way Walk

OPEN: all year except Christmas
ROOMS: 2 double, 1 family; both en suite
TERMS: from €32; single supplement; child reduction

BALLYBUNION

The 19th Lodge
Mr. and Mrs. Beasley
Golf Links Road, Ballybunion, Co. Kerry

Tel: 068 27592 Fax: 068 27830
E-mail: the19thlodge@eircom.net
Web site: www.the19thlodgeballybunion.com

The 19th Lodge is a luxurious 4-star guesthouse in a superb location overlooking Ballybunion Golf Course. The home is only a 2-minute walk to the first tee and a good seven iron to the clubhouse—a Golfer's paradise. It is in pristine condition, beautifully furnished, and has a welcoming ambience. The bedrooms are equipped with rich wood, pretty pastel fabrics, and lace curtains. Bathrooms have bathtubs, and some have power showers. The conservatory, where breakfast is served (available from 6:00 A.M.), overlooks the golf course, as does the lounge.

The owners, Mr. and Mrs. Beasley, are a most accommodating couple who go out of their way to ensure guests have everything they need. Tea or coffee is offered upon arrival, and golf storage and a drying room are made available.

Guaranteed tee times on Ballybunion Old Course are available for residents. The house is not suitable for children. There is no shortage of restaurants and pubs for other meals in Ballybunion. The property is 5 minutes from sandy beaches, salmon fishing, cliff walks, and seawood baths on the beach. This is an extremely good value; a 5-star hotel could not offer more. This is a popular property; early reservations are advised. Private parking.

OPEN: April through November
ROOMS: 8 rooms double/twin/family; all en suite
TERMS: from €60-100; single supplement; child reduction

CAHIRSIVEEN

Cul Draiochta
Ian and Anne Nugent
Points Cross, Cahirsiveen, Co. Kerry
Tel: 066 947 3141 Fax: 066 947 3141
E-mail: inugent@esatclear.ie

Cul Draiochta means "Magic Nook" in Irish, and this is a magical area of the Ring of Kerry. Situated at the foot of the Bentee Mountains overlooking Valentia Harbor, the house was designed as a bed and breakfast and was built to ensure guests have every comfort. The well-appointed, good-sized bedrooms are light and airy. They have cherry wood furniture and pink candy-striped duvets. They are also attractively decorated with coordinating fabrics; all have ortho-pedic beds and overlook the view. All bedrooms have TV, clock radio, and hair dryer.

Owners Ian and Ann Nugent are from a farming family in North Kerry and are very hospitable. They have been in business for nearly a decade and have built up a fine reputation for offering very good value accommodation. Tea or coffee is offered on arrival and other times on request. Excellent breakfasts are served in the conservatory-style dining room overlooking the view, and packed lunches can be provided upon request. The lounge is very comfortable and has multi-channel TV. Routes for walkers are provided. This is an ideal spot for nature lovers. Private parking.

OPEN: all year
ROOMS: 5 double/twin/family; all en suite
TERMS: from €35; single supplement; child reduction

The Final Furlong
Kathleen O'Sullivan
Cahirsiveen, Co. Kerry
Tel: 066 947 3300 Fax: 066 947 2810
E-mail: finalfurlong@eircom.net

This immaculate, warm bungalow sits in a tranquil location on the banks of the River Fertha estuary and enjoys lovely views. It is part of a 40-hectare farm with a suckler cowherd and a Sport Horse Enter-prise. Approved riding stables offer beach gallops and horseback rid-ing in secluded areas of the Ring of Kerry. Guests can also view the ruins of the old Union Workhouse, and a detailed history is avail-able. The rooms are immaculately maintained and attractively deco-rated.

Breakfasts are served on a large refectory table in the dining room. Kathleen O'Sullivan is an excellent cook and enjoys chatting with guests and providing information on the area. Her motto is: "You may come as a stranger, but we hope you will leave as a friend." Group rates are available with special offers during May, June, and Septem-ber. Deep-sea angling packages as well as trips to Skellig Rock from a nearby pier are offered.

DIRECTIONS: Situated 1.5 kilometers from Carhirsiveen on the N70

OPEN: April-November 1
ROOMS: 1 double, 1 twin, triple, family, double/single; all en suite

TERMS: from €28-33; single supplement; child reduction

CASTLEGREGORY

The Shores Guest House
Annette O'Mahoney
Cappatigue, Conor Pass Road, Castlegregory, Co. Kerry
Tel: 066 7139196 Fax: 066 7139195
E-mail: theshores@eircom.net
Web site: www.theshorescountryhouse.com

If you are looking for that special place, Shores House will more than satisfy the most discerning traveler. It stands in lovely grounds on the Conor Pass Road, overlooking Brandon Bay. This luxurious, 5-diamond property, offers superb accommodation, yet has an informal, friendly ambience. Annette O'Mahoney extends the warmest of welcomes, and she has deservedly been the recipient of several awards. Everything is first class, such as the spacious individually decorated bedrooms, i.e. The Gothic, Laura Ashley, and the balcony room. All have elegant furniture, attractive fabrics, power showers, and a TV; many rooms have bay views. Annette is a gourmet cook; a sample menu could be baked Brie in filo pastry, wild Atlantic salmon, and rack of lamb. Delicious desserts could include crêpes and ice cream with a butterscotch sauce and toasted almonds.

Dinners must be pre-booked, special diets are catered with advance notice, served in the summer months. Imaginative breakfasts are served in the dining room overlooking the view. There are miles of sandy beaches and scenic walks close by. An apartment on the waters' edge is available for rent. Dingle is 10 miles away. Private parking.

OPEN: February 15-November 15
ROOMS: 6 rooms twin/double; all en suite
TERMS: from €35-48; single supplement; child reduction

CASTLEISLAND

The Gables B&B
Lilian Dillon
Doneen, Limerick Road, Castleisland, Co. Kerry
Tel: 066 7141060
E-mail: ablesdillon@eircom.net

Web site: www.homepage.net/-gablesbnb

The Gables stands in its own grounds in an attractive landscaped garden with panoramic views of the Castleisland Golf Course. Course fees are modest, and your host Lilian Dillon can arrange for times and tours of the area. There are four spotlessly clean ground-floor bedrooms, all with TV, tea maker, and hair dryer. Three are en suite, and the fourth has a private bathroom.

Excellent freshly prepared breakfasts are served in the dining/sitting room, which features fresh fruit and pancakes as well as a cooked variety. There is a small sunroom for guests to relax in and enjoy the views. Lilian is a very thoughtful host, and the ambience is homely and friendly. On chilly nights, a hot water bottle may be found in your bed. Castleisland, which is 2 miles away, has several venues for evening meals. Private parking.

DIRECTIONS: Situated on the N21 Limerick Road

OPEN: all year except Christmas
ROOMS: 4 rooms double/twin; 3 en suite
TERMS: from €32-34; single supplement; child reduction

DINGLE

Cill Bhreac
Angela McCarthy
Milltown, Dingle, Co. Kerry
Tel: 066 9151358
E-mail: info@cillbhreachouse.com
Web site: www.cillbhreachouse.com

An attractive, spacious residence in a tranquil location, Cill Bhreac overlooks Dingle Bay and Mount Brandon. The house is immaculate, tastefully decorated, and well maintained. Rooms are of a good size and are comfortably furnished. The bedrooms are well equipped with tea/coffee makers, TV, clock radio, and hair dryer. All bedrooms have orthopedic beds and electric blankets. Children are welcome, and cots are provided. There is an extensive breakfast menu (special diets can be catered for) prepared fresh daily, including juices, cereals, cooked choices, and brown bread; you won't need lunch.

The conservatory also overlooks the bay and is a perfect spot in which to relax after a busy day of sightseeing. Guests may also have use of the garden. The ambience is friendly and Angela McCarthy is very helpful, providing lots of assistance with what to see in the area. Close by are facilities for angling, golf, horse riding, sailing, and sandy beaches. Several pubs in the area serve food and have traditional Irish music. Irish is spoken.

DIRECTIONS: Coming in to Dingle on the N86, turn left at first roundabout and left at second roundabout, crossing the bridge. Cill Bhreac is the third house on the left.

OPEN: February 15-November 30
ROOMS: 6 double/twin/family; all en suite
TERMS: from €30 (low season); €40 (high season); single supplement; child reduction

Devane's Farmhouse
Mary Devane
Lispole, Dingle, Co. Kerry
Tel: 066915 1418

A warm welcome awaits you in this family-run farmhouse, which also houses a working dairy farm of 16 hectares nestled at the foot of the mountain with beautiful views all around. The farmhouse is very popular with walkers and tourists, as it is situated on the Dingle Way Walk. The bedrooms are clean, if a little small, but the owners are so hospitable, offering tea and home-baked bread and cake to guests, that room size seems unimportant. There is an extra cot available.

The sitting room leads out to the conservatory, which has stunning views of the bay and mountains. Tea and coffee facilities are provided in the dining room, and hair dryers, irons, and a trouser press are available on request. There are several establishments for evening meals in Dingle, which is just 5 kilometers away.

Guests return here year after year, and visitors new to the property sometimes book in for a night and end up staying for a week or more. Guests may use the garden and are welcome to enjoy the daily farm activities, watch the sheep grazing, or walk in this beautiful area. The farmhouse is located on a small side road, but don't give up; just when you think you have passed it, the farm comes into view. Private parking.

OPEN: April 2-November 1
ROOMS: 3 double/twin, 1 family; 3 en suite

TERMS: from €25-35; single supplement; child reduction

Duinin House
Anne Neligan
Conor Pass Road, Dingle, Co. Kerry
Tel: 066 915 1335 Fax: 066 915 1335
E-mail: pandaneligan@eircom.net
Web site: www.homepage.tinet.ie/~pandaneligan

Duinin, meaning "little fort," is a friendly ranch-style bungalow with beautiful views of the sea and mountains. There is a large front garden with a manicured lawn and lots of pretty flowers and shrubs. Guests enjoy tea outside on warm days or in the conservatory overlooking Dingle Harbour and the valley. The comfortable lounge has a VCR that guests may use, plus an additional lounge for reading or just relaxing after a busy day. All of the bedrooms are on the ground floor, have modern furnishings, large fitted wardrobes, and chairs. The front bedrooms have lovely views. The extensive breakfast menu with fresh baked breads is served in the sunny dining room overlooking the harbor. Golf, fishing, boat trips, beaches, hill walking, and excellent pubs and restaurants nearby. Private parking.
DIRECTIONS: Well signposted in Dingle

OPEN: February 1-November 30
ROOMS: 5 double/twin; all en suite
TERMS: from €33-37.50; single supplement

Greenmount House
John and Mary Curran
Gortonora, Dingle, Co. Kerry
Tel: 066 915 1414 Fax: 066 915 1974
E-mail: mary@greenmount-house.com
Web site: www.greenmount-house.com

Greenmount House, also known as Curran's Bed and Breakfast, stands on an elevated site overlooking Dingle town and the harbor. The wonderful breakfast feasts are a special feature; guests help themselves from an enormous buffet, with choice of fruits, cereals, home-baked breads, muffins, fresh juices, puddings, and other delights, followed by tasty omelets or a traditional Irish breakfast. An added bonus is that it is served in a lovely conservatory/dining room that overlooks the bay. Little wonder the establishment was awarded the Certification of Merit Award.

The rooms are upgraded continually and are tastefully decorated with warm autumn colors in Laura Ashley designs. Rooms have refrigerators and a direct dial telephone. There are seven superior suites and five charming bedrooms. Each suite has a full bathroom, large sitting area, and sea views. There are two lounges for guests' use. The house is maintained beautifully, and John and Mary Curran have been in business for over 25 years. They are from local, long-established families and provide guests with an unlimited amount of knowledge on the area. Plenty of written information is provided. Local amenities include golf, fishing, horse riding, and trips to see Fungi the Dolphin, whom you might even see from your bedroom window.

DIRECTIONS: Well signposted in Dingle

OPEN: February-November
ROOMS: 12 double/twin/family; all en suite
TERMS: from €50-60; single supplement; child reduction

The Lighthouse
Mary and Denis Murphy
High Road, Ballinaboula, Dingle, Co. Kerry
Tel: 066 915 1829
E-mail: info@lighthousedingle.com
Web site: www.lighthousedingle.com

This pleasant two-story spacious house stands in its own grounds overlooking Dingle Harbour. A galleried landing and a pine staircase lead to the spacious bedrooms, all of which have bath/shower combinations; one is on the ground floor. Bedrooms are bright and fresh; they are furnished with pine and have bright, colorful duvets. The lounge and dining room overlook the view.

Breakfast only is served at the Lighthouse, but there are several choices for evening meals in Dingle within walking distance. The Lighthouse offers a high standard of accommodation. Mary Murphy is very helpful indeed, with information for visitors on attractions in this scenic area.

DIRECTIONS: To locate, drive up Main Street to town outskirts, house is on the right

OPEN: February 1-November 30
ROOMS: 1 double, 4 double/single; all en suite
TERMS: from €32.50-40; single supplement

Milltown House
Mark, Anne, and Tara Kerry
Dingle, Co. Kerry
Tel: 66 9151372
E-mail: milltown@indigo.com
Web site: www.milltownhousedingle.com

Milltown House is a charming period house, with views over Dingle Harbour and the golf course. The house is beautifully maintained, elegantly furnished, and offers guests every modern comfort. The tastefully decorated spacious bedrooms, most with coronets, are equipped with direct dial telephones, hair dryer, and a hospitality tray. A superb buffet breakfast, served in the conservatory, includes three choices of home-baked bread, wild honey pancakes, homemade preserves, fruits, etc., plus a full Irish breakfast. Vegetarians are well catered for.

The in-house movie channel features Irish made or Ireland-related movies, including *Ryan's Daughter, Far and Away, Into the West,* and *The Quiet Man.* Robert Mitchum and his family lived in the house while filming *The Quiet Man.*

Milltown House is the recipient of many awards, including a 5-diamond rating, Warm Welcome Award, and the Sparkling Diamond Award.This bed and breakfast would be an excellent choice to stay while exploring this fascinating area.

The Kerrys have a long tradition in the hospitality business and offer guidance on local touring. There are lots of activities close by, including a golf driving range.

DIRECTIONS: Well signposted in Dingle

OPEN: May through October
ROOMS: 9 rooms double/family; all en suite
TERMS: from €65-80; single supplement; child reduction

GLENBEIGH

Mountain View
Anne O'Riordan
Mountain Stage, Glenbeigh, Co. Kerry

Tel: 066 9768541 Fax: 066 976 9768541
E-mail: mountainstage@eircom.net

This yellow bungalow lives up to its name; the setting is spectacular—it stands in an elevated position with magnificent views all round. Bedrooms are colorful and immaculately maintained; three are on the ground floor. The TV lounge overlooks the view. Tasty breakfasts are served in the bright dining room. Owner Anne O'Riordan, a very helpful, accommodating lady, has been in business for five years. Lassie, the sweet collie, is friendly, fitting the quiet, peaceful location.

Safe, sandy beaches 10 kilometers long are only 2 kilometers away, and there are mountains and hill walks, fishing, and horseback riding in the area. The Kerry Way Walk is close by.

DIRECTIONS: Well signposted on the Ring of Kerry

OPEN: April 1-October 31
ROOMS: 2 double, 2 single; all en suite
TERMS: from €35; single supplement; child reduction

Ocean Wave
Noreen O'Toole
Glenbeigh, Co. Kerry
Tel: 066 97 68249 Fax: 066 97 68412
E-mail: oceanwave@iol.ie

Ocean Wave, a luxurious property, stands in a superb location, behind a landscaped garden. It is located on the Ring of Kerry and has wonderful views of Dingle Bay and the mountains. This peaceful haven has the added bonus of the delightful owner, Noreen O'Toole. Noreen has been in business for over 30 years; just about everything has been thought of for her guest's comfort. Her flair for décor and style is evident throughout the house. There are many items of interest, including paintings, photographs, a beautiful chandelier, a mirrored ceiling, and a chess set.

The house is elegantly furnished; the individually decorated large bedrooms, three of which have a Jacuzzi, have rich linens and drapes and coronets made by Noreen. All are en suite and have a TV. The first-floor sitting room is a recommended spot after a busy day of sightseeing; there is also a small balcony. Most rooms have bay views. There is an extensive breakfast menu served in the bright dining room, complete with linen table clothes and napkins. Private parking.

DIRECTIONS: Well signposted on the Ring of Kerry

OPEN: March-October
ROOMS: 3 rooms; all en-suite
TERMS: from €35.00; single supplement; child reduction

GLENCAR

Blackstone House
Breda Breen
Blackstone Bridge, Glencar, Co. Kerry
Tel: 066 976 0164 Fax: 066 976 0164

This spacious, award-winning, old-style farmhouse is situated at the foot of Carrantuohill, Ireland's highest mountain, beside Blackstone Bridge, Licken Wood, overlooking the Caragh River. Walkers will be interested to know it is on the Kerry Way Walk. The clean and cozy bedrooms, which have floral fabrics and pine furniture, are in the oldest part of the house. The sitting room has antique pine furniture and comfortable easy chairs. Breakfast and pre-arranged four-course evening meals are served; wild salmon and home-produced lamb are often on the menu. Special dietary requirements may be met, if pre-arranged. Self-catering is available.

The house has a wine license. The setting is superb, and kindly Breda Breen makes guests feel immediately at home. She offers a hot drink upon arrival. The perfect spot for nature lovers, outdoor activities include nature walks (guides can be arranged), mountain and hill walking, fishing, rock climbing, and canoeing. Also of interest are the ruins of an old smelting works, which can be seen in Blackstone.

DIRECTIONS: Well signposted on the Kerry Way Walk

OPEN: April 1-October 31
ROOMS: 1 double, 2 twin, 2 family, 1 single; 5 en suite
TERMS: from €33-45; single supplement; child reduction

KELLS

Glenville Farmhouse
Marion O'Grady
Gleesk, Kells, Co. Kerry

Tel: 066 947 7625 Fax: 066 947 7625
E-mail: glenvillefarmhouse@eircom.net

Situated in a delightful position, midway between Glenbeigh and Cahirsiveen on the main Ring of Kerry Road, Glenville is a spacious new country house with panoramic views of Dingle Bay. The rooms are well appointed with an attractive bright décor. There is a comfortable TV lounge. Tasty breakfasts are served in the dining room that overlooks the bay and the mountains. For evening meals, the Thatch Tavern, which is very close by, serves a good pint of Guinness®, and there is dancing and good craic. A restaurant is within a 5-minute drive.

There is hill walking on the farm, and fishing trips on Skellig Bay can be arranged. The famous 18-hole champion course at Waterville is just 19 kilometers away.

Transfers can be arranged from the airport or train station, and group or individual tours can be arranged if required.

DIRECTIONS: Well signposted between Glenbeigh and Cahirsiveen

OPEN: April 1-October 31
ROOMS: 1 double, 2 twin, 1 family; 3 en suite
TERMS: from €45; single supplement; child reduction

KENMARE

Ardmore House
Tom O'Connor
Killarney Road, Kenmare, Co. Kerry
Tel: 064 41406 Fax: 064 4140

This luxurious farmhouse is set in beautiful, scenic countryside overlooking the sea. It is warm and inviting, and guests are assured of true Irish hospitality. The immaculate bedrooms are well decorated and have comfortable beds. There are two lounges, one with a TV and an open fire, and one quiet lounge for chatting and/or reading.

Lake and deep-sea angling, pony trekking, and beautiful walks are all available in the area. Kenmare golf course is within $^1/_2$ mile of the house. Scenic farm walks to the cliff and picnic area can also be taken. Private parking.

DIRECTIONS: Situated $^1/_2$ mile from the famous Kenmare golf course

OPEN: March 1-November 30
ROOMS: 2 double, 1 twin, 3 double/single; all en suite
TERMS: from €45; single supplement; child reduction

Muxnaw Lodge
Hannah Boland
Castletownbere Road, Kenmare, Co. Kerry
Tel: 064 41252
E-mail: muxnawlodge@eircom.net
Web site: www.neidin.net

This interesting eighteenth-century house, set in 1.5 hectares of beautiful landscaped grounds, enjoys a lovely position. The house has an informal lived-in atmosphere and is decorated with Laura Ashley wallpaper, a Waterford Crystal chandelier, antique furnishings, and many items of interest. The comfortable TV lounge has the original fireplace and window shutters.

The spacious bedrooms are refurbished in keeping with the character of the house, which has lovely views, original fireplaces, and antique furniture; one bedroom has a brass bed. Telephones are available on request. The all-weather tennis court is available for use by the guests.

This is a wonderful base for touring this beautiful area. A pleasant 10-minute stroll over the bridge takes you into town. Private parking.

DIRECTIONS: On Castletownberehaven Road, within walking distance of town

OPEN: all year
ROOMS: 3 double, 2 twin; all en suite
TERMS: from €45; single supplement; child reduction

O'Donnells of Ashgrove
Lynn O'Donnell
Ashgrove, Kenmare, Co. Kerry
Tel/Fax: 064 41228
E-mail: odonnellsofashgrove@hotmail.com

O'Donnells of Ashgrove is a charming peaceful house set in tranquil surroundings of woodlands, with a view of the Caha Mountains. Lynne O'Donnell is a friendly lady who welcomes guests in her home as friends. She is also a talented artist. Several examples of her work are on display, and there are plans to open an art gallery on the property. In the evening, guests are welcome to relax in the armchairs in front of the fire, or if preferred, to join their family in the spacious furnished TV lounge. There are many antique pieces around, and the house is tastefully furnished. Breakfasts are served in the Jacobean-style dining room with its exposed beams, stone fireplace, and log fire. Guests are encouraged to feel like part of the family. There is a guest sitting room, furnished with a TV and plenty of books. Not suitable for babies or children. Of special interest are Kenmare town, the stone circle, and sea trips around Kenmare Bay. German is spoken. Private parking.

DIRECTIONS: A little tricky to find, phone for directions

OPEN: Easter-October
ROOMS: 1 double/1 twin, 1 en suite; 1 private bath
TERMS: from €36; single supplement

Oldchurch House

Helen McMonigle
Killowen, Kenmare, Co. Kerry
Tel: 064 42054
E-mail: oldchurchkenmare@hotmail.com
Web site: www.kenmare.net/oldchurch/

Close to the town center, situated in a peaceful spot, Oldchurch House is an immaculate, modern spacious house. It has lovely views of the River Sheen, the mountains, and the Kenmare Golf Course. Owner Helen McMonigle, a pleasant lady and talented artist, extends a real Irish welcome, nothing is too much trouble; she enjoys her guests and is happy to assist in every way. She loves to garden and sing, and her paintings are on display around the house. She offers a hot drink and biscuits to guests on arrival.

The entry way has black-and-white tile, and the house is maintained to a high standard.

The four pleasantly decorated bedrooms have en-suite bathrooms, pine furniture, and pretty duvets. There is one ground floor room. All bedrooms have a TV. Guests are welcome to enjoy the garden, which overlooks the thirteenth hole of Kenmare Golf Course. The pleasant lounge has an open fire, and there is a patio and barbeque for guests' use. Private parking.

DIRECTIONS: Well signposted as you approach Kenmare

OPEN: February 1-October 31
ROOMS: 4 rooms double/family/twin; all en suite
TERMS: from €30-35; single supplement; child reduction

Whispering Pines
Mary and John Fitzgerald
Bell Heights, Kenmare, Kerry
Tel: 064 41194 Fax: 064 40813
E-mail: wpines@eircom.net

Whispering Pines is a delightful place to stay, located a 3-minute walk from the town center and a 5-minute walk from the golf course. This modernized period home, with its delightful garden, is set back off the road in quiet and peaceful surroundings. The bedrooms are attractively decorated with matching fabrics and duvets. The charming owners John and Mary Fitzgerald make this a wonderful place to stay; fresh-baked scones and tea are offered on arrival. They are happy to give advice on what to see in the area; this is an ideal location for touring the scenic Ring of Kerry. Several venues for evening meals are within walking distance.
  DIRECTIONS: Well signposted in Kenmare

OPEN: March 1-November 1
ROOMS: 2 double, 2 twin, family; all en suite
TERMS: from €40; single supplement; child reduction

KERRY

Abbey Lodge
John King
Muckross Road, Killarney, Co. Kerry
Tel: 064 34193 Fax: 064 35872
E-mail: abbeylodge@eircom.net
Web site: www.abbey-lodge.com

Abbey Lodge is an attractive building with a stone and brick exterior. It stands in its own grounds and is a 3-minute walk from the town center. The rooms are of a good size, furnished, and decorated to a high standard. John King was formerly in the contracting business and has made creative use of church window supports in two of the bedrooms, most of which have orthopedic mattresses. One bedroom is suitable for disabled visitors. Several rooms have a bath/shower combination. There are several antique pieces of furniture; of special interest are the American oak floors. Throughout the house is a mini art gallery featuring a fine display of prints by the artist William Frandison—John King is constantly adding new prints and paintings to his collection.

This charming property, with its attentive host, has all the facilities of a 4-star hotel. Guests would be well advised to leave their car in the parking lot and walk into town. The guest sitting room has a fire when chilly and a good selection of books. Popular with business people and tourists, this property would be an excellent choice when visiting the Killarney area. Sightseeing tours can be arranged and nearby facilities include golf and horse riding.

DIRECTIONS: Situated in Killarney town

OPEN: all year, except for Christmas
ROOMS: 5 en suite
TERMS: from €60; child reduction; single supplement

KILLARNEY

Carriglea House
The Beazley Family
Muckross Road, Killarney, Co. Kerry
Tel: 064 31116 Fax: 064 437693
E-mail: carriglea@oceanfree.net
Web site: www.carrigleahouse.com

An impressive, Victorian house, Carriglea House is in an elevated position and surrounded by 30 acres of grounds. It is adjacent to a beautiful 10,000-acre national park, within a short drive of Muckross House, and 5 minutes to Killarney. The good-size bedrooms have pine furniture, a bright and tasteful décor, and comfortable beds. Some rooms have a bath and shower. The family room has two double beds, and one room has its own balcony. The Beazleys, a friendly, young couple, have lovely daughters and take pride in their business. It was established as a bed and breakfast in 1932 and has been family run since that time. The comfortable lounge has an original fireplace. Guests will enjoy the peaceful ambience found here and the excellent breakfast provided by the Beazleys. There are four additional rooms in the carriage house, all with their own sitting room.

DIRECTIONS: Easily located off the N71 from Killarney

OPEN: April-November
ROOMS: 8 rooms double/twin/family; all en suite
TERMS: from €34-40; single supplement; child reduction

Kathleen's Country Guest House

Kathleen Sheppard
Tralee Road, Killarney, Co. Kerry
Tel: 064 32810 Fax: 064 32450
E-mail: info@kathleens.net
Web site: www.kathleens.net

Kathleen's Country House is a delightful, family run guesthouse where traditional hospitality and courteous personal attention are assured. The house stands in 3 acres of mature gardens, 1 kilometer from Killarney. It is beautifully maintained and very tastefully decorated; improvements to this immaculate property are ongoing. Kathleen Sheppard's love of art reflects the décor; there is a splendid array of original oil and watercolor paintings, and inspirational verse decorates the walls. The well-appointed bedrooms are elegantly furnished in antique pine and orthopedic beds. Breakfasts only are served in the spacious dining room overlooking the garden. Kathleen's comprises the facilities of a 5-star hotel with the comforts and warmth of an Irish home. Children over two years welcome. Wine license. The house motto of "easy to get to, hard to leave" is endorsed by the many repeat visitors who enjoy the traditional hospitality.

There are three 18-hole golf courses, plus two 9-hole courses within a five-minute drive. Special group rates on request. Private parking.

DIRECTIONS: Well signposted on Tralee Road coming into Killarney

OPEN: March 17-November
ROOMS: 19 rooms double/twin/family; all en suite
TERMS: from €50-70; single supplement; child reduction

The 19th Green Guest House and Restaurant

John and Freda Sheehan
Lackabane, Fossa, Killarney, Co. Kerry

Tel: 064 32868 Fax: 064 32637
E-mail: 19thgreen@eircom.net
Web site: www.19thgreen-bb.com

The 19th Green is an immaculate, well-maintained property situated in quiet and peaceful countryside and just a 5-minute drive from Killorglin and Ring of Kerry Road. Owners John and Freda Sheehan maintain high standards. The large bedrooms are tastefully decorated with comfortable beds; one room is suitable for disabled visitors. The ground floor has been extensively refurbished. The spacious lounge has an open fire in a stone fireplace and overlooks the mountains.

Situated across the road are Killarney's two 18-hole championship courses, sited in mature woodlands. Tee times can be arranged, which is part of the service extended by the accommodating owners. Tours can also be arranged for the Ring of Kerry, Dingle Peninsula, Blarney Castle, etc. The Sheehans are proud of the personal attention guests receive here and make every effort to ensure that guests feel welcome and comfortable. They are pleased to offer advice on the wide range of restaurants in Killarney. The property is not suitable for children.

DIRECTIONS: 5-minute drive from Killorglin and Ring of Kerry Road

OPEN: March 17-November 30
ROOMS: 14 double/twin/family; all en suite
TERMS: from €60; single supplement; child reduction

Knockcullen
Marie O'Brien
New Road, Killarney, Co. Kerry
Tel: 064 33915
E-mail: knockcullen@hotmail.com

Knockcullen, which means hill on top, is an immaculate family home in a private location off the main road, situated only a 2-minute walk from town and the National Park. Marie O'Brien has been in business for over 20 years, and is as enthusiastic as when she started. The rooms are spotlessly clean, are of a good size, and have en-suite facilities. There is a guest lounge with a TV. The house is an ideal touring base for this scenic area. Breakfasts only are served, but there are lots of good pubs and restaurants close by. Marie is interested in walking and mountain climbing and is pleased to assist guests with information and/or planned itineraries. There are landscaped gardens and private parking. From the house, it is 2 minutes to the town center and 5 minutes to bus and railway station.

OPEN: all year
ROOMS: 5 double/twin; all en suite
TERMS: from €30.00; single supplement; child reduction

KILLORGLIN

Grove Lodge
Fergus and Delia Foley
Killorglin, Co. Kerry
Tel: 066 9761157 Fax: 066 9762330
E-mail: info@grovelodge.com
Web site: www.grovelodge.com

This gracious country house stands in 1.2 hectares of beautiful mature gardens and woodlands on the banks of the River Laun and has south-facing views of the Mcgillycuddy Reeks Mountains. The rooms are spacious, and the reception lounge has a restored antique cast iron fireplace. The luxurious bedrooms are tastefully appointed, each have coordinated floral bedding and curtains (one has a lace canopied four-poster bed), and four have balconies. The lodge is delightful in every way; it has high ceilings, a galleried landing, a colorful patio area, and a conservatory. Breakfasts are excellent; guests can help themselves to yogurt, cereal, fruit, and juices, followed by pancakes or a traditional breakfast. Grove Lodge is a superb place to stay when visiting this beautiful region of Ireland. The location is idyllic, it is peaceful and quiet above, and the welcome is wonderful. Blennerville Windmill Centre, Craig Cave, and Killorglin Golf Course are all within driving distance. Private parking.
DIRECTIONS: Well signposted in Killorglin

OPEN: all year, except Christmas
ROOMS: 10 rooms double/twin/family; all en suite
TERMS: from €45-60; single supplement; child reduction

LISPOLE

Hands Dunroman
Noeline Hands
Main Tralee Road, Lispole, Co. Kerry

Tel: 066 9151049
E-mail: info@dunroman.com
Web site: www.dunroman.com

This welcoming and attractive white guesthouse, with views of Conor Mountain, is situated on the Tralee to Dingle Road. There are three very large rooms all with pine wood floors, en-suite facilities, and a TV. There is a guest and games room. This is a "child friendly" house, and the greeting is warm and welcoming. A hot drink and home baking is offered on arrival. Boat trips can be arranged, and Dingle town, restaurants, fishing, and golf are a few minutes away. Private car parking.
    DIRECTIONS: Situated on the Tralee to Dingle Road

OPEN: March-October
ROOMS: double, twin, triple, family
TERMS: from €30-35; single supplement; child reduction

SNEEM

Derry East Farmhouse
Mary and John Teahan
Sneem, Co. Kerry
Tel: 064 45193 Fax: 064 45193
E-mail: teahans@eircom.net
Web site: www.sneem.com/derryeast.html

Derry East is a working beef farm. This is a botanists paradise, with its wild mountain landscape background. The property has its own hard tennis court and a private fish pond stocked with trout. Guests are welcome to use the facilities and to take farm walks. The bedrooms are warm and comfortable, and the bright colorful dining room offers views from all windows.
    Derry East is an ideal spot for a relaxing holiday. Mrs. Teahan is a caring and considerate host, offering guests a truly warm welcome, and is ably assisted in the summer by her children, who are happy to play Irish music for her guests. Private parking.
    DIRECTIONS: Well signposted on the Ring of Kerry

OPEN: April 1-October 31
ROOMS: 1 double, 2 twin, 1 family; all en suite
TERMS: from €35; single supplement; child reduction

Hillside Haven
Helen Foley
Tahilla, Sneem, Co. Kerry
Tel: 064 82065 Fax: 064 82065
E-mail: hillsidehaven@eircom.net

This country house stands in an elevated position set in mature gardens with a magnificent view of the sea, mountains, and glorious countryside. The bedrooms, all on the ground floor, are spotlessly clean and comfortable. All have en-suite bathrooms and a TV.

This is very much a family-run establishment with traditional hospitality and friendly, accommodating owners. Breakfasts are served in the dining room, or, if guests prefer, outside in good weather. A lounge is available to guests.

Walking is one of Helen Foley's hobbies, and she would be pleased to arrange walking holidays for small groups and to outline local walks for individual walkers. Complimentary tea and coffee is available at any time. Light snacks available on request.

DIRECTIONS: Well signposted on the Ring of Kerry

OPEN: May 1-September 30
ROOMS: double, twin, family; all en suite
TERMS: from €35; single supplement; child reduction

Old Convent House
Alice O'Sullivan
Pier Road, Sneem, Co. Kerry
Tel: 064 451 45181
E-mail: conventhouse@oceanfree.net
Web site: www.conventhousesneem.com

Visitors enjoy the Old World atmosphere at the Old Convent House, which is set in its own grounds on the banks of the River Ardsheelaun. The house was built in the middle of the last century as a school for the Presentation nuns, who taught in the local school until 1891. Since that time, it has been in the hands of the O'Sullivan family, who have been careful to preserve the character of the house while offering modern comforts. There are two lounges available to guests.

Tea, coffee, and biscuits are available at all times in the dining room. Upgrades are ongoing; the bathrooms have been enlarged, power showers installed, carpets replaced, and the interior freshly painted. Guests are welcome to make use of the large gardens, and there is access to the river. Fishing enthusiasts may take trips on the Bay from Oysterhead Pier, and Sneem, with its gaily painted houses, is just a pleasant 3-minute stroll away. Alice O'Sullivan is an enthusiastic walker and can provide walking maps and itineraries. Private parking.

DIRECTIONS: Well signposted on the Ring of Kerry

OPEN: November 1-March 15
ROOMS: 5 rooms double/twin/family; all en suite
TERMS: from €30-35; single supplement; child reduction

TRALEE

Ballingowan House
Sheila Kerins
Mile Height, Killarney Road, Tralee, Co. Kerry
Tel: 066 7127150 Fax: 066 7120325
E-mail: ballingowan@eircom.net

This impressive red brick property stands in its own grounds with plenty of parking. The large bedrooms are all en suite, have colorful throws, a TV, and hospitality trays. A pleasant sitting room has comfortable leather furniture, TV/Video, family portraits, and a real fire for chilly evenings. The dining room has an unusual sideboard, and breakfasts are served at separate tables.

The house is bright and clean, with lots of pine doors, and is well maintained. Sheila Kerins enjoys her business and has lots of happy returning guests.

DIRECTIONS: Situated on the Killarney Road to Tralee

OPEN: April 17-September 30
ROOMS: 4 double/family/single; all en suite
TERMS: from €35; single supplement; child reduction

Castlemorris House
Ciarad and Tony Fields
Ballymullen, Tralee, Co. Kerry
Tel: 066 718 0060 Fax: 066 712 6007
E-mail: castlemorris@eircom.net
Web site: www.castlemorrishouse.com

Castlemorris House, a beautiful ivy-clad Victorian house, stands in its own grounds on the edge of town. Built in 1870 by the local regiment of the British Army, the house was used by the commanding officer as his private residence. The house was purchased in 1997 and was recently sold to the new owners Ciarad and Tony Fields. The house was lovingly restored, carefully combining Old World charm with modern comforts. Many original features remain, such as stained glass windows and casement shutters. The coving and fireplace were removed and reinserted after restoration.

A warm and simple elegance pervades, and the ambience is unpretentious. The spacious bedrooms, three with original fireplaces, have king-size beds and are furnished in keeping with the character of the house; two have sloping ceilings and oak beams. The peaceful drawing room has an open fire, which is lit at the first sign of a chill in the air.

There is plenty to interest the visitor, including Samsa Tire (the National Folk Theatre); Irish music can be heard at local pubs. Private parking.

DIRECTIONS: A little tricky to find—take N21 from Limerick, left at the roundabout signed Dingle/Killorglin, $1/4$ mile to a T-junction, take a right. The house is immediately on the right.

OPEN: January 1-December 20
ROOMS: 6 rooms double/twin/family
TERMS: from €40-45; single supplement; child reduction

COUNTY WATERFORD

Waterford is probably best known for its crystal factory, which has regular hours for visits. Situated in the southeast of the country, it is reputedly one of the sunniest spots in Ireland. Waterford has a pretty coastline and more rugged interior, with good farmland. The Nire Vally is good for walking and pony trekking and has wonderful views.

Waterford city has much of interest to visit: Reginald's Tower, a massive circular fortress, is now the civic museum; Christ Church Cathedral, built in 1779; the French church; the Chamber of Commerce, a lovely Georgian building; and the City Hall, which houses two old theaters. All sites are worth seeing. The International Festival of Light Opera is held in Waterford in September.

Dunmore East, Tramore, Annestown, and Dungarvan are all pleasant seaside spots, particularly Dunmore East, which resembles a Devon fishing village. Further south is the Irish-speaking village of Ring, where Irish scholars go to study. St. Declan's Oratory, built in the ninth century, and St. Declan's Well and Temple Disert can be found at Ardmore. The cathedral dates back to the twelfth century and is known for its sculptured figures.

Seven kilometers from Cappoquin is the Cistercian Abbey of Mount Melleray. The Abbey maintains the tradition of monastic hospitality, so it is quite in order to accept a meal if it is offered.

Lismore, in former times a great center of learning, was built by King John in 1185 and once belonged to Sir Walter Raleigh. The gardens are open to the public. The medieval Cathedral of St. Cathach is most attractive and was restored in 1633.

ARDMORE

Ardsallagh Lodge
Elizabeth Kee
Ardsallagh Lodge, Ardmore, Co. Waterford
Tel/Fax: 024 93496

E-mail: ardsallaghlodge@eircom.net
Web site: www.waterfordhouseireland.com/

Ardsallagh Lodge stands in a commanding position above the River Blackwater, with wonderful views over the mouth of the river to the sea. The house was acquired in 2004 and has undergone extensive refurbishment. Nearby, visitors can fish, hill walk, and enjoy coastal drives.

DIRECTIONS: From the N25, take a very small road to the west just before the River Blackwater Bridge, on the east side

OPEN: all year
ROOMS: 4 double, 1 twin; all en suite
TERMS: from €45; single supplement

BALLYMACARBRY

Cnoc-na-Ri Country Home
Richard and Nora Harte
Nire Valley, Ballymacarbry, Co. Waterford
Tel: 052 36239, 087 9477143
E-mail: richardharte@eircom.net
Web site: homepage.eircom.net/~cnocnaricountryhome/

Cnoc-na-Ri, meaning "hill of the kings," is a small country home set in a peaceful, quiet spot in the Comeraghs in the heart of the Nire Valley. It has a welcoming, friendly atmosphere and lovely views. Richard and Nora added a wing to their house especially to cater to visitors. The rooms are very comfortable, well equipped, and two have views. One bedroom has a Jacuzzi bath. Nora, an excellent cook, provides a wide menu for breakfast. This meal is served at separate tables in the dining room, which overlooks the nicely landscaped garden and patio. The patio is a lovely place to sit and absorb the peace that surrounds Cnoc-na-Ri.

Richard and Nora Harte can provide walking maps and packed lunches, and if needed, a local guide is available. Golf, riding, and fishing are also popular pastimes in this area, and traditional music and dance usually can be found in one of the local pubs.

DIRECTIONS: 5 kilometers from Ballymacarbry

OPEN: February 1-November 1
ROOMS: 1 double, 1 twin, 2 family; all en suite

TERMS: from €45; single supplement; child reduction

Glasha Farmhouse
Paddy and Olive O'Gorman
Nire Valley, Ballymacarbry, Co. Waterford
Tel: 052 36108
E-mail: glasha@eircom.net
Web site: www.glashafarmhouse.com

Glasha Farmhouse has won many accolades for its hospitality and quality of accommodation, and it is a large whitewashed building run by enthusiastic, outgoing Olive O'Gorman.

Over the years, the O'Gormans refurbished the old farmhouse and today there are eight en-suite bedrooms of different sizes and designs, all equipped with every possible amenity. Some rooms have Jacuzzi baths, and two are spacious attic-type rooms decorated in bright colors.

Guests have use of an enormous sitting room and sit at separate tables in the dining room. A newer conservatory overlooks the patio area, resplendent with an elaborate fountain and potted plants. The dairy farm stretches around the house. Many rooms have views of the Knockmealdown and Comeragh Mountains. Olive is a great cook and provides dinners by arrangement. The property stretches down to the River Nire, where guests like to fish, and the nearest pub is only a 3-minute walk away.

The Munster Way passes close by, and the nearby mountains are a great place for hill walking. Packed lunches can be provided, and a guide can be made available for those wishing to venture off the beaten track.

DIRECTIONS: Glasha Farmhouse is signposted from Ballymacarbry.

OPEN: closed December
ROOMS: 8 double/twin/family; all en suite
TERMS: from €50; single supplement; child reduction
MEALS: dinner €40; packed lunches

Hanora's Cottage
Mary Wall
Nire Valley, Ballymacarbry, Co. Waterford
Tel: 052 36134 Fax: 052 36540
E-mail: hanorascottage@eircom.net
Web site: www.hanorascottage.com

An absolute haven of peace and tranquility, Hanora's Cottage nestles

at the foot of the Comeragh Mountains, beside the Nire Church and the old schoolhouse, with the Nire River running alongside. The little cottage was built for Seamus Wall's great grandparents in the late 1800s, and Seamus and Mary, the fourth generation of the family, came to live there in 1967 while it was still a two-bedroom cottage. It has come a long way since then. Currently the house has ten spacious, very comfortable bedrooms, with every possible amenity, and all have Jacuzzi baths and king-size beds; superior rooms have double tubs.

Breakfasts at Hanora's are quite a feast. There is an exotic array of fruits and Mary's special porridge, local cheeses, smoked salmon, and a choice of cooked breakfasts. There are a variety of activities for guests—guided or do it yourself walks both strenuous and gentle in the Comeragh Mountains as well as golf and bicycling. After working off breakfast, guests can look forward to Eoin and Judith Wall's dinner. Eoin, Mary's son, trained at Ballymaloe Cookery School and has worked in some renowned restaurants. Later in the evening, join the locals at one of the pubs for traditional music, singing, and dancing.

DIRECTIONS: The house is signposted at Ballymacarbry and is beside the Nire Church by the river.

OPEN: closed for Christmas
ROOMS: 6 double, 4 twin; all en suite
TERMS: from €85; single supplement; not suitable for children
MEALS: dinner €50

CAPPOQUIN

Richmond House
Paul and Claire Deevy
Cappoquin, Co. Waterford
Tel: 058 54278 Fax: 058 54988
E-mail: info@richmondhouse.net
Web site: www.richmondhouse.net

This substantial house was built in 1704 by the Earl of Cork and Burlington and stands in well-maintained parkland. It is a peaceful, comfortable country house, beautifully furnished, and decorated with spacious, bright rooms. Paul Deevy trained as a chef at Ballymaloe, and the restaurant at Richmond House has won several awards for the excellence of its cuisine. Dinner is served in two elegant dining rooms, which are also open to non-residents, and there is a full bar license. Guests have use of two sitting rooms and a conservatory overlooking the garden. The comfortable bedrooms are furnished in keeping with the style of the house. Arrangements can be made for salmon fishing on the Blackwater, and trout fishing on the Blackwater, Suir, and the Bride. Deep sea and coarse fishing are also available. Other amenities nearby include pony trekking, walking, mountain rambling, and golf.

DIRECTIONS: Richmond House is ¹/₂ mile outside Cappoquin on the N72.

OPEN: closed for Christmas and New Year
ROOMS: 6 double, 1 family, 2 single; all en suite
TERMS: from €75; single supplement; child reduction
MEALS: dinner €55 or à la carte

DUNGARVAN

Gortnadiha Lodge
Eileen Harty
Gortnadiha, Dungarvan, Co. Waterford
Tel: 058 46142
E-mail: gortnadihalodge@eircom.net
Web site: www.gortnadihalodge.com

Guests will appreciate old-fashioned hospitality at Gortnadiha Lodge, which has been in the Harty family for several generations. Tom and Eileen Harty have relocated their bed and breakfast from Gortnadiha House to the next-door lodge after some ten years. The lodge, which is surrounded by woodland on an elevated site, has panoramic views of Dungarvan Bay. Gortnadiha Lodge is traditionally and comfortably furnished. The soaps provided are locally made, and until recently, the 300-acre dairy farm made Irish farmhouse cheese.

DIRECTIONS: 3 kilometers from Dungarvan, signposted off the main N25 between Dungarvan and Youghal

OPEN: all year

ROOMS: 2 double, 1 twin; all en suite
TERMS: €45; single supplement; child reduction

Powersfield House
Eunice and Edmund Power
Ballinamuck West, Dungarvan, Co. Waterford
Tel: 058 45594
E-mail: eunice@powersfield.com
Web site: www.powersfield.com

Eunice Power trained in the hotel business in Switzerland, came home, and married a farmer. With three small children, she and Edmund needed to build a house, so they decided to incorporate a family home with a guesthouse. The home they built, finished in 2001, is a classical looking building in the Georgian style, about a mile from Dungarvan. Some land surrounds the house, but most of the dairy and beef farm is a short distance away. Eunice is a bundle of energy and has a love for what she's doing. She is a first-class cook, teaches cookery classes at the house, and has a busy outside catering business. The garden provides organic vegetables for the kitchen. The house is attractively furnished, the décor bright and simple, and the walls adorned with pictures by local artists. The ground-floor bedroom is suitable for wheelchair access.
　　DIRECTIONS: 1 mile from Dungarvan, just off the Clonmel road

OPEN: closed for Christmas
ROOMS: 4 double, 1 twin, all en suite
TERMS: from €55; single supplement; child reduction
MEALS: dinner €27.50, bookable in advance

The Castle Farm
Joan Nugent
Cappagh, Dungarvan, Co. Waterford
Tel: 058 68049
E-mail: castlefm@iol.ie
Web site: www.castlecountryhouse.com

Mountain Castle was the principal seat of the McGraths of Sliabh gCua, one of the two Gaelic families that owned land in this country before the arrival of Cromwell. The accommodation is in a restored wing of the fifteenth-century castle, which stands in lovely countryside with fine views. The oldest section, with the original archway, contains the attractive, long, narrow dining room with its 1.25-meter thick stone walls.

Joan Nugent is a very friendly, welcoming lady and has tastefully decorated and furnished the house. It is very comfortable and has a welcoming sitting room where tea and scones are served on arrival. Dinner is available on request, featuring fruit, vegetables, herbs, and meats from the family farm, and at breakfast, guests are served farm milk and homemade jam.

There are walks through the acre and a half of gardens and fishing on the River Finisk, which flows through the farm. The farmhouse is set on 49 hectares of dairy land, and organized farm groups are accepted.

DIRECTIONS: Castle Farm is signposted at the N72 and R671.

OPEN: April 1-November 4
ROOMS: 2 double, 1 twin, 1 family; all en suite
TERMS: from €47; single supplement; child reduction
MEALS: dinner €30

Sliabh gCua Farmhouse

Jim and Breeda Cullinan
Touraneena, Ballinamult, Dungarvan, Co. Waterford
Tel: 058 47120
E-mail: breedacullinan@sliabhgcua.com
Web site: www.sliabhgcua.com

A warm welcome from Breeda Cullinan awaits the visitor to Sliabh gCua—which literally translated means the Mountain of the Chieftain. It is an attractive creeper clad farmhouse, built in the early part of the twentieth century. Lovely gardens surround the house, and beyond is the beef farm. Every one of the comfortable bedrooms enjoys views of the garden and the Comeragh and Knockmealdown Mountains. Guests have a cozy sitting room for their use, and breakfast is served in the pleasant dining room. Wide-planked wooden floors are exposed and overlaid with rugs in much of the house. Sliabh gCua is a good location for touring the Nire Valley, as well as for walking and riding.

DIRECTIONS: The house is signposted off the R672 between Dungarvan and Clonmel, close to the village of Touraneena.

OPEN: April 1-October 31
ROOMS: 2 double, 1 twin, 1 family; all en suite
TERMS: €45; single supplement; child reduction

DUNMORE EAST

Church Villa
Phyllis Lannon
Dunmore East, Co. Waterford
Tel: 051 383390 Fax: 051 383187
E-mail: churchvilla@eircom.net
Web site: www.churchvilla.com

This whitewashed period house, one of a row of cottages opposite the Church of Ireland church and adjacent to the Ship Bar and Restaurant, is right in the center of the attractive village of Dunmore East. The bright bedrooms have been enlarged and redecorated, some retaining their original fireplaces. There is a guest lounge with a TV, and breakfast is served in the conservatory. There are plenty of eating places in Dunmore East, including the restaurant next door. Church Villa is 10 minutes from the beach and fishing harbor and close to the park where there are caves to explore, and bicycles are available for guests to use.
    DIRECTIONS: In Dunmore East

OPEN: closed for Christmas
ROOMS: 2 double, 2 twin, 1 single, 1 family; all en suite
TERMS: from €33; single supplement; child reduction

McAllister's B&B
Carmel McAllister
4 Wellington Terrace, Dunmore East, Co. Waterford
Tel: 051 383035
E-mail: mcallisterbb@hotmail.com
Web site: www.indunmoreeast.com/stay.php

McAllister's is part of a terrace, standing in a commanding position, in the middle of the attractive village of Dunmore East, looking over the harbor and sea. The front patio is a great place on a sunny day to watch the world go by. The house is about 200 years old and has surprisingly large rooms for its style. A previous owner exposed many of the old stone walls and stripped a lot of the woodwork giving the building a somewhat rustic look. The sitting/dining room is particularly large and pleasing, with a low ceiling and nice views. The family room is like an apartment. Every room except one has a sea view. Carmel McAllister is a friendly lady who gives her guests a warm welcome.
    DIRECTIONS: In Dunmore East

OPEN: June-September
ROOMS: 1 double, 1 double/twin, 1 family; all en suite
TERMS: €35; child reduction

STRADBALLY

Park House
Peg Connors
Stradbally, Co. Waterford
Tel/Fax: 051 293185

Park House is approached up a long driveway through its 300 acres of farmland, a kilometer from the charming little village of Stradbally. A most colorful and beautifully kept garden lies to the front of the house, which dates from the 1800s.

Peg Connors has a good sense of humor and likes to keep an orderly and immaculate home. A long, cheerful dining room, where breakfast is served, lies to one side of the hallway, and a matching-size sitting room is on the other side. The bedrooms are attractively and simply furnished, mostly in pine with bright, fresh colors. Beaches and good restaurants are nearby.

DIRECTIONS: 1 kilometer from Stradbally

OPEN: Easter-November
ROOMS: 4 doubles/twins, 1 single; 2 en suite; 1 public bathroom
TERMS: €35; single supplement

TRAMORE

Cliff House
Pat and Hilary O'Sullivan
Cliff Road, Tramore, Co. Waterford
Tel/Fax: 051 381497
E-mail: hilary@cliffhouse.ie
Web site: www.cliffhouse.ie

Cliff House, built by its owners, stands in landscaped gardens overlooking the sea. Pat and Hilary are friendly and welcoming and run the guesthouse in a professional manner. There are two family suites each consisting of two rooms with en-suite bathrooms, and the remaining rooms are well appointed, most having sea views, with two on the ground floor.

The large conservatory overlooks Tramore Bay and is a popular place to relax and have a cup of tea or coffee. The extensive breakfast menu has some interesting options. Cliff House is within walking distance of Tramore Golf Club and the town center and adjacent to the new leisure center. It is a 10-minute drive from the Waterford Glass Factory.

DIRECTIONS: The house is off the R675 as you exit from Tramore to Dungarvan.

OPEN: April 1-October 31
ROOMS: 3 double, 2 twin, 2 family; all en suite
TERMS: €40; single supplement; child reduction

Glenorney by the Sea
Marie Murphy
Newtown Hill, Tramore, Co. Waterford
Tel: 051 381056 Fax: 051 381103
E-mail: glenorney@iol.ie
Web site: www.glenorney.com

This attractive looking house on the edge of Tramore was built 12 years ago and has a nice front garden. It is very well cared for and has good furniture and decorations. The spacious bedrooms are clean and bright and most have a sea view. The nice, bright sitting room has a TV, open fire, piano, and sea views. Double doors lead into the breakfast room, which has separate tables with linen cloths. The sunroom, garden, and patio area are great places to sit and admire the view over Tramore Bay. Glenorney is within walking distance of the Golf Club and beaches.

DIRECTIONS: On the edge of Tramore

OPEN: March 1-November 30
ROOMS: 2 double, 2 twin, 2 family; all en suite
TERMS: €45; single supplement; child reduction

WATERFORD

Blenheim House
Margaret Fitzmaurice
Blenheim Heights, Waterford, Co. Waterford
Tel: 051 874115
E-mail: blenheim@eircom.net
Web site: homepage.eircom.net/-blenheim/

Blenheim House was built in 1763 and stands in 1.5 hectares of grounds including a deer park and children's play area. Most of the bedrooms have the original Georgian fireplaces. The large lounge with an open fire overlooks the grounds. The Waterford Glass Factory is close by, and other local activities include swimming, riding, golf, and fishing.

DIRECTIONS: 5.5 kilometers from the center of Waterford on the Passage East Road, just a 7-minute drive from the ferry

Foxmount Country House

David and Margaret Kent
Passage East Road, Waterford, Co. Waterford
Tel: 051 874308 Fax: 051 854906
E-mail: info@foxmountcountryhouse.com
Web site: www.foxmountcountryhouse.com

This lovely seventeenth-century house is set in attractive countryside surrounded by its 100-hectare farm, run by David Kent and one of his sons, and is approached up a tree-lined drive.

David and Margaret Kent are a most welcoming, friendly couple and have been many years in the bed and breakfast business. The drawing room is very attractive with an open fireplace and is a nice spot to unwind over tea or coffee in front of a warming log fire. Beautifully presented breakfasts are served in the dining room, which overlooks the garden, at separate tables covered in pretty white linen. Margaret is continuously updating the furnishings and décor. Guests are welcome to use the hard tennis court. It is a pleasant stroll to the atmospheric pub under the bridge.

DIRECTIONS: From Waterford, take the Dunmore East Road; after 3 miles take Passage East Road

OPEN: March 10-November 1
ROOMS: 2 double, 2 twin; all en suite
TERMS: €55; single supplement; child reduction

Sion Hill House and Gardens

Antoinette and George Kavanagh
Sion Hill, Waterford, Co. Waterford
Tel: 051 851558 Fax: 051 851678

E-mail: info@sionhillhouse.com
Web site: www.sionhillhouse.com

The house has a fascinating history and a wonderful, charming atmosphere. It stands high above the river Suir overlooking the city of Waterford. It was built about 1730 for the founder of the famous Pope (shipping) family. The present owners, George and Antoinette Kavanagh, are most delightful and attentive hosts and enjoy relating interesting stories of the house and gardens.

Sion House is full of books and pictures and has a grand piano in the lived in drawing room, and there is a beautiful grandfather clock dating from 1750 in the hall. The wooden floors in the dining room have recently been renovated and the room restored.

The Kavanaghs, who are avid gardeners, were lucky enough to have not only the old plans of the gardens, dating from 1763, but also to inherit the old gardener. Through these two sources, they have been able to restore the lovely garden, which is full of rare and interesting plants, trees, and ferns, and which is open to the public. A great iron bell made locally and hanging at the side of the house is sounded on New Year's Eve. The pleasant, comfortable bedrooms overlook the gardens or river.

DIRECTIONS: Sion Hill is 800-900 meters from Waterford Bridge Roundabout, between Ard Ri Hotel and the Shell petrol station on the N25 Wexford-Rosslare road.

OPEN: closed for Christmas and New Year's
ROOMS: 1 double, 3 family; all en suite
TERMS: from €45; single supplement; child reduction

WOODSTOWN

Gaultier Lodge
Sheila Bagliani
Woodstown, Co. Waterford
Tel: 051 382549
E-mail: castleffrench@eircom.net
Web site: www.gaultier-lodge.com

Gaultier Lodge, an eighteenth-century family home, is hidden behind a high stone wall in the small village of Woodstown, borders the beach, and has wonderful views from practically every room. It is a lovely old house, which although modernized with large, well-appointed bathrooms, still retains its family home atmosphere. One room is particularly impressive with a massive four-poster bed. Tropical looking gardens surround the house, and inside, pictures of hunting scenes hang on the walls. Breakfast is served in the dining room

and the sitting room is a comfortable place to relax.

DIRECTIONS: In Woodstown

OPEN: April 1-October 31
ROOMS: 3 double, 1 twin; all en suite
TERMS: from €60

COUNTY WEXFORD

The most southerly county and one of the main gateways through the port of Rosslare, Wexford is also the warmest part of the whole country, an area of gentle hills, fertile farmland, and a coastline of sandy beaches. Much of Wexford's history is associated with the Norman invasion and the 1798 rebellion.

The Wexford Opera Festival, which takes place in October, is world-renowned and features top international singers. The town throbs with an influx of opera lovers, and many fringe events take place during the festival. It is an attractive town, with narrow, winding streets, and the Maritime Museum and the twelfth-century ruins of Selskar Abbey are of particular interest.

The castle at the attractive market town of Enniscorthy houses the county museum, with an interesting folk section. Worth a visit are the thirteenth-century castle at Ferns, the old town of New Ross, and Dunbrody Abbey, dating from 1182, near Campile. Nearby at Dunganstown is the Kennedy ancestral home.

ARTHURSTOWN

Glendine Country House
Annie Crosbie
Arthurstown, New Ross, Co. Wexford
Tel: 051 389500 Fax: 051 389677
E-mail: glendinehouse@eircom.net
Web site: www.glendinehouse.com

Built in 1830 as the dower house to Dunbrody, Glendine stands above the village of Arthurstown, where the ferry runs to Passage East. It is surrounded by 50 acres of farmland and has lovely views over the estuary. Annie Crosbie, who is a lovely, friendly, cheerful young mother of three sons, inherited the house from her grandparents. The Crosbies did a lot of renovation when they took over the house, and they have managed to preserve many original features. These include the pine floors,

wide back passageway, which runs the length of the house, and the old shutters. It has the feel of a family home and is simply decorated and furnished. A recent addition is four luxury bedrooms all with sea views. Annie grows all her own herbs, strives to serve organic food, and runs a coffee shop in the dining room during July and August. Apart from the 50 acres surrounding the house, Tom works another farm 5 miles away and has horses, sheep, and cattle. There are self-catering units in the converted stables.

DIRECTIONS: In Arthurstown

OPEN: closed for Christmas
ROOMS: 2 double, 2 twin, 2 family; all en suite
TERMS: from €55; single supplement; child reduction
MEALS: light supper and dinner for parties of 6 or more

Marsh Mere Lodge
Claire McNamara and Maria McNamara
Arthurstown, New Ross, Co. Wexford
Tel: 051 389186
E-mail: stay@marshmerelodge.com
Web site: www.marshmerelodge.com

Marsh Mere Lodge stands in a commanding position overlooking Arthurstown, the bay, and small harbor. The front porch is a great place to enjoy a cup of coffee or tea on arrival and watch the world go by. The house was built 50 years ago, but it has the feel of an older home and is full of wonderful pieces—furniture, pictures, and mementoes. The lounge for guests is on the first floor, which is a large, beautifully furnished room overlooking the water and a relaxing place to settle down with a good book.

Marsh Mere is run by Maria McNamara and her daughter Claire. Maria bakes the bread for breakfast, and Claire can take guests for horse-drawn carriage rides around the immediate area, if organized ahead of time. They breed Labrador and corgi dogs. The house is dog friendly. Charming en-suite bedrooms have antique furniture, and each bedroom is named after a picture, which hangs in the room. One bedroom is on the ground floor.

DIRECTIONS: Marsh Mere Lodge is just down the road from the Passage East car ferry.

OPEN: all year
ROOMS: 4 double/twin; all en suite
TERMS: €50; single supplement

BUNCLODY

Meadowside B&B
Phil Kinsella
Ryland Street, Bunclody, Co. Wexford
Tel: 053 9376226 Fax: 053 9375997

Meadowside catches your eye as you drive through Bunclody on the main N80 road. A colorful, flower-decked, old stone building at the southern end of town, it has been owned and run by Phil Kinsella since the late 1980s. Phil is a friendly, organized lady with a lot of energy, who also runs the adjoining flower shop and boutique. The house is spotless with simple bedrooms, a guests' lounge, and breakfast room. All four bedrooms are on the first floor, the two front ones get the road noise, whilst the two at the back of the house have a rural aspect.

DIRECTIONS: In Bunclody

OPEN: all year
ROOMS: 3 triple; all en suite; 1 double with private bathroom
TERMS: from €40

CAMPILE

Kilmokea Country Manor & Gardens
Mark and Emma Hewlett
Great Island, Campile, Co. Wexford
Tel: 051 388109 Fax: 051 388776
E-mail: kilmokea@eircom.net
Web site: www.kilmokea.com/

Kilmokea was built in 1794 as a Church of Ireland rectory and was eventually acquired by David Prince in 1947, who was responsible for creating the seven acres of gardens. In 1997, Mark and Emma Hewlett bought the property and spent an enormous amount of energy renovating and restoring it back to its original charm. They have succeeded in creating a peaceful and elegant retreat. Each room has its own character and theme and offers, to a lesser or greater extent, vistas and glimpses of the magnificent gardens. The downstairs loo, which was formerly a bathroom, has been decorated and equipped with pictures, photographs, and literature, encouraging a long visit! Kilmokea Gardens, which include a formal walled garden full of rare species from all over the world, a woodland garden with exotic plants, and a very large vegetable garden, are open March to October, with the exception of Mondays. The Pink Tea Cup Café is the venue for lunch, dinner, and cream teas, and there is a craft shop. Guests have use of a gym, indoor heated swimming pool, sauna, and aromatherapy sessions. Two ground floor rooms are suitable for guests with pets.

DIRECTIONS: From New Ross, take the R733 to Campile and follow the signs to Kilmokea Gardens

OPEN: February 1-November
ROOMS: 5 double, 2 twin, 2 family, 1 single; all en suite
TERMS: from €80; single supplement
MEALS: lunch; dinner à la carte

ENNISCORTHY

Ballinkeele House
John and Margaret Maher
Ballymurn, Enniscorthy, Co. Wexford
Tel: 053 9138105 Fax: 053 9138468
E-mail: john@ballinkeele.com
Web site: www.ballinkeele.com

Built in 1840, this impressive country house still belongs to the Maher family four generations later. Approached up a sweeping avenue through game-filled parkland, it is set in 140 hectares of farmland. Apart from such modern conveniences as bathrooms and heating, the restored house remains much as it was built, with a distinctively Victorian flavor, thanks to the fourth generation. The master bedroom, which has a four-poster bed, is the same shape as the drawing room below. The bedrooms are very large and furnished and decorated to a high standard, and a welcoming glass of sherry awaits guests.

The Mahers are a friendly, hospitable couple and Margaret produces delicious dinners, if booked in advance, which include produce from the garden and fresh local ingredients. Meals are served by candlelight in the elegant dining room, and  the house has a wine license. Breakfast, which is organized by John, can include hot pancakes and homemade jams. The former billiard room has reverted to a big drawing room with a TV. Visitors are welcome to walk around the old walled garden, the lake, and grounds. There is also a croquet lawn.

DIRECTIONS: From the N11, turn in Oilgate at signpost

OPEN: February 1-November 30
ROOMS: 5 double/twin; all en suite
TERMS: €80; single supplement
MEALS: dinner €45

Clone House
Betty Breen
Ferns, Enniscorthy, Co. Wexford
Tel/Fax: 053 9366113
E-mail: info@clonehouse.ie
Web site: www.clonehouse.ie

This attractive, creeper-covered, 300-year-old farmhouse is in a quiet location on nearly 120 hectares of mixed farmland. Guests can fish on the Bann River, which runs through the property, feed the lambs, see calves being born, or just go for wonderful walks. The Breens bought the property about 40 years ago, and gradually did it up. Betty is particularly gifted at landscaping and has created a lovely garden. Guests are treated as friends and enjoy such luxuries as breakfast in bed, served at any time, using home grown or reared produce. The house is very comfortable and has been attractively furnished. Two of the rooms have balconies, which are very popular with guests. There is a comfortable sitting room and dining room. Baby-sitting is available. Many guests come to buy horses, others to visit a local herbalist, others to hunt, or just to relax.

DIRECTIONS: Clone House is signposted on the N11 at Ferns, 3 kilometers away.

OPEN: April 1-September 30
ROOMS: 3 family en suite; 1 family and 1 twin with private bathrooms
TERMS: €45; single supplement; child reduction

Salville House
Gordon and Jane Parker
Enniscorthy, Co. Wexford
Tel/Fax: 053 9235252
E-mail: info@sallvillehouse.com
Web site: www.salvillehouse.com

This lovely old house, built in the mid-nineteenth century, stands in its own grounds (with grass tennis court and croquet lawn) overlooking the River Slaney and the Blackstairs Mountains. The interior is light and bright with spacious, simply furnished rooms, and wooden floorboards. Salville House has a good reputation for its food, and dinner, by arrangement, is served at one long table in the dining room. Guests are welcome to bring their own wine, and they have use of a comfortable drawing room. The house is just outside the cathedral town of Enniscorthy, noted for its thirteenth-century castle. There are a number of golf courses in the area, good walking in the Blackstairs Mountains, and fine beaches along the Wexford coastline. There is also a self-catering unit available.

DIRECTIONS: From Enniscorthy, take the N11 towards Wexford, after a mile take the first left after the hospital, go up the hill, and turn left. The house is the third on the left.

OPEN: all year
ROOMS: 2 double en suite; 1 double with private bathroom; apartment with 2 rooms sharing bathroom
TERMS: €55; single supplement; child reduction
MEALS: dinner €40

Woodbrook
Giles and Alexandra FitzHerbert
Killanne, Enniscorthy, Co. Wexford
Tel: 053 9255114
E-mail: fitzherbert@eircom.net
Web site: www.woodbrookhouse.ie

Woodbrook is a lovely, large, Georgian house, first built in the 1770s but damaged in the rebellion of 1798. Giles and Alexandra FitzHerbert, who both have ties to South America, have lived here with their four children since 1998 and have worked on improvements to the house. The rooms are spectacularly large, and the first floor central corridor is particularly impressive, with the two outstanding features of the house being the "flying staircase" and the enormous drawing room.

It is set in lovely parklands, gardens, and woods and is part of a farm that provides a house cow and a small herd of purebred Hereford cattle. The FitzHerberts on occasion arrange opera performances on the grounds, there is a grass tennis court, and the walled garden produces organic fruit and vegetables for sale and for home consumption. Good home-cooked dinners are available, if booked in advance, and the house carries a selection of wines. There are lovely walks on the nearby Blackstairs Mountains, and riding, fishing, and golf are all available in the area.

DIRECTIONS: 2 miles from Kiltealy and 2 miles from Killane, off the R730

OPEN: May-September and for the Wexford Festival (October)
ROOMS: 3 double, 1 twin; 3 en suite; 1 private bathroom
TERMS: €75; single supplement; child reduction
MEALS: dinner €35

GOREY

Carraig View
Martina Redmond
Ballycale, Gorey, Co. Wexford
Tel/Fax: 055 21323
E-mail: carraigview@eircom.net

Set in a wonderful position with panoramic views and a beautiful garden, Carraig View offers superb accommodation. Martina Redmond is an extremely attentive and helpful host who enjoys interior design and gardening. All the rooms are on the ground floor, and the bedrooms are a good size. The dining room/lounge has an open fire, and breakfast is served overlooking stunning countryside.

DIRECTIONS: 2 miles from Gorey on the R741, also signposted on the N11 at Clough

OPEN: closed for Christmas

ROOMS: 1 double, 1 family; both en suite
TERMS: €37; single supplement; child reduction

INCH

Perrymount House
Peter and Anne Donnelly
Inch, Gorey, Co. Wexford
Tel: 0402 37387 Fax: 0402 21906
E-mail: perrymountholidays@eircom.net
Web site: www.perrymountholidays.com

Built by Colonel Perry in 1798,
Perrymount has been in Peter
Donnelly's family for the last
100 years. The Donnellys offer
delightful hospitality with both
comfortable en-suite bedrooms
in the house and very pretty
self-contained cottages in the
courtyard. Peter runs the most
picturesque dairy farm, some-
times with the help of his three young sons. Anne is an enthusiastic and very successful gardener and provides delicious food that is
traditionally Irish and mostly home produced. This is a paradise
for children. They are made very welcome, and there are all sorts
of safe play areas for them and pets to play. There is a lovely view
over the hills and walks down to a large pond full of ducks and
geese. Guests have use of bicycles, walking maps, and washing and
drying facilities, as well as the use of a fridge, freezer, and
microwave.

DIRECTIONS: Signposted off the N11, just south of Inch

OPEN: April 1-November 1
ROOMS: 1 double, 1 twin, 3 family; all en suite
TERMS: €40; single supplement; child reduction
MEALS: high tea; dinner

KILLURIN

Healthfield Manor
Mayler and Loretto Colloton
Killurin, Co. Wexford

Tel/Fax: 053 9128253
Web site: www.healthfield.8k.com

The story goes that back in the 1400 to 1500s there was a plague in Wexford, and consequently, the water was undrinkable. Healthfield, which has its own well, was the nearest place to the city with good water—hence the name. Built in 1820, this country house is reached up a long driveway through its 40 hectares of farmland, which supports organically reared sheep and is bordered by mature shrubs and wonderful rhododendrons. At the top, there are spectacular views of the river Slaney. The entrance to the house is through a small conservatory and beyond is the very large drawing room. The bedrooms are incredibly spacious—the "Five Acre Suite" has its own sitting room and two bedrooms. All but one room have the lovely front view over the grounds to the river. Packed lunches can be prepared with notice.

DIRECTIONS: Healthfield is 8 kilometers from Wexford and is signposted on the Killurin road.

OPEN: Easter-Halloween
ROOMS: 2 twin, 1 family; 1 en suite; 2 private bathrooms
TERMS: €45; single supplement; child reduction
MEALS: packed lunch

KILMORE

Ballyhealy House
Betty Maher-Caulfield
Ballyhealy Beach, Kilmore, Co. Wexford
Tel: 053 9135035 Fax: 053 9135038
E-mail: betty@ballyhealyhouse.com
Web site: www.ballyhealyhouse.com

Once the seat of Wexford's High Sherriff, this house is very close to the sea and a pleasant beach. The present owner, Betty Maher-Caulfield, acquired the then ruined eighteenth-century house ten years ago and has created the sort of holiday house of childhood dreams. There is swimming and sea fishing and a feeling of freedom and happiness for people of all ages. The bedrooms are very spacious, some with enough beds for a family of four or five, and all have a sea or castle view. Children and pets are especially welcome.

DIRECTIONS: 2 miles from Kilmore

OPEN: all year
ROOMS: 3 family; all en suite
TERMS: €45; single supplement; child reduction

ROSSLARE HARBOUR

O'Leary's Farm
Philomena O'Leary and Family
Killilane, Kilrane, Rosslare Harbour, Co. Wexford
Tel: 053 9133134
E-mail: info@olearysfarm.com or polearyfarm@eircom.net
Web site: www.olearysfarm.com

O'Leary's Farm is well worth negotiating the narrow lanes from the main N25 road. Parts of the original 200-year-old farmhouse were destroyed by fire some 30 years ago—various pieces have been added since, resulting today in a substantial building orientated to the sea, a mere 5-minute stroll away. The attractions here are many, most importantly cheerful Philomena O'Leary who owns and runs the farm with husband Gabriel. Surrounded by its 100 acres of farmland (beef and barley) and with sweeping sea views, it is a peaceful place well off the beaten track. The farm's free range hens provide eggs for breakfast; jams and marmalades are homemade, and sausages and bacon are produced locally. The bedrooms are simply furnished, and breakfast is served in the spacious, but cozy dining room at separate tables. The old coach house, which, during its lifetime, has also been the turnip house (where turnips were mangled) and potato house, has recently been converted into a charming, small self-catering unit—which has its own beach access.
    DIRECTIONS: Signposted off the N25

OPEN: closed for Christmas and New Year's
ROOMS: 2 double, 1 twin, 2 family, 1 single; all en suite
TERMS: from €25; single supplement; child reduction

TAGOAT

Churchtown House
Patricia Cody
Tagoat, Rosslare, Co. Wexford
Tel: 053 9132555 Fax: 053 9132577
E-mail: info@churchtownhouse.com

Web site: www.churchtownhouse.com

Set in 3.25 hectares of parklike grounds, this attractive house dates from 1763. Patricia and Austin Cody have worked miracles in transforming Churchtown House to what it is today. When they bought it, it had been inhabited by one old man, who used a kitchen with stairs up through a cupboard to one room above. The spacious rooms have been tastefully decorated and furnished, and a bedroom on the ground floor is suitable for wheelchairs. There are two comfortable drawing rooms and three dining rooms, one of which is a conservatory-like room with windows all around looking out over the garden. Good old-fashioned cooking and local ingredients are what make dinners at Churchtown House memorable. These need to be booked in advance and are available Tuesday through Saturday, and there is a wine license. Activities such as bird watching, golf, fishing, swimming, walking, and riding are available locally.

DIRECTIONS: Churchtown is on the R736.

OPEN: March 17-November 1
ROOMS: 5 double, 5 twin, 1 family, 1 single; all en suite
TERMS: from €55; single supplement; child reduction
MEALS: dinner €43

WEXFORD

Broom Cottage
John and Theresa Devereux
Rosslare Road, Drinagh, Wexford, Co. Wexford
Tel: 053 9144434

This attractive, creeper-clad, eighteenth-century farmhouse set back a little from the main road is part of a 56-hectare beef, sheep, and tillage farm. Eleven hectares of the land lie around the house.

Broom Cottage has been in the same family for the last 200 years and an extension was added 25 years ago. It offers comfortable, clean, well-equipped bedrooms, and guests have use of a TV lounge and conservatory. Breakfast is served in the dining room. The accommodation is good value, and it is convenient for the Rosslare car ferry.

DIRECTIONS: 3 kilometers from the center of Wexford on the Rosslare road

OPEN: June 1-September 1
ROOMS: 4 double/twin; all en suite
TERMS: €35; single supplement; not suitable for children

Clonard House
Kathleen Hayes
Clonard Great, Wexford, Co. Wexford
Tel/Fax: 053 9143141
E-mail: info@clonardhouse.com
Web site: www.clonardhouse.com

This elegant Georgian farmhouse, part of a 48-hectare dairy farm, is set in idyllic surroundings with a clear view of Wexford harbor. Clonard House was completely renovated and retains many of its original features, such as cornices, ceiling roses, and the dining room fireplace. Since then, there has been a continuous program of updating and refurbishing to maintain its already high standard. The bedrooms are extremely attractive, with traditional and antique furnishings, and some have four-poster beds. The lounge has plenty of room to relax in after a busy day sightseeing. There is a games room in the basement for guests. This is a lovely, peaceful house with a lot of character (and a stairway to nowhere!).

DIRECTIONS: Signposted off the N11 ring road, 1 kilometer away

OPEN: June-October
ROOMS: 3 double, 3 twin, 1 family, 1 single; all en suite
TERMS: from €45; single supplement; child reduction

Killiane Castle
Jack and Kathleen Mernagh
Drinagh, Wexford, Co. Wexford
Tel/Fax: 053 9158885
E-mail: killianecastle@yahoo.com
Web site: www.killianecastle.com

This eighteenth-century house is attached to the tower of a fourteenth-century castle and is part of a dairy farm. Killiane Castle is down a quiet country lane and is very handy for the Rosslare ferry, which is only a 10-minute drive away. The Mernaghs are constantly striving to keep up standards and regularly redecorate the house, which is attractively furnished. The first floor bedrooms are particularly large. Coffee or  tea are available in a small ground floor lounge, and another sitting room is a nice place to relax. For those catching early morning ferries, breakfast is provided. There is a hard tennis court and four self-catering apartments at the back of the house.

DIRECTIONS: Killiane Castle is signposted on the N25 between Wexford and Rosslare.

OPEN: March-November
ROOMS: 4 double, 3 twin, 1 family; all en suite
TERMS: €50; single supplement; child reduction

THE WEST AND NORTHWEST

COUNTY CLARE

Two hundred castles and 2,300 stone forts dating to pre-Celtic times testify to County Clare's turbulent past. Although Shannon Airport lies on the southern border, most of the county is underpopulated by tourists. Scenery varies from the barren terrain of the Burren, in spring the area is covered in a profusion of northern and southern plants, to the scenic lakes and hills of Slieve Bernagh, wonderful walking country, and the towering Cliffs of Moher.

The country is bordered by the sea to the west and the Shannon Estuary to the south and east. One of the principal sights of the county capital Ennis, situated on a bend of the River Fergus, is the Franciscan Ennis Friary, noted for sculptures and decorated tombs.

A bridge crosses the Shannon at Killaloe. Nearby is a twelfth-century cathedral built on the site of an earlier church. It has a magnificent door and splendid views from the top of the square tower.

Across the Shannon lies Bunratty Castle, well known for its medieval banquets. Dating from 1460, it was once occupied by the father of William Penn, founder of Pennsylvania. A Folk Park in the castle grounds displays examples of houses from the Shannon area. Iniscealta Island on Lough Derg can be reached by boat from the attractive village of Mountshannon. There are five old churches, a round tower, saints'graveyard, hermit's cell, and a holy well.

Moohaun Fort, one of the largest Iron Age forts in Europe, is to be found at Newmarket on Fergus. Both Knappogue Castle, another venue for medieval banquets, and Quinn Abbey are venues close to Craggaunowen.

Of special interest to both botanists and historians is the Burren. Once densely populated, this savagely rocky area is rich in prehistoric and historic monuments. Its limestone holds a wealth of exquisite, delicate plant life thriving in a myriad of tiny crevices.

The Burren Display Centre explains the fauna and flora of these 500 square kilometers and the remains of ancient civilizations. The ruined Leamaneh Castle is near Kilfenora, which is on the edge of the Burren. Between Kilfenora and Ballyvaughan is Ballykinvarga, one of Ireland's finest stone forts, and southeast of Ballyvaughan is Aillwee Cave, which dates to 2 million B.C.

The road from Lisdoonvarna, Ireland's foremost spa town, leads to the impressive Cliffs of Moher, which stretches for nearly 9 kilometers. Liscannor is famous for the Holy Well of St. Brigid, which is an important place of pilgrimage.

Lahinch is a small seaside resort best known for its championship golf course, and to the south is Spanish Point, where many ships of the Spanish Armada were wrecked.

Around the village of Quilty, seaweed can be seen drying on the stone walls. The coast south of Kilkee is every bit as spectacular as the Cliffs of Moher, with caverns and strange rock formations.

BALLYVAUGHN

Dolmen Lodge
Philip and Mary Kyne
Tonarussa, Ballyvaughn, Co. Clare
Tel: 065 707 7202 Fax: 065 707 7202
E-mail: dolmenlodge@eircom.net

This elegant, modern farmhouse stands in open, scenic countryside and has stunning views of the Burren and Galway Bay. It is part of a working cattle farm, and there are some interesting rock formations on the land.

The bedrooms are large, have dainty duvets, and a light pastel décor. The dining room, where breakfast is served, overlooks the view, as does the lounge. There are some interesting antiques about the home, including a grandmother clock in the hallway.

Dolmen Lodge offers a high standard of accommodation at modest prices. It is a superb choice for people touring this beautiful area. Breakfast only is served, but Ballyvaughn, where there are venues for food is 1 kilometer away. Philip and Mary Kyne have created a friendly, homely atmosphere, and they will be happy to assist with choosing venues for evening meals and to give advice on what to see and do in the area. Two friendly Springer spaniels live here, Chloe and Frankie. Private parking.

DIRECTIONS: Signposted on the N67 Ballyaugvaughn-Galway Road

OPEN: March 17-October 20
ROOMS: 5 rooms double/twin/family; all en suite

TERMS: €35-37.50; single supplement; child reduction

BUNRATTY

Bunratty Castle Mews
Dolores and Gary O'Toole
Low Road, Bunratty, Co. Clare
Tel: 061 369766
E-mail: bcmews@eircom.net
Web site: www.bunrattycastlemews.com

This charming bed and breakfast property stands in its own grounds and attractive garden. A short walk will bring you to Bunratty Castle, shops, and restaurants. All rooms are on the ground floor, and the recent updating and renovating provides extremely comfortable luxurious accommodation. The themed bedrooms include Irish, African, and Mediterranean décor.

The rooms are spacious, have quality linens, fluffy towels, and power showers. Some rooms are wheelchair friendly, have a LCD TV, tea makers, and hair dryers. Hospitality begins on arrival with a hot drink and homemade tasties. To unwind after a busy day, there is a HoMedics® massage chair.

Rooms range from standard to superior, but whatever your choice you are assured of a comfortable night's rest. The owners, Dolores and Gary O'Toole, have been in the hospitality trade for many years and know how to make guests feel at home. There is a patio for dining or relaxing and a lounge. Light meals are available. An extensive breakfast starter buffet followed by a traditional Irish breakfast, keeps you going all day. Special diets are catered for with advance notice. Children under 12 sharing with parents are free, and there is a small charge for breakfast. Internet access and private parking are available. Shannon Airport is 10 minutes away, and Cratloe Woods and country walks are close by.

OPEN: all year except Christmas
ROOMS: 11 rooms double/twin/family; all en suite
TERMS: €37-45; single supplement; children under 12 sharing are free; special breaks for three nights or more

Bunratty Grove
Joe and Maura Brodie
Castle Road, Bunratty, Co. Clare

Tel: 061 369579 Fax: 061 369561
E-mail: bunrattygrove@eircom.net

Bunratty Grove is ideally placed for visits to nearby Bunratty Castle. Bookings for the famous banquets at the castle can be made here. The house is within minutes of Shannon Airport, as well as the tourist favorites of fishing, golf courses, and Irish heritage sites.

All bedrooms are equipped with a multi-channel TV, hair dryer, and telephone, as well as tea and coffee making facilities and private parking.

OPEN: all year
ROOMS: 4 double, 3 twin, 2 family; all en suite
TERMS: €35; single supplement; child reduction

Tudor Lodge
Carmel and Michael Dennehy
Hill Road, Bunratty, Co. Clare
Tel: 061 362248 Fax: 061 362569
E-mail: tudorlodge@esatclear.ie

This gracious and elegant home stands in a secluded, peaceful wooded setting where guests awaken to the sound of birds singing. The house was in a derelict condition when it was purchased and has been beautifully restored into a comfortable and quite luxurious home. The tiled entryway is full of plants, and the bedrooms are furnished and decorated to a high standard. The bathrooms are large and have powerful showers. There is a very comfortable lounge, with blue leather furniture, which leads out to a conservatory overlooking the well-tended garden. The accommodating and helpful owners, Carmel and Michael Dennehy, both local people who provide lots of information for guests on what to see and do in the area, are an added bonus.

Reservations can be made for the medieval banquet at Bunratty Castle, which is within walking distance, as is Durty Nellie's pub, which serves lunch and dinner. Shannon Airport is a 15-minute drive.

OPEN: February 1-November 30
ROOMS: 5 double/twin/triple; all en suite
TERMS: €35; single supplement; child reduction

DOOLIN

Atlantic Sunset House
Val and Brid Egan
Doolin, Co. Clare
Tel: 065 707 4080 Fax: 065 707 4922
E-mail: sunsethouse@esaatclear.ie
Web site: www.atlanticsunsetdoolin.com

You can be sure of a warm welcome at this comfortable house, which stands on its own grounds, 1 mile from Doolin village, where Irish music can be heard most nights. Brid Egan has been in business for over 18 years. People feel very much at home here; one guest commented, "Your home is a pleasure."

The large bedrooms, all with pine furniture, have a TV and tea makers. The rooms are decorated with soft pastels and have pretty quilts of pinks, blues, and cream. The dining room, where delicious breakfasts are served, feature kippers, French toast, cheese plate, yogurt, omelet, and traditional fare.

The Moher stone floors are of special interest, as are the many items on display, including several harps made by Brid's father-in-law, various pots, and dolls. A sitting room is also available. This would be an ideal spot from which to visit the Cliffs of Moher, The Burren, and Lisdoonvarna.

OPEN: all year except Christmas
ROOMS: 6 rooms double/twin; all en suite
TERMS: €33-35; single supplement; child reduction

Harbour View
Jonathen and Cathy Normoyle
Doolin, Co. Clare
Tel: 065 7074154
E-mail: clarebb@eircom.net
Web site: www.harbourviewdoolin.com

This large attractive house, with arched windows, stands in its own grounds in an elevated position. There are extensive scenic views, and some rooms have views of the Atlantic Ocean.

Cathy and Jonathen Normoyle are a young enthusiastic couple, who have been busy upgrading and making improvements to the property. The result is a well-run spotlessly clean house, offering a good standard of accommodation.

All of the en-suite, spacious bedrooms are on the ground floor, have comfortable beds, and cream and gold bed covers. The showers are of a good size, and all have a TV, tea makers, and a hair dryer.

A substantial breakfast is served in the bright dining room, featuring fruits, cereals, and yogurt, with a cooked breakfast to follow. Doolin is 1 mile away. The Irish Musical Festival takes place here every February. Music can be heard just about every night at one of the local pubs. Doolin is well known for its Irish music and is a popular venue for Irish music enthusiasts. Private parking is available.

DIRECTIONS: Located on the R478 off the N67

OPEN: from mid February-mid November
ROOMS: 6 rooms double/twin/family; all en suite
TERMS: €35-38; single supplement; child reduction

KILLALOE

Carramore Lodge
Eileen Brennan
Roolagh, Killaloe, Co. Clare
Tel: 061 376704

This spacious country house stands in $1^1/_2$ acres of landscaped rounds, overlooking Lough Derg. The good-sized, bright, and fresh bedrooms are luxuriously furnished, immaculately maintained, and have either mountain or lake views. All rooms have en-suite facilities, a TV, and tea making facilities.

Carramore Lodge is popular with tourists and outdoor enthusiasts; there are lovely walks close by, and the property is convenient to golf, horse riding, and fishing. Evening meals are not served, but there are several restaurants and pubs in Killaloe that are within walking distance. Imaginative tasty breakfasts are served at separate tables in the dining room/lounge. These great morning meals include smoked salmon, home-baked brown bread, fruit, a good choice of cooked items, and plenty of tea and coffee.

DIRECTIONS: Carramore Lodge is situated 30 minutes from Shannon Airport and is easily located on the Limerick to Ballina road, just before the village.

OPEN: March 1-October 31
ROOMS: 4 double/twin/family; all en suite
TERMS: from €35.00; single supplement; child reduction

KILRUSH

Clarke's Bed and Breakfast
Michael and Mary Clarke
Killmer Road, Kilrush, Co. Clare
Tel: 065 90552250 Fax: 065 90552250
E-mail: clarkekilrush@hotmail.com
Web site: www.clarkekilrush.com

Set back from the main road, behind a black wrought iron gate and secluded garden, this Georgian-style two-story house offers quality accommodation in a peaceful setting. Hospitality begins on arrival, with an offer of a drink and home-baked cakes, and continues throughout the stay. Good-sized bedrooms have colorful bedding, attractive curtains, and comfortable beds. All rooms are en suite and have a TV, clock radio, hospitality tray, and hair dryer. Rooms to the back of the house overlook the Shannon Estuary. The extensive breakfast menu includes freshly squeezed orange or grapefruit juice, muesli or porridge, fresh fruit, yogurt, and omelets with Kilrush mushrooms. A full traditionally cooked variety is also served. Breakfast can be taken in the dining room or the conservatory, which leads out to the gardens and terrace. There is also a TV lounge.

Michael and Mary Clarke are happy to share their knowledge of the area, and a video on West Clare is available to guests. Opposite the house are the Vandeleur Gardens. Private parking.

DIRECTIONS: Situated on the N67, a short drive to the Tarbert Ferry

OPEN: all year except Christmas
ROOMS: 4 rooms double/twin; all en suite
TERMS: €32-34; single supplement; child reduction

LAHINCH

Auburn House
Cathy and Nanno Vuyk
School Road, Lahinch, Co. Clare
Tel: 065 7082890
E-mail: auburnhse@eircom.net
Web site: www.auburnhouse.ie

The large attractive corner house stands in its own grounds, across from a popular surfing beach. In summer, hanging baskets and flowering tubs abound. Safe sandy beaches can be found very close by.

Guests can expect a high standard of furnishings and comfort. The spacious bedrooms, all on the ground floor, have a light pastel décor and comfortable beds. Three have views, a TV is available on request, and all are en suite. A freshly prepared breakfast, with home-baked brown bed, is served in the sitting/dining room overlooking the sea.

The owners, a delightful young couple named Cathy and Nanno Vuyk, formerly ran a hotel but went into the bed and breakfast business to extend a more personal service. The ambience is warm and friendly. They have two lovely children, Laoise and Emma. Auburn House is a 2-minute walk from the town, and the Lahinch Golf Club is close by. French, German, and Dutch are spoken. Private parking.

OPEN: all year except Christmas
ROOMS: 7 rooms double/twin/family; all en suite
TERMS: €30-37; single supplement; child reduction

Grovemount House
Sheila and Gerard Linnane
Lahinch, Co. Clare
Tel: 065 7071431 Fax: 707 7071823
E-mail: grovmnt@gofree.indigo.ie

This handsome, spacious house stands in its own grounds in an elevated position with wonderful views of the surrounding countryside. The house is pleasantly furnished and well maintained. The large bedrooms are spotlessly clean, have pine furniture, and white Dorma bedding. All have en-suite facilities, direct dial phones, tea makers, a hair dryer, and a TV. There is a guest lounge.

Sheila Linnane is a helpful lady, who is always happy to give advice on local activities and to recommend venues for evening meals. This is a comfortable place to stay, the ambience is friendly, and the Irish welcome from Sheila and Gerard is warm and inviting.

Ennistymon, a market town, is a popular destination for tourists and is famous for its nineteenth-century shop fronts. A popular spot for golfers, the Lahinch Golf Course, is 2 kilometers away and is within easy driving distance of the Cliffs of Moher and The Burren. Traditional Irish music can be heard in Linnane's Pub, a popular venue in Kilfenora. Private parking.

OPEN: May 1-October 31
ROOMS: 5 rooms double/twin/family/triple

TERMS: from €32-42; single supplement; child reduction

Moy House
Antoin O'Looney
Lahinch, Co. Clare
Tel: 065 7082800 Fax: 065 7082500
E-mail: moyhouse@tinet.ie
Web site: www.moyhouse.com

A classic country house with views of beautiful Lahinch Bay, Moy House is approached up a long drive and is peacefully set in 15 acres of parklike grounds and mature woodland. Built in the eighteenth century as home to Sir Augustine Fitzgerald, it overlooks beautiful Lahinch Bay. Before the restoration, which took place over a three-year period, Moy House stood empty for 10 years and was derelict. Antoin O'Looney purchased the house and undertook the daunting job of restoration. The results are stunning, the original oak floors were used, and part of the stone stable wall can be seen.

The house is beautifully maintained. The bedrooms are luxurious and individually designed, using a combination of styles from past and present. All have a TV, tea makers, and a hair dryer. All bedrooms are furnished and decorated with beautiful fabrics, most have working log-burning fireplaces, and all but two have sea views. The bathrooms are equipped with toiletries, dressing gowns, large fluffy towels, and most have shower/bath combinations. One bedroom features the original well from which the water was drawn. The house is not suitable for children under 12 years.

Gourmet candlelit dinners are served in the elegant dining room overlooking the bay. Everything is prepared with fresh local produce, and fish, meats, and mouth-watering homemade desserts are presented with flair and style. The gracious drawing room has a real fire where guests can enjoy a pre- or after-dinner drink. Antoin pampers and spoils her guests. Single and group rates are available on request. The rooms range from deluxe doubles or twins to elegant suites.

DIRECTIONS: Situated on the coast road, 1¹/₂ miles from Lahinch Golf Course

OPEN: all year, except Christmas, and from November-March 1, weekends only
ROOMS: 9 double/twin/family/single; all en suite

TERMS: from €175-360 per room, depending on room style and season; single supplement

LISDOONVARNA

Fermona House
Vera Fitzpatrick
Bog Road, Lisdoonvarna, Co. Clare
Tel: 065 707 4243
E-mail: fermona@eircom.net

This pleasant cream and green bungalow is set back off the road in a quiet location, close to the Spa Wells, and is a 5-minute walk from town. The bedrooms and en-suite facilities are quite spacious and are individually decorated in soft colors of blue and peach. All bedrooms are on the ground floor. There is a cozy TV lounge with a stereo that guests may use. The house is exceptionally well maintained and everything is spotlessly clean.

Owner Vera Fitzpatrick loves her work and enjoys meeting new people and sharing her home with them. Breakfasts are served at separate tables, freshly cooked to order, and there are several establishments in town for evening meals. Doolin, the Cliffs of Moher and The Burren, golfing, pony trekking, and hill walking are all close by. Private parking.

OPEN: April-October
ROOMS: 5 rooms double/twin/family
TERMS: €28-34; single supplement; child reduction

Lisdoon Lodge
Bernie and Oliver Connolly
Lisdoonvarna, Co. Clare
Tel: 065 7075849
E-mail: lisdoonlodge@eircom.net
Web site: www.lisdoonlodge.com

This charming bed and breakfast is a 5-minute walk from Lisdoonvarna and is delightful in every way. There are nine pretty guest rooms; two are on the ground floor. All have large bathrooms, power showers, a TV, hair dryer, tea trays, and a radio.

Bernie and Oliver have been in the house for four years, three of which were taken up with extensive refurbishment. Bernie, a natural decorator, has done an amazing job. Bedrooms have canopies, coronets, lace, and soft shades of lavender and blue, with a doll to greet you in each room. The family room has four beds, and a "Romantic Room" is available for special occasions.

An extensive menu, served in the bright dining room, offers a good choice for breakfast. Bernie and Oliver, a warm and helpful couple, greet you with a hot drink and home-baked goods. Lisdoon Lodge is a good value bed and breakfast; to ensure a reservation, we recommend advance booking.

DIRECTIONS: Easily located on the Kilfenora/Ennis road

OPEN: all year, except Christmas
ROOMS: 9 rooms double/twin/family; all en suite
TERMS: €35-45; single supplement; child reduction

Woodhaven
Irene Vaughan
Doolin Coast Road, Lisdoonvarna, Co. Clare
Tel: 065 7074017
Email: woodhavenbb@eircom.net

This bright terracotta-painted house stands in its own grounds in a peaceful location. It is a spacious well-maintained property, well located for the Doolin Ferry, Cliffs of Moher, and the Doolin Caves. All five en-suite rooms are bright and cheery, have electric blankets, a hair dryer, and modern furnishings. A TV lounge is available to guests.

Irene Vaughan has been in the hospitality business for many years; although she did venture into retirement, she missed meeting people and went back into business. Irene is a delightful lady who is always welcoming and happy to share her knowledge of the area. An excellent well-presented breakfast includes home baking. Private parking.

DIRECTIONS: Situated off the N67/R477, 1 kilometer from Lisdoonvarna

OPEN: all year
ROOMS: 5 rooms double/twin/single
TERMS: €32-34; no single supplement in single room; child reduction

COUNTY DONEGAL

County Donegal is a large county with a spectacular variety of scenery and an indented coastline of bays, beaches, cliffs, and peninsulas set against a backdrop of mountains, moors, and lakes. It has many archaeological sites and much evidence of the old Irish culture and traditions. Irish is still spoken in areas north and west of Killybegs, an important fishing port. Donegal takes its name from the fort the Vikings established called Dún na nGall, the fort of the Foreigners. The town was built by Sir Basil Brooke and is on the estuary of the River Eske, a busy place, good for buying tweeds. Brooke refurbished the castle, with its great square tower, once the stronghold of the O'Donnels, in 1610. Bundoran is one of Ireland's best-known seaside resorts with a good golf course and famous beaches. Farther north is Ballyshannon, long a center of importance because of its river; the town winds up a steep hill above the River Erne.

Beyond Killybegs, the coastal scenery becomes wild and spectacular. Kilcar is a center for the hand-woven tweed industry, as is Ardara. The scenery at Glencolumbkille is magnificent, with its blend of hills and sea. The late Father MacDyer organized a cooperative movement to keep young people from emigrating and established a folk museum. Portnoo and Narin are other popular seaside towns for holidaymakers. Letterkenny is the largest town in Donegal, dominated by St. Eunan's Cathedral, built in the modern Gothic style between 1890 and 1900. The winding road approaching Doocharry from Fintown is known as the "corkscrew," bringing you through the Gweebarra Glen to the sea. Aranmore Island is the most populated and largest of a series of islands that can be reached by ferry from Burtonport, an attractive, unspoiled fishing port. Gweedore, situated in the spectacularly wild country, is a major holiday center. Follow the road of remarkable scenic beauty by Loughs Nacung and Dunlewy into the Derryveagh Mountains.

The Irish-speaking areas of Gortahork and Falcarragh are good places from which to start a climb of Muckish Mountain. There is a fine beach at Dunfanaghy, a good place to explore the granite promontory of Horn Head. Between Creeslough, attractively situated on Sheephaven Bay, the Carrigart is the romantic Doe Castle, almost surrounded by the sea.

Gull Peninsula has wonderful views of Melmore Head, Horn Head, and Muckish Mountain. Milford is a pretty town from where the Fanqad Peninsula, with its sandy beaches, can be explored. The tranquil village of Rathmullan, famous for its historical associations, is beautifully situated with a sandy beach. The road between here and Ramelton is also in a lovely location and is a planned planter's town, begun early in the seventeenth century.

ARDARA

Woodhill House
John and Nancy Yates
Ardara, Co. Donegal
Tel: 074 9541112 Fax: 074 9541516
E-mail: yates@iol.ie
Web site: www.woodhillhouse.com

Woodhill House is in a wonderful position up a valley from Ardara. It is an historic country house standing on a site dating from the seventeenth century, overlooking the Donegal Highlands. It was formerly the home of the Nesbitts, Ireland's last commercial family. The present owners purchased the house about 16 years ago. The two front rooms are large and have wonderful views. Six ground-floor rooms are in the restored carriage house, ideal for folks who value their privacy. All have wheelchair access. There is a friendly informal atmosphere, and the house is surrounded by 1.5 acres of gardens, including a walled garden open to guests.

The high-quality restaurant is open from March to the end of October, and there is a licensed bar. Excellent French style cuisine is served, using fresh Irish produce and fish from Killybegs, Ireland's principal fishing port. There are several other options for eating in Ardara, and Irish music is often heard at most of Adare's 13 bars. The area is well known for its Donegal tweeds and woolen goods. The Wildlife Reserve is well worth a visit, and there are excellent bathing beaches, pony trekking, and golfing close by. Private parking.

OPEN: January-October
ROOMS: 23 rooms double/twin/family/single; all en suite

TERMS: from €48-65; single supplement; child reduction

BALLYSHANNON

Inis Saimer House
Sharon McGuinnes
Portnason, Bundoran Road, Ballyshannon, Co. Donegal
Tel: 071 985 1418
E-mail: Sharonmcguiness@eircom.com

This charming, listed Victorian residence, of terracotta colors and colonnades, has river or ocean views from all rooms. Woodland walks can be taken from the garden, where the wall dates back to the 1600s. The orchard provides fruit for the homemade jams served at breakfast. There is plenty of Old World charm here, the furnishings are mostly antique, and some of the bell pulls are in working order. After eight years of restoration, Inis Saimer opened for business in 1977.

The ambience is relaxed, peaceful, and informal. Sharon McGuinnes, a delightful lady, thoroughly enjoys chatting to her guests and is helpful in every way. The large bedrooms have rich Victorian colors, a TV, and hospitality trays; one has an original Victorian bath and shower. The room with a private bathroom has a "loo with a view". There is a drawing room with a TV and a fireplace and a separate dining room, where guests can order from the menu. The smoked salmon and home-baked bread are a treat, and Sharon's delicious omelets are the house specialty. There is plenty to keep you busy in the area—Belleek Pottery, golf, fishing, and coastal walks. Ballyshannon is within a 10-minute drive.

OPEN: March 1-November 1, other dates on request
ROOMS: 4 doubles
TERMS: from €35; single supplement; child reduction

BRUCKLESS

Bruckless House
Joan and Clive Evans
Bruckless, Co. Donegal
Tel: 074 9737071 Fax: 074 9737070
E-mail: bruck@iol.ie
Web site: www.iol.ie/~bruc/bruckless.html

This classic eighteenth-century house stands in a secluded spot in an

award-winning garden and cobbled yard and is a well-known Connemara Pony Stud Farm. It offers gracious living and guests are
encouraged to sit around and chat with the owners, who are happy
to share their knowledge of the area. The bedrooms are large and elegantly furnished. The spacious drawing and dining rooms overlook
green lawns and the sea. Both rooms have turf fires that are lit at the
first sign of a chill in the air. Most guests are happy with the houses'
"TV-free zone."

In this beautiful and unspoiled area of Ireland's Atlantic coast,
there are many archaeological sites to explore. Fishing, golf, and
horseback riding are also available. Private parking.

DIRECTIONS: Bruckless House is 12 miles west of Donegal town.

OPEN: April-September
ROOMS: 2 double, 2 single, 2 en suite
TERMS: €60-65; single supplement; child reduction

BUNDORAN

Bay View
Vincent and Ann McGrath
Main Street, Bundoran, Co. Donegal
Tel: 071 98412237
E-mail: bayviewbundoran@eircom.net

This impressive Victorian House faces the sea and has safe lockup
parking. The property is well maintained and several original features
remain, including marble fireplaces, cornices, and a ceiling rose. The
bedrooms have coordinated colorful bedding, direct dial phones, a
TV, hair dryers, and electric blankets. Tea makers are available, as
are ironing facilities, cots, and fax facilities. The McGraths take pride
in their business, and rooms are upgraded as needed. They are an
amiable and helpful couple and are happy to recommend places for
evening meals. Some of the rooms have sea views, as does the large
bright dining room and lounge. The ground-floor bedrooms have en-
suite facilities. There are standard rooms with private or shared bathrooms. Golf concessions are available.

OPEN: all year except Christmas
ROOMS: 25 rooms double/twin/family/single
TERMS: from €30; single supplement; child reduction

DONEGAL

Bay View
Marian Bennett
Ardara, Donegal, Co. Donegal
Tel: 075 41145 Fax: 075 41858
E-mail: chbennett@eircom.net

This handsome property overlooking the bay stands in a beautiful land-scaped garden, half a mile from Adare. Owner, Marian Bennett extends a warm welcome, offering tea and scones upon arrival. There are four extremely comfortable, spacious, well-equipped bedrooms, mostly with pine furniture, colorful fabrics, and cozy duvets. All the rooms have en-suite facilities and satellite TV. There is one twin-bedded ground-floor room.

Breakfast is served in the bright yellow and green dining room. Guests will enjoy Marian's award-winning breakfast featuring home-baked breads and scones. The house is well maintained and offers a high standard of accommodation. Guests are well taken care of here and are encouraged to sit back, relax, and enjoy the scenery. Adare is a Tweed and Heritage town, and there is an 18-hole golf course at Narin. Private parking.

OPEN: February-November
ROOMS: 5 rooms double/twin/single; all en suite
TERMS: €35; single supplement; child reduction

Island View House
Bernadette Dowds
Ballyshannon Road, Donegal Town, Co. Donegal
Tel: 074 9722411
E-mail: dowdsb@indigo.ie

Island View House stands in an elevated position, in $^3/_4$ of an acre of grounds, 1 kilometer from the town center. Bernadette Dowds is a friendly host, and the house is beautifully kept. The spacious family room has an oversized shower. All bedrooms are individually decorated in Victorian colors and have rich bed covers of white, green, yellow, and red. The ground-floor room has a pine wood floor and ceiling; all have en-suite facilities, a TV, hair dryer, and tea makers. Tasty breakfasts are served on fine china and lace tablecloths at separate tables.

Vegetarian and special diets are catered for with notice. There are books and puzzles for guests' use. The well-furnished lounge overlooks the sea. Private parking.

OPEN: all year
ROOMS: 2 double, 1 twin, 1 family; all en suite
TERMS: €35; single supplement; child reduction

St. Ernan's House
Brian O'Dowd
St. Ernan's Island, Donegal, Co. Donegal
Tel: 074 972 1065 Fax: 074 972 2098
E-mail: res@sainternans.co
Web site: www.sainternans.com

St. Ernan's, a classic Georgian house, was built in 1826 by John Hamilton, a nephew of the Duke of Wellington. It is situated on what was an island, is now linked to the mainland by a short causeway, and covers some 3.25 hectares. It is an elegant lovely country house in a beautiful location, offering peace and tranquility in wonderful surroundings. It has been in the O'Dowd's hands since 1987 and is licensed.

The individually styled rooms are well proportioned and spacious; most bedrooms have views of the sea and countryside. Dinner featuring fresh produce is beautifully presented in the large dining room; the elegant drawing room, with a log fire, is an informal spot in which to relax after a busy day. This property is for guests who are seeking quality accommodation combined with peace and tranquility. St. Ernan's is the right choice. Not suitable for children under six.

OPEN: Easter-October
ROOMS: 10 rooms double/twin/family; all en suite
TERMS: €120; single supplement; child reduction

DUNFANAGHY

Rosman House
Roisin McHugh
Dunfanaghy, Co. Donegal
Tel: 074 9136273 Fax: 074 9136273
E-mail: rosman@eircom.net

Web site: www.rosmanhouse.ie

Rosman House, an attractive modern dormer bungalow, stands in a superb spot with spectacular views of Horn Head, Muckish Mountain, and Sheephaven Bay. It has a large well-landscaped garden and is within walking distance of the village. Roisin McHugh, formerly a teacher, takes great pride in her establishment, and her husband runs the 40-hectare dairy and sheep farm. Improvements are ongoing, and the house has been freshly decorated. The spacious lounge opens onto a patio and gardens.

The bedrooms are individually decorated with coordinated floral color schemes. There are four ground-floor rooms. Their magnificent breakfasts are well known and are served in the elegant dining room on separate tables overlooking Horn Head. There are some enjoyable scenic walks nearby and an 18-hole golf course.

DIRECTIONS: Through Dunfanaghy village on the Falcarragh Road, turn right, immediately after Art Gallery

OPEN: all year
ROOMS: 1 double, 2 twin, 2 family; all en suite
TERMS: €34; family prices on request; single supplement; child reduction

GLENCOLUMBKILLE

Corner House
J.P. Byrne
Cashel, Glencolumbkille, Co. Donegal
Tel: 074 973 0021

Corner House is situated in the center of the village and, as the name implies, located on the corner. Mrs. Byrne is a pleasant and considerate host, and her son runs the pub.

The house looks quite modest from the outside but is surprisingly spacious inside. It has an enormous dining room and a small upstairs lounge. The house is well maintained; the bedrooms are average in size, immaculate, fresh, and bright.

The surroundings are beautiful and a great spot for hill walking. A lovely old grandfather clock stands in the hallway. There is an interesting doll collection displayed in a cabinet on the landing.

OPEN: June 1-end September
ROOMS: 2 double, 2 twin; all en suite

TERMS: €30; single supplement; child reduction

GWEEDORE

Min-a-Locha
John and Kathleen Duggan
Brinaleck Post Office, Bloody Foreland, Gweedore, Co. Donegal
Tel: 074 9532279
E-mail: minalocha@eircom.net

This purpose-built modern bungalow, although it does have a second story, overlooks what is said to be one of the best views in Ireland, the Bloody Foreland, and the Atlantic Ocean. The house was purpose-built for B&B and offers every comfort in a peaceful and tranquil setting. The bedrooms have a medieval décor and are of a good size, as are the bathrooms. The beds have attractive colorful duvets. Kathleen Duggan, who extends a warm welcome and prides herself on personal attention to her guests' needs, made all of the curtains and bed covers. The spacious lounge has a Victorian-style fireplace where turf fires burn on cool evenings. Breakfasts are served in the bright and airy dining room overlooking the view and include home-baked bread and scones.

There are sandy beaches, hill and coastal walks, cycling, and day trips to the islands. This is a perfect place from which to explore the dramatic and rugged area. A baby-sitting service can be arranged. Traditional Irish music can be found at several local venues.

DIRECTIONS: Call for driving directions

OPEN: April 1-October 31
ROOMS: 3 double, 1 twin, 1 family; 4 en suite
TERMS: €30; single supplement; child reduction

INISHOWEN

McGrory's
The McGrory Family
Culdaff, Inishowen, Co. Donegal
Tel: 074 9379104
E-mail: mcgr@aircom.net
Web site: www.mcgrorys.ie

McGrory's is a family-run establishment and provides first-class accommodation. The bedrooms are all of a good size and most have cherry wood furniture, comfortable beds, attractive fabrics, and duvets. All have a TV, a direct dial telephone, a hair dryer, tea makers, and a luggage rack; rooms in the oldest part of the house have exposed stone walls.

McGrory's is also a pub and restaurant. The McGrory family is musical, and Mac's Backroom Bar has earned an excellent reputation as one of Ireland's finest live music venues. Opening acts from around the world have appeared at Mac's, as well as Ireland's top performers, Altan and Paul Brady, the Saw Doctors, and Kieran Goss to name but a few.

Concessions are given to McGrory's residents who attend a gig at the Backroom Bar. Live music is performed every Wednesday and Saturday—quite a success story for a village in Donegal with a population of just 300 people.

The Front Bar hosts traditional sessions on Tuesday and Friday. Fresh local seafood features heavily on the menu in the restaurant, as well as steaks and lamb. Vegetarian and special diets are catered for. Angling and golf are close by; special golfing rates have been negotiated with Ballyliffen Golf Club.

DIRECTIONS: McGrory's is easily located in Culdaff village.

OPEN: all year
ROOMS: 17 double/twin; all en suite
TERMS: €55; single supplement; child reduction

INVER

Cloverhill House
Terry and June Coyle
Cranny, Inver, Co. Donegal
Tel: 074 9736165 Fax: 074 9736165

Cloverhill House is approached by a private drive bordered with high yew hedges and is an attractive long, low, modern whitewashed house in an elevated position, which has lovely river views.

The extensive gardens are beautiful and there are fruit trees and strawberry fields. There is an enormous and very pleasant sitting/dining room with a turf fire. The bedrooms are spacious and well furnished; three are on the ground floor. An annex bedroom with en-suite bathroom is available, ideal for guests who prefer privacy.

A 10-minute walk brings you to a sandy beach and fishing river.

Fishing, golfing, and mountain climbing activities are available locally. Private parking.

OPEN: February-November
ROOMS: 3 double, 2 twin, 1 single; 2 en suite
TERMS: from €30-35 for double/twin; single supplement; child reduction

KILLYBEGS

Bannagh House
Phyllis Melly
Fintra Road, Killybegs, Co. Donegal
Tel: 074 9371108
E-mail: bannaghhouse@eircom.net
Web site: www.bannaghhouse.com

This modern house stands in an elevated position in a small front garden and has wonderful views of the harbor, town, and near and distant hills. Killybegs is a large fishing port, and the harbor is busy with enormous fishing boats, making this an ideal place for fresh fish.

The lounge and dining room also have bay views. There is a TV lounge. The bedrooms, all on the ground floor, are well appointed and tastefully furnished. All are en suite and have a TV and hair dryer. Phyllis Melly works hard at creating a comfortable home for guests and is happy to give advice on local activities and recommend local restaurants. Private parking.

OPEN: March 30-October 31
ROOMS: 4 rooms double/twin/family; all en suite
TERMS: €32-35; single supplement; child reduction

Hollycrest Lodge
Ann Keeney
Donegal Road, Killybegs, Co. Donegal
Tel: 074 97 31470
E-mail: hollycrest@hotmail.com
Web site: www.littleireland.ie/hollycrestlodge

Guests continue to enjoy the relaxing atmosphere and warm welcome found here at this attractive Georgian style house, which sits off the road in a large well-maintained garden. Guests are welcome to make use of the garden, a pleasant spot in which to relax on fine days. Ann Keeney, a very personable lady, enjoys meeting people, and nothing is too much trouble to ensure her guests are comfortable. The house is well maintained and decorated and furnished to a high standard. The color-coordinated bedrooms are on the ground floor, one of which has a brass bed.

There is a guest lounge with a TV and a separate dining room where filling breakfasts are served. Evening meals are not served, but there are plenty of eating establishments close by. Private parking.

DIRECTIONS: N56 from Donegal to Killybegs, situated on right-hand side of road 2 kilometers from Killybegs

OPEN: February 1-November 30
ROOMS: 3 double, 1 twin, 1 single; 3 en suite
TERMS: from €33 for en suite; €30 for standard; single supplement; child reduction

Tullycullion House
The Tully Family
Tullycullion, Killybegs, Co. Donegal
Tel/Fax: 074 9731482
E-mail: tullys@gofreeindigo.ie
Web site: www.tullycullion.com

This delightful country house stands in 2 acres of grounds and well-landscaped gardens, in a secluded peaceful location, with wonderful views all round. It is an extremely good value, offering luxurious accommodation and 4-star facilities at modest prices. The Tully family is charming and takes great pride in their business, going out of their way to ensure their guests' needs are met. The kettle is always on the boil, and tea and cake are served in the conservatory on arrival.

The five bedrooms are individually decorated, have comfortable beds, quality linens, toiletries, and a TV. All bedrooms have en-suite facilities, with the exception of the additional room, which adjoins the family room and is ideal for families or friends traveling together. There are some interesting stenciled wood floors and walls throughout the house.

A banquet breakfast that includes a buffet starter, followed by potato waffles, pancakes and syrup, scrambled eggs, and smoked salmon, etc. is served in the elegant dining room. The dining room has an open fire and leads onto the conservatory, both overlooking scenic countryside views. Three sweet donkeys form the friendly welcoming committee—Cora, Abbey, and Connie. Guests return often for the tranquil ambience and the warm hospitality found at Tullycullion House. Early reservations recommended. Killybegs, the famous fishing port, with a variety of shops and venues for meals, is a 5-minute drive. Private parking.

DIRECTIONS: The house is well signed just before entering Killybegs on the Donegal to Killybegs Road.

OPEN: April 1-October 31
ROOMS: 5 rooms double/twin/family; all en suite
TERMS: €32-42; single supplement; child reduction

LETTERKENNY

Glenswilly B&B
Christopher and Eileen McGinley
New Mills, Letterkenny, Co. Donegal
Tel: 074 9137525

This 300-year-old house is surrounded by gardens in a peaceful location. The owner, Eileen McGinley, is an outgoing, colorful lady. Little wonder she has guests visiting from Canada, where she ran a bed and breakfast for 32 years. Her talent is obviously interior decorating and design. Guests who like to step back in time will love the old-fashioned ambience. The parlorlike lounge has a Victorian-style fireplace and is full of items of interest, including paintings and china. The rooms are unique, all with four-posters, one of which is king size. The fabrics are in rich colors of gold, green, and red. All are en suite and have a TV. The house is furnished in keeping with the character, some of which was shipped over from Canada. Guests will enjoy the tea and home-baked cakes offered upon arrival. This is an amazing place to stay; plan on staying awhile. Letterkenny is just over 4 miles away.

OPEN: all year including Christmas
ROOMS: 4 rooms double/twin/single
TERMS: €32.50; €35.00 single; not suitable for children under 10

Rinneen Country Home
Mary McBride

Woodlands, Ramelton Road, Letterkenny, Co.Donegal
Tel: 074 91 24591
E-mail: rinneencountryhome@eircom.net

Rinneen, which means "little plot of land at the top of the hill," has panoramic views of Lough Swilly, the mountains and green hills where contented sheep graze. This is a bright modern country home. Three rooms are upstairs, two of these command a fantastic view of the woodlands and water, all have a TV and power showers. There is a gas fire in the lounge that overlooks the view.

An additional bonus is Mary McBride, a former recipient of the Lyons Tea Irish Welcome Award and a congenial and helpful host, who is almost always on hand to assist with itineraries and who is particularly interested in literature. There are good choices at breakfast, served in the bright dining room. A wide choice of eating venues can be found in Letterkenny.

DIRECTIONS: Take the Ramelton Road from Letterkenny and travel for 5 kilometers to Fingerpost indicating Rinneen Country House, 1 kilometer from there to the house.

OPEN: February 20-December 20
ROOMS: 2 double, 1 family, 1 single
TERMS: €32.50; single supplement; child reduction

White Gables
Cabrini McConnellogue
Derry Road, Letterkenny, Co. Donegal
Tel: 074 9122583

White Gables is a spacious house in an elevated position overlooking the river and the town. There is a pleasant view from the dining room/lounge, which has a small sitting area and a table for breakfast that faces the window. The small bedrooms are clean and simply furnished; two are on the ground floor.

There is a pleasant garden where guests may sit on fine days and a conservatory with comfortable wicker furniture.

OPEN: all year
ROOMS: 3 double, 2 twin, 1 single; 3 en suite
TERMS: from €28 for double/twin; €63 for family room; single supplement; child reduction

LIFFORD

Fernbank
Elizabeth McLaughlin
Redcastle, Lifford, Inishowen, Co. Donegal
Tel: 074 9383032 Fax: 074 9383164

Fernbank, built in 1970, with later additions, is an extremely good value and is situated in an elevated position with spectacular views of Lough Foyle. Elizabeth McLaughlin, who is from Buncrana, has been offering her special brand of hospitality for 30 years; there is a home-away-from-home atmosphere, and the house is immaculate.

A hot drink is available at just about any time, and Elizabeth is happy to give advice on what to see and do in the area. The bedrooms are all on the ground floor and some have lough views. The sitting room and dining room have pine ceilings, and the rooms are bright and cheery. Greencastle, with its maritime museum and award-winning fish restaurant, is 11 kilometers away. Private parking.

DIRECTIONS: Situated on the main Derry-Moville Road, 9 miles from Muff

OPEN: all year
ROOMS: rooms, 3 double, 1 twin; all en suite
TERMS: €35; single supplement; child reduction

The Hall Green Farmhouse
Mervyn and Jean McKean
Port Hall, Lifford, Co. Donegal
Tel: 074 9414318 Fax: 074 914138
E-mail: jeanmckean@eircom.net
Web site: www.thehallgreen.co.uk

This traditional farmhouse dates back to 1611 and is situated on a working beef farm. The house has views over the River Foyle and on to the Sperrin Mountains. Salmon fishing is available on the River Foyle that runs through the farm. The bedrooms are tastefully decorated and have electric blankets, hair dryers, and other extras. The house is mainly furnished in antiques with marble fireplaces in the dining and drawing rooms. The house is centrally heated with modern conveniences throughout, yet it is one of the oldest inhabited houses in Ireland and retains the charming architecture of the past.

Guests are welcome to relax in the garden or go for a walk on the banks of the River Foyle. The farmhouse is in a good central position for touring Donegal, Glenveagh Castle and National Park, Slieve League, and the Giant's Causeway in County Antrim.

Golf, walking, bird watching, and a fully equipped leisure center are close by. A visit to the Lifford Old Courthouse, Visitor and Clan Centre is worthwhile. This is a friendly house with a home-away-from-home atmosphere. Your hosts will gladly help organize your itinerary and advise on local restaurants for your evening meal. Guests arrive as strangers but leave as friends. Private parking.

OPEN: January 6-December 15; off season by request
ROOMS: 1 double, 2 family, 1 double/single; 2 en suite
TERMS: €35 en suite, €32 standard; single supplement; child reduction

MOVILLE

Admiralty House
Suzanne McFeely
Carrownaffe, Moville, Co. Donegal
Tel: 074 9382529

Admiralty House, a beautifully restored Georgian house, was in a derelict condition when the McFeelys purchased it. Restoration took over two years; the result is a beautiful country house set in a pleasant wooded garden, with views of Lough Foyle. The entryway is very attractive and has marble floors, as does the lounge. There are rich colors throughout and stained-glass windows depicting various sea scenes. The house is furnished in keeping with its character; the owners found most of the pieces at various venues around the country. The bedrooms are individually decorated and are warm and comfortable. The conservatory, with its wicker furniture, is a new addition to the house. A bonus at Admiralty House is the warmth of the friendly owners, who are extremely helpful and provide a portfolio of places to visit.

Breakfasts only are served, but there are plenty of places to eat in Moville, an 8-minute walk away. Of local interest is Greencastle Maritime Museum, a Norman Castle and Napoleonic fort. Private parking.
DIRECTIONS: Take the Derry Road from Moville. The house is yellow and white and overlooks Lough Foyle.

OPEN: June 1-September 30

ROOMS: 2 double, 1 twin, 1 family
TERMS: €30; single supplement; child reduction

RAMELTON

Ardeen
Anne Campbell
Ramelton, Co. Donegal
Tel: 074 9151243 Fax: 074 9151243
E-mail: ardeenbandb@eir.com
Web site: www.ardeenhouse.com

This splendid country house built in 1845 is situated on its own grounds overlooking Lough Swilly. It stands in a well-tended, pleasant lawned front garden in a peaceful and tranquil spot. Improvements are ongoing. The spacious bedrooms are individually and elegantly decorated in lemon, blue, and buttermilk; they all have patchwork quilts made by the owner, Anne Campbell. The drawing and dining rooms are furnished with antiques and have open fires.

The house at one time belonged to a private nurse of King George V and, more recently, to two doctors. Anne Campbell is an excellent host who knows just how to make her guests feel at home. She formerly ran a village shop but now concentrates on running her very successful bed and breakfast. There is a tennis court for guests' use. There are three self-catering cottages available from Easter to October.

There are several places for an evening meal in Ramelton, which has been designated a National Heritage town and is a pleasant short stroll away. The county Genealogical Center is located in the old Meeting House, which is one of the oldest Presbyterian churches in Ireland. Private parking.

OPEN: Easter-October
ROOMS: 2 double, 1 twin, 1 family, 1 single; 3 en suite
TERMS: €35-40; child reduction; single supplement

COUNTY GALWAY

Galway contains the widely renowned area of Connemara, which stretches northward from Galway city up to Killary Harbour and is bordered on the east by beautiful Lough Corrib, which boasts an island for every day of the year.

Galway, the "city of the tribes", and the nearby popular resort of Salthill, which overlooks the famous Galway Bay, have lovely beaches, a promenade for walking, and lots of restaurants, making this an ideal holiday spot. Wild Connemara has inspired song and poetry. Today, Galway, Connemara, and the west of Ireland are a haven for ancient customs and culture. You will hear lilting and evocative Irish music in the pubs and often the Irish language being spoken. Travel offshore and you become immersed even deeper into Ireland's traditional way of life, with trips to Innishbofin, County Clare, Achill, and the Aran Islands. There is plenty to see and do in the west of Ireland, such as pony trekking, golfing on dramatically located golf courses, and angling (which is well catered for with abundant salmon and trout in clean waters).

If you are interested in sixteenth-century castles, visit the ruins of Ardamullivan Castle, 7.5 kilometers south of Gort, an O'Shaughnessy stronghold, and Fiddaun Castle, 7.5 kilometers south southwest of Gort, is another of their strongholds.

Clarinbridge is a popular place in September, when it hosts the Oyster Festival. Portumna, a market town, is at the head of Lough Derg. For the more adventurous, a climb up the Slieve Auchty Mountains is well worth the view. Two castles worth seeing are well preserved Derryhivenny Castle, 4.5 kilometers northeast of Portumna, built in 1653, and Pallas Castle, 9 kilometers from Portumna on the Loughrea Road.

Ballinasloe's well-known October Horse Fair lasts for eight days and includes carnival events and show-jumping exhibitions.

ARAN ISLANDS

Ard-Mhuiris
Cait Flaherty

163

Kilronan, Aran Islands, Co. Galway
Tel: 099 61208
E-mail: ardmhuiris@eircom.net

This friendly and warm house, with stunning Galway Bay views, is situated in a peaceful location. Cait Flaherty, born on the island, is a hospitable lady, who is happy to outline local walks and share her knowledge. She enjoys painting, and there are several pieces of her work on display. A sitting room has a TV and tea-making facilities. The en-suite rooms are neat and clean.

   Guests will enjoy the open countryside and the convenience of the restaurants and pubs at the Harbour, which is a 3-minute walk away. Guests arriving at the Harbour can be met with prior notice. Private parking.

OPEN: March 1-November 1
ROOMS: 6 rooms, all en suite; 4 on ground floor
TERMS: from €35; single supplement; child reduction

Man of Aran Cottage
Joe and Maura Wolfe
Kilmurvey, Inish Mor, Aran Islands, Co. Galway
Tel: 099 61301 Fax: 099 61324
E-mail: manofaran@eircom.net
Web site: www.manofarancottage.com

Man of Aran Cottage has a thatched roof and stands on an acre of ground. It was built by Robert Flaherty and used as the film set for *Man of Aran*. There is plenty of Old World charm, and the cottage is well maintained and the accommodation comfortable. The sitting room is a good place for guests to gather and share their day's experiences.

   Excellent breakfasts and prebooked dinners are on offer at the Man of Aran Cottage's own restaurant (for guests only) featuring fresh organic vegetables from the garden. Joe and Maura Wolfe are adept at making guests feel at home and are happy to help in any way to ensure guests have a comfortable stay. Parking available.

   DIRECTIONS: The house is approximately 4 miles from the harbor.

OPEN: March-November
ROOMS: 3 rooms double/twin; 1 en suite; 2 standard
TERMS: from €37-40; single supplement; child reduction
MEALS: breakfast; dinner availability arranged in advance

CASHEL

Cashel House
Dermot and Kay McEvilly
Cashel, Connemara, Co. Galway
Tel: 095 31001 Fax: 095 31077
E-mail: info@cashel-house-hotel.com
Web site: www.cashel-house-hotel.com

Situated at the head of Cashel Bay, this gracious, nineteenth-century country house is set in 20 hectares of award-winning gardens and woodland walks. It has gained an international reputation for good food and luxurious comfort in a quiet, relaxing atmosphere. General and Madame de Gaulle spent two weeks of their Irish holiday here in 1969.

Carefully cooked fresh garden and sea produce, such as lobsters, clams, mackerel, salmon, and scallops, are its specialties. There is a carefully chosen wine list. Meals are tastefully presented in the elegant dining room with open turf fires. Special diets may be catered for with advance notice.

The house is furnished with antiques and other fine treasures, and the bedrooms are beautifully appointed. There are several areas in which to sit, including a conservatory and patio area. Guests may walk along the seashore, through woods and streams, or drive through beautiful scenic Connemara.

Luxury and tranquility combine with the romantic setting to create a magical experience. Cashel House is an excellent choice for a special occasion or honeymoon.

DIRECTIONS: Driving $1^1/_2$ miles west of Recess, turn south on N59—Cashel House signposted from there

OPEN: February 5-January
ROOMS: 35 double/twin/family; 32 en suite
TERMS: from €190-390 per room; single supplement; child reduction
MEALS: full dinner and lighter meals

CLARINBRIDGE

Springlawn B&B
Maura McNamara
Stradbally, Clarinbridge, Co. Galway
Tel: 091 796045 Fax: 091 796045

E-mail: springlawn2@hotmail.com
Web site: www.surf.to/springlawn2.com

This attractive house with dormer windows stands in a hectare of land in the heart of oyster country. Springlawn has been awarded the Irish Hospitality Award three times. Clarinbridge holds an annual Oyster Festival on the weekend of the second Sunday in September.

There is a wooded area behind the house, and the sea is within walking distance. The good-sized bedrooms are maintained to a high standard and have modern comfortable furnishings. Maura McNamara, who has been running her successful bed and breakfast for over 11 years, takes a personal interest in her guests and is happy to provide information on golf, fishing, and pony trekking, all of which are within a 15-minute drive. There is a TV lounge and a separate dining room where breakfasts and light meals are served at modest prices. For evening meals, there are several restaurants close by. There is no public phone, but guests may use the owner's on request.

DIRECTIONS: Springlawn is 1 mile off the N18 on the Limerick side of Clarinbridge village.

OPEN: March 1-November 30
ROOMS: 3 double/twin/family; all en suite
TERMS: €30-34; single supplement; child reduction

CLIFDEN

Buttermilk Lodge
Patrick and Catheriona O'Toole
Westport Road, Clifden, Connemara, Co. Galway
Tel: 095 21951 Fax: 095 21953
E-mail: buttermilklodge@eircom.net
Web site: www.buttermilklodge.com

Buttermilk Lodge is a charming property situated in an elevated position and a 5-minute walk to Clifden. Guests are advised at the front door to "Ring the Cowbell and I will be with you in a moo." This is a very welcoming and friendly property. Owners, Patrick and Catheriona O'Toole opened for business in July 1997 and have been busy with happy guests since that time. This is a very pleasant and relaxing place to stay. There are 12 delightful bedrooms, all furnished in pine, with luxurious white quilts and comfy beds. All rooms have en-suite showers, a TV, hair dryer, tea makers, phones, and ironing facilities. Three are on the ground floor, named after local lakes; the house is named after the closest, Loch Ime—Buttermilk Lake. All have countryside views.

Breakfasts are a banquet; the buffet offers freshly baked pastries, scones, bread, fruits, and juice, followed by a choice of a full-cooked Irish or Connemara smoked salmon, homemade pancakes, etc., or you can try the delicious "daily special." A guest comments, "Back again, kept dreaming about the breakfast."

There is an upstairs lounge that has a turf fire, books, board games, and a computer, where you can check e-mail, with free broadband Internet. Drying facilities are provided.

A special New Year's Package is available. Advance reservations only. Private parking

DIRECTIONS: Buttermilk Lodge is located 400 meters north of Clifden on the N59, Westport Road.

OPEN: March-December
ROOMS: 12 rooms double/twin/family/single; all en suite
TERMS: from €40-50 March/April/May/June and September/October/November; €50-70 July/August/December

✓ Mallmore House
Alan and Kathleen Hardman
Clifden, Co. Galway
Tel: 095 21460
E-mail: info@mallmore.com
Web site: www.mallmorecountryhouse.com

This lovingly restored Georgian house (formerly the home of the Darcy family, the founders of Clifden, and His Excellency, the Archbishop of Tuam) is set in 14 hectares and is within walking distance of the sea. The house overlooks the bay, and most of the bedrooms have lovely views. The spacious bedrooms, equipped with a TV, are on the ground floor; they are comfortable and tastefully decorated with period paper. The large lounge has a turf fire and is a peaceful place in which to relax after a busy day. Award-winning breakfasts are served in a separate dining room, and for other meals, there are several establishments in Clifden.

Kathleen Hardman is a considerate and helpful host and guests are assured of personal attention. The world-famous Connemara ponies are bred at Mallmore and can be seen in the grounds, and the woodland is a haven for a great variety of wildlife.

DIRECTIONS: 1 mile from Clifden on the Ballconneely Road

OPEN: March 7-October 1
ROOMS: 3 double, 2 twin, 1 family; all en suite
TERMS: €40; single supplement; child reduction

Ocean Villa
Carmel Murray
Sky Road, Kingstown, Clifden, Co. Galway
Tel: 095 21357 Fax: 095 21357
E-mail: oceanvilla@eircom.net
Web site: www.oceanvillaireland.com

Ocean Villa is situated in a wonderful position overlooking sea and hills. The house is immaculately maintained, and the welcome is warm and friendly. Carmel Murray is a most hospitable host who greets guests with a hot drink upon arrival and is happy to spend time assisting them in every way. The bedrooms are warm, of a good size, have level access, comfortable beds, and tea-making facilities. There are two lounges, one with a TV.

This is a peaceful and tranquil location and there is plenty to see and do from here.

Three cats, a horse, cows, and calves reside on the property. Golf, mountain climbing, pony trekking, fishing, and beach walks, all of which can be arranged by your hosts, are close by.

DIRECTIONS: Take a left turn at center of Clifden for Sky Road, pass for Ocean Villa

OPEN: March 1-October 31
ROOMS: 6 double/twin/family; all en suite
TERMS: €35; single supplement; child reduction

The Quay House
Paddy and Julia Foyle
Beach Road, Clifden, Co. Galway
Tel: 095 21369 Fax: 095 21608
E-mail: thequay@iol.ie
Web site: www.thequayhouse.com

Quay House is the oldest building in Clifden, built over 200 years ago for the Harbour Master. Since that time, it has been a Franciscan Monastery and a convent. A charming couple, Paddy and Julia Foyle, run it, and the ambience is informal and comfortable. The spacious bedrooms are individually themed and have antique furniture, original paintings, and large bathrooms with both shower and bath. Several bedrooms have working fireplaces, most of them overlooking the harbor. The studios have balconies and small fitted kitchens. All bedrooms have a TV, a phone, and tea makers. Two ground-floor bedrooms have wheelchair access.

Quay House is full of items of interest, including family portraits, period furniture, and other treasures. The house was in a dilapidated condition until Paddy and Julia undertook the job of tastefully refurbishing the house, skillfully combining modern amenities with Old World charm. A tiger's head greets guests in the entry hall, and Buster the pug also resides here. This is a wonderful place to stay; guests have every comfort. The house has a good selection of wines.

Breakfast is served in the conservatory overlooking the garden, a great spot from which to start the day. Special diets can be catered for at breakfast. There are several establishments in the area for evening meals.

OPEN: mid March-end October
ROOMS: 14 rooms, double/twin/family; all en suite
TERMS: from €70-90; single supplement; child reduction

CLONBUR

Ballykine House
Ann Lambe
Clonbur, Co. Galway
Tel: 094 9546150 Fax: 094 95460150
E-mail: ballykine@eircom.net
Web site: www.ballykinehouse-clonbur-cong.com

Ballykine house is situated on the road between the picturesque villages of Cong and Clonbur and is known as the gateway to Connemara. The house continues to maintain its high standard and offers good value accommodation. It overlooks the famous fishing lake of Lough Mask.

Approached via a long private driveway, it has its own private grounds of gardens and lawns surrounded by beautiful woodlands. The oldest part of the house belonged to the Guinness family; the family purchased the house and land in 1940, with an addition in 1992. There is a wine license. Mr. and Mrs. Lambe are a very congenial couple who have created a warm and inviting atmosphere. There is a cozy sitting room with open fire and a conservatory to relax in with tea and coffee makers provided. The house is beautifully maintained, and all bedrooms have a TV.

There are wonderful forest walks (guides can be provided) as well as walks to the summit of magnificent Benlevi. The immediate area is a fisherman's paradise. There is a very pleasant lakeside walk available. Restaurants are within walking distance of the house. Golf is available at famous Ashford Castle and Ballinrobe.

DIRECTIONS: Take N84 from Galway to Cong; from Cong, take R345 to Ballykine House

OPEN: April 1-November 1
ROOMS: 5 twin/family/double; all en suite
TERMS: from €35; single supplement; child reduction

CONNEMARA

Cregg House
Mary O'Donnell
Galway Road, Connemara, Co. Galway
Tel: 095 21326 Fax: 095 21326
Email: cregghouse1@eircom.net
Web site: www.cregg-house.com

This immaculate dormer bungalow stands in an elevated position on half a hectare of grounds. The house has a spectacular view of Roundstone Bog and the mountains beyond. Mary O'Donnell maintains her high standards, and the bedrooms are individually decorated with soft pastel colors. The O'Donnells have been offering their special brand of hospitality for over 13 years. Guests feel very much at home here and enjoy chatting round the turf fire, which is lit at the first sign of a chill in the air. Excellent breakfasts include fresh fruit, homemade yogurt, and soda bread. An ideal base from which to tour Connemara, there is a fishing river less than 5 minutes away, and golf and horseback riding are also available. Private parking.

DIRECTIONS: On N59, main Galway Road

OPEN: March 1-November 1
ROOMS: 3 double, 2 twin, 1 family; 5 en suite
TERMS: €28-35; single supplement; child reduction

Killary House
Fiona King
Leenane, Connemara, Co. Galway
Tel: 095 42254
E-mail: kinghillaryhouse@eircom.net

Killary House has lots of character and is situated on 800 acres, part of a working sheep farm, overlooking Killary Harbour. This is an idyllic location for families and folks interested in outdoor activities. After 35 years in the business, Fiona King is still an enthusiastic host. Leenane is a small village that served as the location for *The Field*, a film starring Richard Harris. Evening meals are not served, but there are plenty of establishments close by that serve good food. Special diets are catered for at breakfast. The bedrooms are all spacious and furnished. Tea-making facilities are available in the bedrooms. There is also a very large sitting room with a TV. The welcome here is warm; guests return here often, enjoying the informal ambience and Fiona's hospitality. There are lovely views all round the property and pleasant walks can be taken round the farm. Private parking.
DIRECTIONS: Signposted at Leenane

OPEN: March-October
ROOMS: 6 rooms double/family/twin; 5 en suite
TERMS: €30-35; single supplement; child reduction

Screebe House
Marcus Carey
Camus, Connemara, Co. Galway
Tel: 091 574110 Fax: 091 574179
E-mail: bookings@screebehouse.ie
Web site: www.screebehouse.ie

This secluded, magical, rugged listed Edwardian estate comprises 32,000 acres and stands in the beautiful, wild Connemara countryside. It overlooks Camus Bay and has its own harbor and lovely gardens. Although Screebe House is primarily a fishing and shooting lodge, there are lots of activities on offer for outdoor enthusiasts. Walks can be taken, where you can see red deer, rare flora, and many birds.
The nine spacious bedrooms, all en suite, except for the two top

floor single bedrooms, have antique furniture and comfortable beds. There are three large public rooms, a library/sitting room, drawing room, and separate dining room. There are several items of interest about, including some original paintings. Food is a specialty of the house; the chef prepares imaginative evening meals featuring fresh seafood, meats, and fresh local produce, followed by homemade desserts. Special diets catered for with advance notice.

OPEN: May 1-September 30
ROOMS: 9 double/twin/family/single; all en suite except for 2 singles on top floor sharing a bathroom
TERMS: from €75; single supplement; not suitable for children

GALWAY

Carraig Beag
Catherine and Paddy Lydon
1 Burren Heights Knocknacarra, Salthill, Galway, Co. Galway
Tel: 091 521696
E-mail: thelydons@eircom.net

This luxurious red brick house is just off the promenade and has peek views of the bay.

The bedrooms are of a good size and are furnished with every comfort in mind. The house is well furnished, and there is an elegant dining room, which has a beautiful crystal chandelier, marble fireplace, attractive wood doors, and a handsome staircase.

The owners, Catherine and Paddy, are an additional bonus; they are a very helpful couple and superb hosts. They often take walks along the promenade in the evening; guests may join them, but beware you might find it hard to keep up.

This good value bed and breakfast offers a good standard of accommodation at modest prices and is well situated for all the local amenities. Private parking.

DIRECTIONS: Follow the signs for Salthill, turn right after the Spinnaker House Hotel into Knocknacarra Road, Carraig Beag is the second house on the right.

OPEN: March-October 1
ROOMS: 3 rooms double/twin/family; all en suite
TERMS: from €40-50; single supplement; child reduction

The Connaught
Colette and Tom Keaveney
Barna Road, Salthill, Galway, Co. Galway
Tel: 091 525865
E-mail: tcconnaught@eircom.net
Web site: www.connaughtbandb.com/

This pleasant, friendly residence is set back off the road in an elevated position. Galway town is within walking distance, or you can take the city bus, which runs at 30-minute intervals. It is a well-maintained house decorated to a high standard. The rooms are nicely furnished, have orthopedic beds with electric blankets, a TV, and hospitality trays. The lounge has rich red carpeting, and there is a bright dining room where an extensive menu of fruits and a full Irish breakfast can be enjoyed.

An extremely cordial and helpful couple, the Keaveneys do everything to ensure guests are comfortable and well taken care of. There is a warm and friendly atmosphere; guests feel relaxed and very much at home here. There are many interesting family photographs on display, as well as other items of interest. Private parking.

DIRECTIONS: Drive along the promenade in Salthill, with Galway Bay on the left. Continue until you reach a T-junction, turn left at Barna Road. The house is approximately 500 yards on the right.

OPEN: March 15-November 1
ROOMS: 6 rooms double/twin/ family; all en suite
TERMS: from €45-50; single supplement; child reduction

Killeen House
Catherine Doyle
Bushy Park, Galway, Co. Galway
Tel: 091 524170 Fax: 091 528065
E-mail: killeenhouse@ireland.com
Web site: www.killeenhousegalway.com

This charming house, built in 1840, is approached by a tree-lined lane. It is nestled in 10 hectares of beautiful landscaped gardens that extend down to Lake Corrib. Catherine Doyle is a wonderful host with a flair for décor and a passion for antiques.

The house has been tastefully refurbished, combining all modern comforts without detracting from the original ambience. The elegant drawing room has the original marble fireplace and an interesting teapot collection. The rooms are enormous and luxuriously appointed. One room reflects the Victorian era, and another the Edwardian. As a guest once commented, "These must be the most comfortable beds in Ireland." There are direct dial phones and tea-making facilities in the bedrooms, all with bath and shower.

A varied breakfast of fresh fruit, home-baked bread, juice, cereals, plus a full Irish choice is presented in the elegant dining room. For those who enjoy gracious living in a tranquil atmosphere, Killeen House is an excellent choice. A path from the house leads down to the shores of Lough Corrib. Private parking.

DIRECTIONS: Situated on the N59 4 miles from Galway

OPEN: March-October; closed for 2008
ROOMS: 6 rooms double/family/twin; 5 en suite
TERMS: from €75.00; single supplement; not suitable for children under 12

Rose Villa
Kevin and Maire O'Hare
10 Cashelmara, Knocknacarra Cross, Salthill, Co. Galway
Tel: 091 584200 Fax: 091 584200
E-mail: kevin.ohare@ireland.com
Web site: www.rosevillabnb.com

This handsome large, bright, and airy house has views of the Bay and Bird Sanctuary and stands in a peaceful spot on the road to Connemara. The bedrooms are individually decorated, well furnished, have comfortable beds, and Dormer duvets. All have en-suite bathrooms, tea makers, and a TV. Hair dryers are available on request.

Excellent breakfasts include fresh fruit, yogurt, and a freshly cooked version served at separate tables in the bright sunny dining room.

Of interest is a selection of prints of the Custom House Trinity College that are on display. There is a comfortable lounge where a gas fire is lit at the first sign of a chill in the air, and there is a balcony for guests' use. Kevin and Maire O'Hare work as a team to maintain their high standards. Kevin usually greets guests, provides lots of local information, and is happy to share his knowledge of the area.

DIRECTIONS: Follow the signs to Salthill for Knocknacarra Cross

OPEN: all year
ROOMS: 4 double/twin; all en suite
TERMS: €35; single supplement; child reduction

KILKIERAN

Hillside House
Barbara Madden
Kylesalia, Kilkieran, Carna, Co. Galway
Tel: 095 95 33420
E-mail: hillsidehouse@oceanfree.net
Web site: www.connemara.net/hillside

Hillside House, a haven of peace and tranquility, is nestled between the mountains and the sea overlooking Kilkieran Bay. The elevated position enhances the stunning views, one guest commented, "We will keep this place in our heart." The exceptionally well-maintained, stylish bedrooms are beautifully furnished, tastefully decorated, and equipped with a TV, radio, hair dryer, and tea makers. All have balconies overlooking the view. There are areas to sit outside, and tea can be taken on the verandah. There is an extensive breakfast menu served in the bright and charming dining room.

An additional bonus is the delightful owner, Barbara Madden, who has created a warm home from home ambience. Little wonder she is the proud recipient of a 4-diamond award.

There are coastal walks, hill walks, and sandy beaches nearby.

DIRECTIONS: Situated 200 meters off the Coast Road #340 towards Carna in the heart of Connemara

OPEN: April 1-September 30
ROOMS: 4 rooms double/twin/triple; all en suite
TERMS: from €33-35

LEENANE

Delphi Lodge
Peter and Jane Mantle
Leenane, Co. Galway
Tel: 095 42222 Fax: 095 42296

E-mail: stay@delphilodge.ie
Web site: www.delphilodge.ie

This magnificent, beautifully restored 1830s house is exceptionally well maintained and is now one of the finest sporting lodges in Ireland. Set in 400 hectares with three loughs in a stunning lakeside location, surrounded by ancient woodlands and towering mountains, Delphi Lodge is the ultimate Connemara retreat.

The house has antique pine furniture, and the spacious bedrooms have lovely views. Originally the sporting estate of the Marquis of Sligo, Delphi Lodge is now the home of Peter and Jane Mantle. Jane is a Cordon Bleu cook, who specializes in local seafood.

The lodge has a strong emphasis on salmon and trout fishing. Delphi is one of the finest fisheries in Ireland. Fly-fishing for salmon is available but must be prebooked. The fishing season runs from spring to September. Outside the season, the lodge is popular with shooting parties, ramblers, and golfers. Horseback riding and hunting can be arranged. A huge snooker room and a magnificent library are open to guests. Superb and uncrowded beaches are within a 20-minute drive, and Delphi Lodge is conveniently placed for visiting Westport and all the sites of Connemara. Superb evening meals are served at a huge oak table, and the wine cellar is extensive. French is spoken. There are 2, 3, and 7 half-board packages available.

OPEN: January 5-December 10
ROOMS: 12 rooms double/twin; all en suite; 4 charming cottages available for self catering
TERMS: €100; single supplement; not suitable for young children
MEALS: dinners extra

Glen Valley House
Josephine O'Neill
Glencroff, Leenane, Co. Galway
Tel: 095 42269
E-mail: gvhouse@yahoo.com

This friendly, award-winning, modest farmhouse is found down a rather bumpy road in a remote location amidst lovely countryside. Nestled in the foothills of Lettershanbally Mountain, Glen Valley is a working farm and a warm, friendly house. The rooms are spacious, clean, and filled with old-fashioned furniture. The small cozy lounge has turf fires.

This is an ideal base for those who enjoy hill walking. Pony trekking is available on the farm, which is run by Mrs. O'Neill. Substantial breakfasts are provided, and Mrs. O'Neill is happy to make recommendations and dinner reservations for the restaurants that can be found a short drive away. Private parking.

DIRECTIONS: N59 Clifden Road, 4 ¹/₂ miles from Leenane Village

OPEN: May 1-November 20
ROOMS: 2 double, 2 twin, 1 family; 3 en suite; 1 private bath
TERMS: €37.50; single supplement; child reduction

OUGHTERRARD

Corrib View Farmhouse
Ethel and Rita Lea
Lough Corrib, Oughterrard, Co. Galway
Tel: 091 552345 Fax: 091 552880
E-mail: corribvw@gofree.indigo.ie

This secluded 200-year-old Georgian-style farmhouse bordered by shrubs and trees, stands in lovely gardens, with panoramic views of Lough Corrib. This a wonderful place where you can unwind and enjoy the stunning scenery. The pitted rock formation, created over thousands of years by acid water, and the beautiful summer lilies are an added bonus. The bedrooms are of a good size, the family room is very large, and all have en-suite facilities. The rooms have comfortable old-fashioned furniture, and the ambience is warm and friendly. There is a guest sitting room, and private tennis courts are available. Fishing boat and boatmen can be hired. Oughterrard Golf Course and pitch and putt courses are a few minutes walk. The ruins of Aughnanure Castle are close by, and a boat ride will take you to the fifteenth-century monastic ruins. Private parking.

OPEN: February 1-November 30
ROOMS: 6 rooms double/twin/family; all en suite

Corrib Wave Guest House
Michael and Maria Healy
Portacarron, Oughterrard, Co. Galway

Tel: 091 552147 Fax: 091 552736
E-mail: cwh@gofree.indigo.ie
Web site: www.corribwave.com

Corrib Wave House is a 3-star guesthouse situated in picturesque surroundings, overlooking the lake and Connemara Mountains. This is a
peaceful retreat, part of a working sheep farm of 10 hectares. The
bedrooms, all of which overlook the view, have been upgraded with
sturdy seating made by owner Michael Healy and have good-sized
bathrooms, a television, and hair dryer. The lounge has an open fire,
and there is a separate dining room where breakfast and excellent
meals, if prearranged, are served. Special diets are catered for with
advance notice. A conservatory and patio are available to guests. This
is an ideal spot for people who enjoy the outdoors; there are lovely
walks close by, as well as salmon, trout, and coarse fishing. There are
boats for hire and ghillies can be arranged. Swimming can be enjoyed
on the lake, and there is an 18-hole golf course within a kilometer.
Special breaks can be arranged. Private parking
   DIRECTIONS: Easily found of the N59 1 kilometer east of
Oughterrard. The house is conveniently located near Galway and
Connemara.

OPEN: February 1-November 30
ROOMS: 6 rooms double/twin/family; all en suite
TERMS: €40-45
MEALS: prebooked dinners are available

Waterfall Lodge
Kathleen Dolly
Oughterrard, Connemara, Co. Galway
Tel: 091 55168
E-mail: kdolly@eircom.net
Web site: www.waterfalllodge.net

This superb period residence stands in a secluded setting, only a minute's walk to the village. There is a mature garden with rare shrubs
and plants and a cascading waterfall; the beautiful grounds are ablaze
with color in spring and summer. The river Owen Riff runs through
the property, and private game fishing for salmon and trout is available to guests. The house is furnished with antiques, including a
grandfather clock, and the tastefully furnished bedrooms are reached

by a pitch pine stairway. Two have four-poster beds; all are en suite and have a TV. An extensive breakfast is served in the elegant dining room at separate tables. The spacious lounge has a cast-iron and marble fireplace, and guests may help themselves to tea and coffee at any time.

Kathleen Dolly is a delightful lady and is very knowledgeable about the area. This is a warm, friendly, and popular establishment; early reservations are recommended. Private parking

OPEN: all year except Christmas
ROOMS: 6 rooms double/twin/family; all en suite
TERMS: €40-45; single supplement; child reduction

ROUNDSTONE

Errisbeg Lodge
Shirley King
Errisbeg, Roundstone, Co. Galway
Tel: 095 35807
E-mail: errisbeglodge@eircom.net
Web site: www.errisbeglodge.com

Errisbeg Lodge, named after the mountain, stands on 30 acres, amid several acres of traditional Connemara Gardens. Situated on the mountain slopes, overlooking two Atlantic Beaches, it is a nature lover's paradise. There are Connemara Ponies, rare wild flowers, plenty of beautiful walks, and for artists, an opportunity to capture the local beauty on canvas. The ground floor's well-maintained en-suite bedrooms are equipped with clock radios, hair dryers, and an information pack.

Some of the rooms have king-size beds and are of a good size. There is a sitting room, and although Errisbeg Lodge is a TV-free zone, there is a video and plenty of books available.

Shirley King is a friendly and helpful lady who enjoys her bed and breakfast business. She is happy to offer advice and recommend things to do and places for meals. French is spoken. Shirley has been in business for many years and has built up a steady clientele. Advance reservations are highly recommended. Private parking.

OPEN: February 1-November 30
ROOMS: 5 double/twin; all en suite
TERMS: €37.50-47.50; single supplement; child reduction

SPIDDAL

Cala 'n Uisce
Moya Feeney
Greenhill, Spiddal, Co. Galway
Tel: 091 553324 Fax: 091 553324
E-mail: moyafeeney@iolfree.ie

Cala 'n Uisce means "little harbor," which is apt, as the house is in a picturesque setting facing the bay. The house was designed by owner Padraig Feeney and has leaded windows and a red brick exterior. High standards are found here, and the house continues to be exceptionally well maintained. There are three ground-floor bedrooms attractively decorated with coordinated fabrics; all bedrooms have tea making facilities and a TV. Many interesting paintings of local scenes, by Mrs. Feeney and other family members, are on display throughout the house. The lounge, which has a turf fire, leads out onto a patio. The dining room, where tasty breakfasts are served on pretty china and linen tablecloth-covered tables, overlooks the bay. Padraig Feeney's father was a cousin of John Ford, who directed *The Quiet Man*. This is an Irish-speaking area, and the Feeney family speaks Irish. Cala 'n Uisce is a most comfortable and peaceful place; beautiful bog areas and sea walks are close by. No pets.
   DIRECTIONS: Situated 2.5 kilometers west of Spiddal village

OPEN: April-October
ROOMS: 5 double/twin; all en suite
TERMS: from €34; single supplement; child reduction

Cloch na Scith-Thatched Cottage
Nancy Hopkins-Naughton
Kellough, Spiddal, Co. Galway
Tel: 091 553364 Fax: 091 553890
Web site: www.thatchcottage.com

This cozy, 130-year-old, traditional thatched cottage overlooking Galway Bay is part of a working farm and has played host to actress Julie Christie and the Swedish ambassador. There are thick stone walls, uneven floors, plenty of history, and Old World charm. Owner, Nancy Hopkins-Naughton offers one of the warmest welcomes in Ireland. She is a delightful, down-to-earth host, and guests are greeted with a hot drink on arrival, often with homemade cake. The family are Irish speaking and into Irish music. The lounge/dining room has turf fires, and a Galway wedding shawl that belonged to Nancy's grandmother hangs on the wall. Breakfast and four-course home-cooked dinners, if ordered in advance, are served on blue willow china on old pine tables. Guests may bring their own wine.

Nancy is an absolutely delightful lady; there are no petty rules, and guests are treated as friends, so it is little wonder that many guests are repeat visitors. Bedrooms are comfortable with firm beds; two are on a lower floor and one room is quite large with its own bathroom. The beach is 2 minutes away and there are maps provided for folks interested in walking. Cloch na Scith has been featured on the television program *Unusual Holidays in Ireland.* A one bedroom self-catering cottage is available.

OPEN: all year except Christmas
ROOMS: 1 double, 1 twin, 1 single; all en suite
TERMS: €34 low season; €36 high season; single supplement; child reduction

Col Mar House
Maureen Keady
Salahoona, Spiddal, Co. Galway
Tel: 091 553247 Fax: 091 553247

This comfortable secluded country home stands in mature gardens and private woods, 150 yards off the road. The rural and peaceful setting is close to the sea and the beach. Bog walks with lovely views can be taken. Col Mar House is well maintained, with new windows recently installed. Special diets can be catered for at breakfast. There are plenty of venues for evening meals close by. The bedrooms are of a good size, have comfortable beds, and are furnished in keeping with the house; tea-making facilities are provided in rooms. Children are welcome here. There is a playground, cot, and a highchair available. Guests are welcome to enjoy the garden.

There is a sandy beach, golf, and fishing nearby, and this location is handy for touring Connemara. Maureen Keady is a warm and hospitable host, a hot drink is offered on arrival, and there is a good supply of information on what to see and do in the area. Private parking.
DIRECTIONS: Situated 1.5 kilometers west of Spiddal

OPEN: May-September

ROOMS: 5 double/twin/family; all en suite
TERMS: from €33; single supplement; child reduction

TUAM

O'Connor's Guesthouse
Josephine O'Connor
Kilmore, Tuam, Co. Galway
Tel: 093 28118 Fax: 093 26525
E-mail: kilmorehouse@mail.com
Web site: www.ebookireland.com/oconnors.htm

This warm and friendly bungalow, part of a working farm, stands in extensive grounds and large gardens. Guests are welcome to enjoy the garden on fine days. Josephine O'Connor has been running her business for 30 years; she enjoys meeting people and welcomes visitors from all over the world. The bedrooms, all on the ground floor, have garden views and are prettily decorated with soft pastels. All have ensuite showers and a TV. A tasty breakfast, prepared to order, features homemade bread and scones and traditional Irish fare.

This is a good value accommodation. Josephine is happy to help with itinerary planning and genealogy. A cozy guest lounge is available, and there is an interesting teapot collection. There is a restaurant within walking distance for evening meals. The house is easily located and well signed. Private parking.

DIRECTIONS: Situated off the Galway/Tuam Road, 1 mile from Tuam

OPEN: all year except Christmas
ROOMS: 5 rooms double/twin/family/single; all en suite
TERMS: €34.00; single supplement; child reduction

COUNTY LIMERICK

Bordered on the north by the expanses of the Shannon, Limerick is a peaceful farming county with its fair share of relics from the past. Limerick city's origins go back to the days of the Vikings. Always a principal fording point for the Shannon River, it has played an important part in Irish history, particularly during the 1690s. Old English Town and the old Irish area across the river are the most interesting parts of the city to explore, particularly the Georgian architecture around St. John's Square. The most noteworthy sight to visit is the Granary, a restored eighteenth-century warehouse, which houses the tourist office as well as restaurants, shops, and an exhibition gallery. King John's Castle with its massive rounded tower, St. Mary's Cathedral, dating from 1172, and the Hunt Collection at the National Institute for Higher Education can also be visited. Adare has some splendid ruins to see, the finest one being the Franciscan Friary. Others include the Trinitarian Abbey, the Augustinian Abbey, and St. Nicholas Church. It is a most attractive town, with pretty thatched cottages and lovely views of Desmond Castle and Adare Manor on the river. It is thought the "limerick" may well have come from Croom, which was the meeting place of eighteenth-century Gaelic poets, who wrote extremely witty verse.

ADARE

Carrabawn House
Bridget Lohan
Killarney Road, Adare, Co. Limerick
Tel: 061 396067 Fax: 061 396025
E-mail: carrabawnhouse@eircom.net
Web site: www.carrabawnhouseadare.com/

Carrabawn House is situated on the edge of Adare Golf Course, just a few minutes away from the picturesque village of Adare, stands in beautiful gardens, and is delightful in every way. Bridget Lohan takes immense pride in her guesthouse and is the proud recipient of many awards, including the prestigious Environmental Award for the Best Kept Business Premises. The bedrooms, some with garden views, have individual décor and are named after local counties. They are tastefully decorated with rich pastels, have quality furnishings, 4-star amenities, satellite TV, direct dial telephones, and tea makers. The en-suite bathrooms are fully tiled and have power showers. Breakfasts are served in the conservatory overlooking the garden and comfortable sitting room.

Bridget enjoys her guests, and is happy to sit and chat, and gives advice on places of local interest. The hospitality here is of the highest standard. There are several venues for dinner in the village, and Bridget would be happy to make recommendations.

OPEN: all year except Christmas
ROOMS: 8 rooms double/twin/family; all en suite
TERMS: €45-50; single supplement; child reduction

Clonunion House
Mary and Michael Fitzgerald
Limerick Road, Adare, Co. Limerick
Tel/Fax: 061 396657
E-mail: clonunionhouse@eircom.net
Web site: www.adarevillage.com

This traditional eighteenth-century farmhouse is 100 meters off the main road in tranquil surroundings and is part of a working sheep, beef, and tillage farm. At one time, it was the stud farm belonging to Lord Dunraven, and interested guests can see the Horse Cemetery, with its horseshoe-shaped headstones, where several stallions are buried.

This house is furnished with antique and traditional furniture: three bedrooms have original fireplaces, one has a high bed, and all are clean and comfortable. Mary, is a kindly lady, she takes excellent care of her guests, and provides a substantial breakfast. There are plenty of venues for evening meals and Irish music in Adare, reputedly one of Ireland's prettiest villages, which is 2 kilometers away.

DIRECTIONS: Turn right at the roundabout Croom Road for 200 meters, first service road on the left

OPEN: April 1-October 31
ROOMS: 3 rooms double/twin/family; all en suite

TERMS: €37.50; single supplement; child reduction

GLIN

Glin Castle
Bob Duff
Glin, Co. Limerick
Tel: 068 34173 Fax: 068 34364
E-mail: knight@iol.ie
Web site: www.glincastle.com

This magical property, although a castle, with all the delights of living in a bygone era, is first and foremost a home. People do live here, and the ambience is welcoming and informal. From the moment of arrival, when a member of staff warmly greets you, you know they are happy to have you as their guest.

Glin Castle stands on the banks of the River Shannon, surrounded by 500 acres of woodland, gardens, and a dairy farm. It has been in the FitzGerald family for over 700 years; originally built as a long thatched house, it has been transformed throughout the years into an impressive castle. The interior has a large assortment of portraits, paintings, prints, and many other works of art. Of special interest are a set of bayonet holders decorated with the FitzGerald arms, an embroidered settee, the work of Veronica FitzGerald, a mahogany games table dating from 1750, and a fine example of mid-eighteenth-century Irish seat furniture, an upholstered armchair and chair with Shepherd's crook arms. This is only the tip of the iceberg.

When making a reservation, be sure to allow time to enjoy all the treasures to be found in the castle. The luxurious, beautifully furnished bedrooms range from standard to superior, but whichever your choice, you will not be disappointed. All rooms have modern amenities, quality toiletries, and large fluffy towels and bathrobes. There is a library, a handsome drawing room, and a charming dining room, where gourmet meals are served. All diets are catered for; reservations are required. For the discerning visitor looking for that special place, Glin Castle has to be a first choice. No children under 10. Private parking.

DIRECTIONS: Located $1/2$ an hour from Shannon Airport and Ballybunion Golf course

OPEN: March 1-November 30

ROOMS: 15 double/twin; all en suite
TERMS: from €310

Knights Haven
John and Josephine O'Donovan
Tarbet, Glin, Co. Limerick
Tel: 068 34541
E-mail: knightshaven@eastclear.ie
Web site: www.knightshaven.com

This large country house stands in a peaceful position overlooking the River Shannon and rolling hills. It is part of a working dairy farm that children are welcome to explore.

This is a child friendly property; three delightful children, James, Hazel, and Patrice, live here, as does Tiny the dog, and swings and slides are available.

The bright and clean bedrooms have white furniture, patchwork or blue and white quilts, one has a king-size bed, and two have river views. Four of the rooms are en suite, one has a private bathroom, and all have a TV, radio, and tea makers. There is also a guest lounge. Breakfasts feature fresh eggs from the farm's chickens. Tony Jacklin, the golfer, and family enjoyed the friendly ambience and appreciated the use of the barbecue. Private parking. Glin Castle and the Equestrian Centre are adjacent to the farm, and the Tarbert Ferry is 3 kilometers away.

OPEN: all year
ROOMS: 5 double/twin/family; 4 en suite, 1 with own bathroom
TERMS: €35; single supplement; child reduction

LIMERICK

Trebor
Joan McSweeney
Ennis Road, Limerick, Co. Limerick
Tel: 061 454632 Fax: 061 454632
E-mail: treborhouse@eircom.net
Web site: homepage.eircom.net/~treborhouse/

Trebor, which is the name of the owner's son spelled backwards, is a well-maintained, comfortable turn-of-the-century townhouse. The bedrooms are immaculate and tastefully decorated with color-coordinated wallpapers and fabrics. Breakfast includes freshly squeezed orange juice, muesli or porridge, and homemade breads, followed by a cooked breakfast. Mrs. Joan McSweeney takes excellent care of her guests and is happy to give advice on what to see and do in the area. Trebor is popular with cyclists. Drying facilities are available.

OPEN: March-November 1
ROOMS: 5 rooms 2 double, 1 twin, 2 family; all en suite
TERMS: €32-35 low season; €35-50 high season; single supplement; child reduction

MUNGRET

Shanville B&B
Noreen Walshe
Loughanleach, Mungret, Co. Limerick
Tel: 061 353887
E-mail: shanvillehouse@eircom.net

Shanville, a two-story red brick house, with colonnades to the front, stands in its own grounds, displaying an attractive front and rear garden. Noreen Walshe takes care of the garden, which guests are welcome to enjoy on warm days.

The house is well maintained and offers good value accommodation. The rooms are decorated in warm terra-cotta colors. The large family room has a double, two single beds, and a TV.

All bedrooms have en-suite facilities, hair dryers, and tea makers. Breakfasts consist of fruit, yogurt, cheese, homemade brown bread, and traditional fare. The cozy dining/sitting room has a real fire that is lit on chilly evenings. There are several venues for evening meals within a short drive.

OPEN: all year except Christmas
ROOMS: 3 double/twin/family; all en suite
TERMS: from €35; single supplement; child reduction

NEWCASTLE WEST

Ballingowan House
Carmel O'Brien
Newcastle West, Co. Limerick
Tel: 069 62341 Fax: 069 62457
E-mail: ballingowanhouse@tinet.ie

The light and airy Georgian House, known to the locals as the "pink house," stands back a good distance from the road behind a well-landscaped front garden. The bedrooms are quite spacious, colorfully coordinated, and have multi channel TVs. Two have a bath and shower, and some have views overlooking peaceful countryside. One bedroom is on the ground floor. The lounge is bright with a blue and terra cotta décor, interesting coving, and a marble fireplace. The conservatory area, which is full of colorful potted plants in summer, is a good spot in which to relax with a book and a cup of tea.

Breakfast only is served, and tea is offered upon arrival and by request at other times. The owners are most accommodating and guests receive lots of personal attention; there is plenty of information on what to see and do in the area. Self-catering units are also available. Private parking.

DIRECTIONS: Easily located on the main road going through Newcastle. Look for the pink house.

OPEN: all year
ROOMS: 6 rooms double/twin/family; all en suite
TERMS: €31-34; single supplement; child reduction

COUNTY MAYO

County Mayo is a maritime county, with the Atlantic Ocean making deep inroads into its coastline on the west and on the north. The sea influences the shape of its beauty, from the long, narrow fjord of Killary Harbour to the island-studded Clew Bay. Castlebar is the county town of Mayo and a good center for touring. The most interesting building in the town is now the art center and the education center. It was formerly a chapel, the cornerstone of which was laid by John Wesley in 1785.

Westport is a gem of a town. The architect is unknown—some locals believe him to be a French architect left behind from Humbert's expedition in 1798. The main feature is the Octagon, a fine piece of planning. In the center stands a Doric pillar, mounted on an octagonal granite base, on which the statue of George Glendenning once stood. Innisturk Island can be visited from Roonah Point. It is an exceptionally attractive island with a lovely harbor; there is a glorious beach on the south side. Killary Harbour is a striking example of a fjord. Its 8-kilometer sweep cuts deep into the surrounding mountains.

Knock Fold Museum pays tribute to the area's forefathers. The collections and exhibitions on show help us to understand what life was like for our ancestors.

An area and attraction well worth visiting is the Ceide Fields Centre, which recreates the life of a Stone Age farming community and overlooks spectacular cliffs on the north Mayo coast. At over five thousand years old, this is one of the world's most ancient field systems. Mayo's blanket bogs have preserved many elements of life in that far-off era.

ACHILL ISLAND

Aquila
Kay Sweeney
Sraheens, Achill Island, Co. Mayo
Tel: 098 45163
E-mail: kay.sweeney@aquila-house.com

This cozy, clean, modern bungalow is situated in an elevated position and has magnificent views of Achill Sound and the Corraun Mountains. The ground-floor bedrooms are well appointed, prettily decorated, and have comfortable beds. Cots are available. There is a comfortable sitting room and lounge with a TV/VCR and an open turf fire.

The house is located near five Blue Flag beaches and two outdoor pursuit centers. Self-Catering is available. Private parking.

DIRECTIONS: Drive onto Achill Island, take the second left turn; house is signposted

OPEN: March 1-September 30
ROOMS: 2 double, 1 twin, 1 family, 1 single; all en suite; no upstairs rooms
TERMS: €33; single supplement; child reduction

BALLINA

Belvedere House
Mary Reilly
Foxford Road, Ballina, Co. Mayo
Tel: 096 22004

This spacious, modern two-story house stands in its own grounds, a 10-minute walk from the town center. Bedrooms have orthopedic beds, are of a good size, attractively decorated, and clean. There is a very large dining room and lounge with a TV and fireplaces. The owners are attentive and work hard to maintain the high standards. Breakfast only is served, but there are many fine eating establishments in the area.

Ballina is situated on the lower reaches of the River Moy, directly between Lough Conn/Cullen and Killala Bay. Bicycles are available for hire locally. For guests who would like a day trip to Dublin, there is a reliable local bus service. Ballina is a bustling town, and there are several venues where traditional Irish music can be heard. Private parking.

DIRECTIONS: On main Dublin Road—N6, heading to Ballina

OPEN: January 3-December 15
ROOMS: 2 double, 2 twin, 2 family; 5 en suite
TERMS: from €33; single supplement; child reduction

BELDERRIG

The Hawthorns
Carmel Murphy

Belderrig, Co. Mayo
Tel: 096 43148 Fax: 096 43148
E-mail: camurphy@indigo.ie

Located in the picturesque village of Belderrig (between Ballina and Bellmullet), beside the sea and small fishing port, this clean and cozy bungalow stands in an open area with wonderful views of Ben Head and the Twang Mountains. There are cliff walks close by, and the sea is a 5-minute walk away.

Owner Carmel Murphy is a local lady who enjoys sharing her knowledge of the area with interested guests. The house is within driving distance of the Ceide Fields. The bedrooms, all on the ground floor, are spotlessly clean. The lounge has a turf fire that is lit on cool days, and breakfasts are served in the bright dining room. Vegetarians can be catered for. This is a pleasant family home—the Murphys have three children. Self-catering is available. Baby-sitting can be arranged.

OPEN: all year
ROOMS: 2 double, 1 twin; 2 en suite
TERMS: €30; single supplement; child reduction

CASTLEBAR

Primrose Cottage
Monica and Teresa Nealon
Pontoon Road, Castlebar, Co. Mayo
Tel: 094 9021247

If you are looking for that "special place" to stay, Primrose Cottage, standing behind a very pretty garden, would be a first choice. Sisters Monica and Teresa are a delightful team, taking excellent care of their guests in their home-from-home cottage. They have traveled extensively and wanted to ensure that all the comforts they found lacking during their travels were provided. There are lots of items of interest throughout the house, including paintings of local scenes, candles, dolls, and books. The bedrooms are of a good size, with pine furnishings, electric blankets, comfortable beds, tea makers, hair dryers, and a portfolio of what to see and do in the area. The ground-floor room has a king-size bed. Two rooms are en suite, and one has its own adjacent luxury bathroom. Warm terry-cloth bathrobes are provided in all rooms.

There is an imaginative breakfast menu that is prepared to order, and homemade scones and preserves are offered. Monica and Teresa are very knowledgeable about the area and are happy to assist with itinerary planning.

DIRECTIONS: Situated on the edge of town off R310

OPEN: January 1- December 18
ROOMS: 3 rooms double/twin; 2 en suite; 1 with own bathroom
TERMS: €33; single supplement

CHARLESTOWN

Ashfort
Carol and Philip O'Gorman
Galway/Knock Road, Charlestown, Co. Mayo
Tel: 094 925470
E-mail: ashfort@esatclear.ie

Ashfort is an impressive two-story Tudor-style house set off the road in spacious grounds.

The bedrooms are well appointed and have rich wood furnishings. The house is decorated to a high standard and has plush carpets and a luxurious lounge.

This is an ideal base from which to explore this unspoiled area of the west of Ireland; there are lots of places to see and things to do in the area. Owners Carol and Philip O'Gorman are a warm and friendly couple who are always happy to assist guests with itinerary planning and reservations for evening meals. Guests are greeted with a hot drink upon arrival. The bedrooms are roomy and comfortable. Ashfort is modestly priced for the comfort and high standards found here. Private parking.

OPEN: March 1-December 31
ROOMS: 2 family, 3 double/single; all en suite
TERMS: from €28.50; single supplement; child reduction

CONG

Ashfield House
Christina and Pariac Dunleavy
The Neale, Cong, Co. Mayo
Tel: 094 954759
E-mail: ashfield@mayo-ireland.ie
Web site: www.mayo-ireland.ie

Ashfield House is a large, attractive yellow house standing behind a rock wall and a pretty garden. The inside is just as pleasant as the outside with oak and Canadian maple floors. There are four appealing rooms individually decorated in soft pastels of green, yellow, and pink. All the rooms have en-suite power showers. Breakfast is served in the conservatory; the menu includes omelets, pancakes, fruit, cereals, and a full Irish variety. There is a real fire in the lounge on chilly days. Christina and Pariac Dunleavy are a hospitable couple; they have two delightful children, Colm and Orla. Westport and Knock Airport are within an easy drive. Cong is a 5-minute drive. Private parking.

DIRECTIONS: Located off the R345

OPEN: all year except Christmas
ROOMS: 4 rooms double/twin/family/single; all en suite
TERMS: €30- 35; single supplement; child reduction

CROSSMOLINA

Kilmurray House
Madge and Joe Moffat
Castlehill, Crossmolina, Co. Mayo
Tel: 096 31227
E-mail: madgemoffat@yahoo.com
Web site: www.kilmurrayhouse.com

Kilmurray House is a large welcoming farmhouse on 22 hectares of dry stock farmland, beautifully situated under Nephin Mountain. It is hard to believe that the house was in ruins before Joe and Madge Moffat restored the interior, cleverly providing modern comforts while retaining the feel of a bygone era.

The original oak staircase and wooden doors have been retained, as has the fireplace in the lounge, which was made by a local craftsman. The house is the recipient of three awards: Farmhouse of the Year, the BHS, and the Bord Fáilte Award. The bedrooms are large and tastefully decorated with matching fabrics and antique and traditional furniture.

All rooms have a double and single bed; the single rooms share a close-by bathroom. A turf fire burns in the lounge on chilly days. It's an ideal base from which to explore this scenic area, and a fisherman's delight, the farm has its own boat for guests' use on Lake Corrib.

There are several pubs and restaurants in the area for evening meals. Irish musical evenings are less than 0.5 kilometers away. The Heritage Museum for tracing ancestry is 2.5 kilometers away. Baby-sitting is available. Private parking.

DIRECTIONS: Signposted from Crossmolina

OPEN: April 1-October 1
ROOMS: 8 rooms double/twin/family/single; 6 en suite
TERMS: from €32-34; single supplement; child reduction

ERRIS

Hillcrest House
Evelyn Cosgrove
Main Street, Bangor, Erris, Co. Mayo
Tel: 097 83494

This is a modern, cozy bungalow located in the center of the village, very close to the Owenmore River. Mr. and Mrs. Cosgrove are a very congenial couple. Mr. Cosgrove was born in the village and can provide lots of information on local events. The restaurant, which is part of the house, is very popular with the locals. Special diets are catered for if prebooked. Mrs. Cosgrove, who does all the cooking, has built up an excellent reputation for providing good food.

The bedrooms are comfortable and hot water bottles are provided. This is a popular spot with fishermen, with river and lake fishing close by.

DIRECTIONS: On the N59 from Mulrany to Belmullet

OPEN: all year
ROOMS: 2 double, 2 twin
TERMS: from €33; single supplement; child reduction

KILLALA

Beach View House
Mary O'Hara
Ross, Killala, County Mayo
Tel: 096 32023

Beach View House as the name indicates has bay views and is within a 2-minute walk of Blue Flag beaches. The quiet, peaceful spot is ideal for bird watching and outdoor activities. Mary O'Hara is a good-natured host; her guests are well taken care of and made to feel at home. The bedrooms, all on the ground floor, have soft pastel colors of green, blue, and pink, with coordinated duvets and curtains all made by Mary. Hair dryers are available. All rooms have garden views.

There is a turf fire in the lounge that has a TV and VCR, and tea is available on request. Breakfast only is served, but there are plenty of choices for food within a close drive. Mary has been offering her special brand of hospitality since 1981, with many visitors returning for yet another peaceful break. Private parking.

DIRECTIONS: Northbound from Killala take the first right off the R314.

OPEN: all year except Christmas
ROOMS: 4 rooms double/single/family; all en suite
TERMS: €30; single supplement; child reduction

KNOCK

Ashford Manor B&B
Olivia McGreal
Claremorris Road, Knock, Co. Mayo
Tel: 094 9388514
E-mail: omgreal@oceanfree.net

Ashford Manor is a large, attractive house with hanging baskets, potted plants, and leaded windows. The house is beautifully maintained and immaculately kept. The entryway has rich carpets, and the relaxing sitting room has tasteful furniture and luxurious red carpet. The bedrooms are of a good size and are well furnished.

Breakfasts are excellent and are cooked on the Aga. On fine days, guests can enjoy a cup of tea outside where seating is provided. Private parking.

OPEN: February-November
ROOMS: 2 double, 2 twin, 2 family; all en suite
TERMS: from €35; single supplement; child reduction

LOUISBURGH

Rivervilla
Mary O'Malley
Shraugh, Louisburgh, Co. Mayo
Tel: 098 66246
E-mail: rivervilla@eircom.net
Web site: www.rivervillamayo.com

Rivervilla is a neat and clean bungalow situated in a peaceful and secluded spot along the banks of the Runrowan River, on a 10-hectare sheep farm. Salmon and trout fishing are available as well as some lovely walks. A real home-from-home atmosphere pervades, and home-baked breads and free-range eggs are a feature at breakfast. There are some excellent restaurants in Louisburgh for other meals.

The bedrooms are carefully decorated; some have glorious views of Shreffy Mountain and Croagh Patrick. Of special interest is the Great Famine and Granville Interpretive Centre. A scenic walk takes you to the village of Shraugh.

DIRECTIONS: Signposted on Louisburgh-Westport Road R335, or via Chapel Street, via Louisburgh Pass Spar shop; continue past O'Malleys Builders, the house is signposted from there.

OPEN: May 1-October 31
ROOMS: 4 rooms double/twin/family/single; 2 en suite; 2 standard
TERMS: €32.00-45; single supplement; child reduction

WESTPORT

Altamount House
The Sheridan Family
Altamont Street, Ballinrobe Road, Westport, Co. Mayo
Tel: 098 25226

Altamont House is a pre-Famine wisteria-covered farmhouse situated within a 5-minute walk of the town center. The standards continue to improve at this pleasant, welcoming house, established as the first guesthouse in the area. It has an excellent reputation for offering good service at reasonable prices. The welcome is always warm and inviting.

The spotless bedrooms are prettily decorated, and the rooms to the rear of the house overlook the lovely garden, as does the lounge, which has an open fire. A sun lounge and patio have been added. The prizewinning gardens are a popular spot with guests. Breakfasts are served in the attractive dining room, and when possible, there are fresh flowers on the table. Evening meals can be had at several good pubs and restaurants close by. Private parking.

OPEN: March-November
ROOMS: 2 double, 3 twin, 1 family, 2 double/single; 5 en suite
TERMS: from €35 for en suite; child reduction; single supplement

Ben Gorm Lodge
John and Mary Gavin
Murrisk na Bol, Westport, Co. Mayo
Tel: 098 6479
E-mail: gormlodge@eircom.net
Web site: www.bengormlodge.com

Situated 10 minutes east of Westport, this country house, with a green and white exterior, stands in an elevated position and has sea and mountain views. It is close to Croach Patrick and Clew Bay. Outside seating is provided for picnics, or for guests just to unwind and enjoy the scenery.

The house has lots of pine and light, neutral colors. All rooms have sea views. The well-maintained bedrooms are en suite, and there is a sitting room on the first floor that has a TV and a fireplace.

A short walk takes you to the beach, and for the hardy, there are mountains to climb. Pubs and restaurants for evening meals can be found close by. Discounts available for long stays. Secure parking available.

OPEN: Easter-October
ROOMS: 1 double, 1 twin; 1 family; all en suite
TERMS: from €35; single supplement; child reduction

Bertra House
Margaret Gill
Thornhill, Murisk, Westport, Co. Mayo
Tel: 098 64833; 098 64968
E-mail: bertrahse@eircom.net
Web site: www.dirl.com/mayo/westport/bertra-house.htm

This modern, award-winning bungalow set at the foot of Croagh Patrick, known as Ireland's Holy Mountain, has fine views overlooking Clew Bay. Five minutes brings you to a Blue Flag sandy beach, with hill walking, golf, and fishing close by. This is a very peaceful location, there are cattle in the fields, and the welcome is warm and friendly. The ground-floor bedrooms are tastefully decorated with wallpaper and have firm beds. Margaret Gill makes all the curtains and bed covers. The sunshine room is yellow and gold, all but one room is en suite, which has a private bathroom. TV and tea makers are provided. Breakfast includes home-baked soda bread, yogurt, cereals, and fruit, followed by a cooked variety served family-style.

Margaret is an attentive host, who has been in business for 25 years. Guests enjoy the beautiful surroundings and the informal atmosphere. Private parking.

OPEN: March 1-October 31
ROOMS: 4 double/twin/family; 3 en suite
TERMS: €32-35; single supplement; child reduction

Brook Lodge
Michael and Noreen Reddington
Deerpark East, Newport Road, Westport, Co. Mayo
Tel: 098 26654
E-mail: brooklodgeb&b@eircom.net

This spacious house is situated in a quiet residential area 2.5 kilometers from the town center. This is a relaxed and friendly house, and guests are encouraged to make themselves at home. Owners Michael and Noreen Reddington are extremely pleasant. Breakfast can be provided if required, or if you prefer, a cooked breakfast is available until 10:00 A.M.

The lounge has a turf and coal fire in the restored Victorian fireplace, a pleasant spot in which to unwind after a busy day. The bedrooms are of a good size, have a soft pastel décor, and are tastefully furnished. There is a nice selection of pubs and restaurants in town, a 5-minute walk away. Private parking.

DIRECTIONS: Third turn to right after petrol station on N59 to Newport

OPEN: March 1-November 30
ROOMS: 4 twin; all en suite
TERMS: from €35; single supplement; child reduction

Cloneen house
C. Reidy
Castlebar Street, Westport, Co. Mayo
Tel: 098 25361

Easily located in the heart of Westport, Cloneen House has a terracotta, deep south exterior, and a large colorful display of flowers on the balcony and at the front of the house.

The bedrooms are decorated with autumn colors and coordinated fabrics and bedspreads made by Mrs. Reidy. All have a TV, telephone, hair dryer, and ironing facilities. Well-presented breakfasts are served at separate tables in the bright dining room; there is also a very large lounge. The Irish Museum is close by and should be on your list of things to see. All the town amenities are within walking distance, and there is a wide choice of venues for evening meals. Private parking.

OPEN: all year except Christmas
ROOMS: 16 rooms double/twin/family; all en suite
TERMS: €40; single supplement; child reduction

Moher House

Marian O'Malley
Liscarney, Westport, Co. Mayo
Tel: 098 21360
E-mail: moherbandb@eircom.net
Web site: www.moherhousewestport.com/

Marian O'Malley is a delightful lady who knows just how to make her guests feel at home, offering a cup of tea and some of her delicious home-baked scones upon arrival. Marian is the recipient of the Irish of the Welcomes Award. The house stands in an award-winning garden. All en-suite bedrooms are well maintained, with duvets, electric blankets, hot water bottles, and a TV. Excellent breakfasts, dinner, and light meals are served. The cozy sitting room has a real fire burning in the marble fireplace.

Moher House is located off the Western Way Walking Trail, and a pickup and drop service is available to the trail. The more adventurous can climb Croagh Patrick Mountain, with its magnificent view of 365 islands.

Fishing is available in Moher Lake, across the road from the house. Transport to the pub in the evening is also offered.

DIRECTIONS: Take N59 heading south out of Westport on Westport/Clifden Road

OPEN: March 17-October 31
ROOMS: 1 double, 2 twin, 1 family; all en suite
TERMS: €33; single supplement; child reduction
MEALS: dinner €20

Seapoint House

Carol O'Malley
Kilmeena, Westport, Co. Mayo

Tel: 098 41254 Fax: 098 41903
E-mail: info@seapointhouse.com
Web site: www.seapointhouse.com

Seapoint House is situated in a beautiful, unspoiled setting overlooking an inlet of Clew Bay. The house has quality, comfortable accommodation. Two deluxe bedrooms are available, one has a Jacuzzi bath, and a third room has disabled access. Most of the rooms have views of the sea and mountains. There is a very large lounge and fireplace, a reading room, and a tastefully decorated dining room, which leads out onto a sun porch. Fishing, sailing, walking, and an 18-hole golf course are available nearby, and there is a pony for children to ride. Baby-sitting can usually be arranged.

OPEN: April 1-October 31
ROOMS: 2 double, 2 twin, family; all en suite
TERMS: from €37-45; single supplement; child reduction

WESTPORT HARBOUR

Riverbank House
Kay O'Malley
Rosbeg, Westport Harbour, Co. Mayo
Tel: 098 25719

An inviting, spacious house with attractive black shutters, flower baskets, and window boxes, Riverbank House is situated in a peaceful spot adjacent to a river. The rooms are a good size and are clean and comfortable with modern furnishings. There is a relaxing guest lounge with an open fire. Kay O'Malley is pleased to help guests plan activities or day trips. Freshly prepared tasty breakfasts with home-baked bread are served in the sunny dining room; evening meals are not available, but there are several choices for evening meals close by. Local amenities include shooting at the Tirawley Game Reserve, bathing, boating, trout and salmon fishing, and golf.
    DIRECTIONS: On T39/R335, turn left at the harbor

OPEN: April 1-October
ROOMS: 4 double, 2 twin, 2 family; 6 en suite
TERMS: €35-37.50; single supplement; child reduction

COUNTY SLIGO

County Sligo is located in one of the most beautiful and least explored regions of Ireland, surrounded by rugged mountains and rolling hills. The landscape is a patchwork of picturesque lakes, lush forests, and sparkling rivers, its coastline dotted with peaceful coves.

Sligo's seaside resorts stretch along the coast from Innishcrone to Mullaghmore, with sandy beaches, fishing, golfing, beautiful walks, and horseback riding—there is so much to do in this uncrowded corner of Ireland.

Explore the Glenriff Horseshoe, the Ladies Brae, visit Lissadell House, and for the more adventurous, climb to the summit of Queen Maeve's Cairn. Tour the loughs—Arrow, Gill, Easky, Gara, Glencar, Templehouse, and Talt—and feast your eyes on Sligo's beauty. W.B. Yeats, the poet, is buried at Drumcliffe. He called Sligo "The Land of Heart's Desire," and after you have visited, you will too.

BALLYMOTE

Temple House
Roderick and Helena Perceval
Ballymote, Co. Sligo
Tel: 071 9183329 Fax: 071 9183808
E-mail: enquiry@templehouse.ie
Web site: www.templehouse.ie

Temple House is approached through an impressive gateway bordered by white iron railings. The drive meanders through parkland to this large Georgian mansion. It is set in 400 hectares of farmland and woodland, and there is a large garden where organic vegetables are grown for the evening meal. This estate has been in the Perceval family since 1665, the present house having been redesigned and refurbished in 1864. The entrance through a portico leads to a large entry hall. This in turn leads to a second, larger hall, off which is an enormous dining room and three sitting rooms with open fires. The larger room has lovely views over the garden to the lake and ruins of a castle, built by the Knights Templar in 1200. The enormous bedrooms are furnished with antiques and family portraits. Refurbishment is ongoing, new carpets have been installed, and the bathrooms modernized with power showers.

Mrs. Perceval does the cooking; Mr. Perceval runs the farm, which is stocked with sheep, Kerry cattle, and poultry, providing the kitchen with fresh meat, bacon, eggs, vegetables, and fruit. Almost everything is homegrown and homemade, including yogurt, jams, and cream cheese. Evening meals, if pre-arranged are served at 7:30 P.M.; special diets are catered for. Three friendly Labradors live here. Wonderful walks can be taken from here and boating is available on the lake. Private parking.

OPEN: April 1-November 30
ROOMS: 3 double, 1 twin, 1 single; all en suite
TERMS: €80 for private bathroom; €90 for en-suite room

DRUMCLIFFE

Benbulben Farm
Anne Hennigan
Barnaribbon, Drumcliffe, Co. Sligo
Tel: 071 9163211 Fax: 071 9173009
E-mail: hennigan@eircom.net

This large, modern house nestles in the foothills of Benbulben Mountain, in a well-tended landscaped garden, surrounded by a 36-hectare sheep farm. There are unparalleled views and 250 square kilometers of beautiful Yeats country; his last resting place is Drumcliffe Churchyard, which is within view of the farm.

This is very much a family home, and the Hennigans are very congenial people, offering a hospitality tray upon arrival. The rooms are spotlessly clean and simply furnished with fitted wardrobes and firm beds, and most have views. This is perfect walking country (there is a nature walk on the farm), and there are 30 mapped hill walks in the vicinity. Transport can be arranged to take visitors to starting points and back to base in the evening. If you're looking for a tranquil holiday, you may wander round the farm, visit the small museum on the property, and enjoy some local lane walks. There is a TV lounge and a bright dining room where breakfasts are served.

Sligo has some fine early megalithic tombs. Benbulben Farm would be a good base from which to explore this scenic area. Private parking.

DIRECTIONS: Take the N15 from Sligo, turn right at Drumcliffe Creamery; signposted

OPEN: April 1-October 1
ROOMS: 3 double, 2 twin; 5 en suite
TERMS: from €33; single supplement; child reduction

Serenity B&B
The Kelly Family
Doonierin, Kintogher, Rosses Point, Co. Sligo
Tel: 071 914 3351
E-mail serenitysligo@eircom.met
Web site: www.serenitysligo.com/

This is a haven of tranquility, a wonderful "away from it all" property. It stands in extensive grounds, surrounded by magnificent scenery with stunning views of the Bay and the Benbulben Mountains. You will receive a warm welcome from Brendan Kelly, a local history buff, who enjoys sharing his knowledge of local events. He has a great sense of humor and is an entertaining gentleman. Ask him to share the history of St. Columba's Church at Drumcliffe, the final resting place of William Butler Yeats, whose great-grandfather was rector in the early years of the nineteenth century. This "little bit of heaven" provides a high standard of accommodation, with curtains and quilts made for the house. The largest bedroom has Georgian and Victorian furniture and patchwork quilts. Breakfast, with home-baked bread, is served at separate tables in the conservatory. Private parking.

OPEN: March 1-October
ROOMS: 2 double, 2 twin; all en suite
TERMS: €35-40; single supplement

Yeats Lodge B&B
Michael and Geraldine Gibbons
Drumcliffe, Co. Sligo
Tel: 071 91 73787
E-mail: gibbonsg@eircom.net
Web site: www.yeatslodge.com

This impressive, five-peak stone-built house is surrounded by the gorgeous scenery of Yeats Country, with the Benbulben Mountains as a backdrop. Michael and Geraldine Gibbons, and the house, are delightful in every way. Geraldine is an artistic lady, and a selection of her paintings can be seen around the house. The spacious rooms have pine furniture and are named after local places of interest. All are en suite, with a TV, hospitality trays, and hair dryer.

There are two lounges and a separate dining room where a delicious breakfast of French toast, fruits, cereals, and juice, followed by a full Irish breakfast, is served from 8:00 A.M. to 10:00 A.M. A "Welcome to our Nest" sign indicates the warmth of the welcome. This is a perfect "get away from it all" retreat. If you are looking for a special place to unwind and charge your batteries, this has to be the place for you. A bar and restaurant is 300 meters away, 8 kilometers to Sligo town. Horse riding is close by. Private parking.

OPEN: February 1-October 31
ROOMS: 5 rooms double/twin/family; all en suite
TERMS: €35; single supplement; child reduction

SLIGO

Aisling
Des and Nan Faul
Cairns Hill, Sligo, Co. Sligo
Tel: 071 916074
E-mail: aislingsligo@eircom.net

This immaculate bungalow, whose name means "Irish Dream," stands in its own grounds in an elevated location on the south side of Sligo.

The bedrooms are average in size and are comfortably furnished. They are all on the ground floor and have a TV and dressing gowns. Des and Nan Faul are a very congenial and accommodating couple who work together as a team. Nan cooks breakfast, while Des enjoys chatting with guests and helping them plan daily activities. Breakfast only is served, but there are plenty of eating establishments in Sligo. There is a comfortable lounge with a coal fire.

OPEN: all year
ROOMS: 2 double, 2 twin (double, single bed in each room)
TERMS: €67; €73 per room with en suite; single supplement; child reduction

Lissadell
Mary Cadden

Mail Coach Road, Sligo, Co. Sligo
Tel: 071 9161937

This red-brick new house is within walking distance of the town center and offers a high standard of accommodation. The rooms are of a good size, well furnished, and tastefully decorated. Mary Cadden formerly ran a bed and breakfast establishment of the same name in the area for several years and brings her expertise to this property. Mary is friendly, accommodating, and willing to help her guests in every way to ensure they have a comfortable stay. Freshly prepared breakfasts are served, but there are several establishments within walking distance for evening meals. Lissadell is a good base from which to explore Yeats Country.

OPEN: all year
ROOMS: 2 double, 1 twin; all en suite
TERMS: from €36; single supplement; child reduction

Lough Gill House
Florrie Gilmartin
Pearse Road, Sligo, Co. Sligo
Tel: 071 9150045 Fax: 071 9150639
E-mail: loughgillbandb@eircom.net
Web site: www.loughgillhouse.net

This ivy-covered, modern, two-story house, with its home-away-from-home feel, is within walking distance of the town center. The house is comfortably furnished, and the four pleasantly decorated bedrooms are en suite and have a TV and tea makers. Guests are welcome to join the owners, Shane and Florrie Gilmartin, in their sitting room. Breakfasts are served on cobalt blue china at separate tables in the dining room. There is horse riding and pony trekking on site. Close to the beach. Parking available.
    DIRECTIONS: Situated on N4 Dublin/Galway Road

OPEN: all year except Christmas
ROOMS: 4 double/twin/family/single; all en suite
TERMS: €38; single supplement; child allowance

St. Martin de Porres
Mary Goldrick
Keadow Road, Carraroe, Sligo, Co. Sligo
Tel: 071 9162 793

E-mail: stmdeporres@eircom.net

This attractive, well-maintained bungalow stands behind a beautiful landscaped garden. The comfortable spotless bedrooms are of a good size, tastefully decorated in soft greens, pinks, and creams. All have a TV and en-suite facilities. The family room has wheelchair access to the bathroom.

This is a peaceful home, and guests are welcome to enjoy the gardens, furniture is provided. Mary Goldrick has been in business since 1972, and many customers return for her warm Irish welcome. She is a keen gardener and works hard maintaining the high standards found at this delightful bungalow. Tea and coffee are offered in the evening. Yeats, the poet, was buried in the Drumcliffe churchyard. A Yeats Festival takes place here on July 22. Private parking.

OPEN: all year including Christmas
ROOMS: 4 rooms double/twin/family/single; all en suite
TERMS: €32-35; single supplement

Tree Tops
Doreen MacEvilly
Cleveragh Road, Sligo, Co. Sligo
Tel: 071 9160160 Fax: 071 9162301
E-mail: treetops@iol.ie
Web site: www.sligobandb.com

This well-maintained, spacious, modern, attractive house stands in a secluded location with an interesting garden and fishpond. An 8-minute walk will take you to the town center.

The immaculate bedrooms are large, tastefully decorated, and well furnished and have orthopedic beds. There is a large collection of Irish prints and paintings on display.

Wholesome breakfasts are served in the dining room/lounge, which has period furniture. There are some lovely walks and views close by. Tree Tops would be a good choice from which to explore this interesting area.

OPEN: January 10-December 10
ROOMS: 2 double, 1 twin, 2 family; all en suite
TERMS: €37; single supplement; child reduction

Walrey
Margaret Reynolds
Rosses Point Road, Sligo, Co. Sligo
Tel: 071 917 7327

This large inviting house is in a secluded setting, set back off the road behind a mature garden. The rooms are spotlessly clean, have floral décor, a TV, tea makers, and a hair dryer. Two bedrooms have an en-suite shower and two have a bath and shower.

There is an elegant lounge for guests' use and a bright dining room overlooking the garden. Margaret Reynolds is a friendly helpful host and is happy to recommend restaurants and give advice on what to see and do. Guests are well looked after in this warm and inviting home. Rosses Point and most amenities are close by, as are golfing and beaches. Private parking.

OPEN: all year except Christmas
ROOMS: 4 rooms double/triple/twin; 2 en suite, 2 with bath and shower
TERMS: €36; single supplement; child reduction

TUBBERCURRY

Cruckawn House
Joe and Maeve Walsh
Ballymote Road, Tubbercurry, Co. Sligo
Tel: 071 9185188 Fax: 071 9185188
E-mail: cruckawn@esatclear.ie
Web site: www.sligotourism.com/cruckawn/

This welcoming home is set back off the road and stands in its own grounds overlooking a golf course; there are clubs and caddies for hire, and the green fees are moderate. Maeve Walsh is a friendly, outgoing lady who knows how to make her guests feel at home and greets them with a complimentary hospitality tray. Maeve is also director of the North West Tourism Organisation and an expert on local attractions. The rooms are a little small but are spotlessly clean and comfortable. There is a pleasant TV lounge and a separate dining room where freshly prepared, substantial breakfasts are served. There are several establishments close by for evening meals. Separating the dining room from a small sun lounge are sliding glass doors with the family crests of the owners' families engraved in the middle of each door. Laundry facilities are provided. Local amenities include salmon and trout fishing, game shooting, mountain climbing, horseback riding, and pony trekking. Tubbercurry is quite a lively place, traditional Irish music and dance can be enjoyed Tuesday and Thursday and on weekends from May to September. Private parking.

OPEN: Easter-November
ROOMS: 5 double, 2 twin, 2 family; all en suite
TERMS: €35-40; single supplement; child reduction

Pine Grove
Teresa Kelly
Ballina Road, Tubbercurry, Co. Sligo
Tel: 071 9185235

This attractive, white and green house with Georgian-style windows stands in a pretty front garden on the edge of town on Ballina Road. Mrs. Kelly is a good cook, and a tasty substantial breakfast is served in a large dining room overlooking a patio. The house has comfortable old-fashioned furniture. There is a TV lounge with an open fire. There is no license, but guests are welcome to bring wine if they wish. This is a popular venue and reservations are recommended. On pleasant days, guests are welcome to use the garden. Knock Airport is 11 miles away.
    DIRECTIONS: Situated on Ballina Road, 300 meters off N27

OPEN: all year
ROOMS: 1 double, 2 twin, 2 family; all en suite
TERMS: €32-35; single supplement; child reduction

THE MIDLANDS

COUNTY CARLOW

One of the smallest counties in Ireland, Carlow lies just below Wicklow and is an area of rich farmland.

The county town Carlow has had an eventful history, which includes being captured by Cromwell in 1650. Now the town manufactures beet sugar and has quite a few noteworthy sights, including the ruins of a Norman castle, a Gothic Revival Catholic church, the Carlow Museum, and the fine courthouse with a Doric portico fashioned after the Parthenon.

There is a ruined twelfth-century church at Killeshin, with a fine Romanesque doorway, and fourteenth-century Ballymoon Castle, which has apparently never been occupied.

BAGENALSTOWN

✓ **Kilgraney House**
Bryan Leech and Martin Marley
Bagenalstown, Co. Carlow
Tel: 059 9775283 Fax: 053 9775595
E-mail: info@kilgraneyhouse.com
Web site: www.kilgraneyhouse.com

Bryan Leech and Martin Marley have created a most delightful fantasy world in their charming Georgian house overlooking the lovely Barrow valley. Kilgraney House is full of wonderfully chosen pieces of fabric, furniture, and art from around the world, with a strong Philippine influence, and each of the seven comfortable bedrooms is furnished and decorated with unique imagination. This is a delightful place to spend a weekend, and in fact, Bryan and Martin specialize in creating memorable weekend getaways. Guests can experience wonderful home-cooked six-course dinners using exotic products and homegrown fruits, herbs, and vegetables. Breakfast, served in the sunlit morning room, offers both traditional and healthy options. There are two courtyard suites, which can be used for B&B or self-catering. Guests can visit the herb garden, play croquet, or enjoy the aromatherapy center. The house has a wine license.

DIRECTIONS: Just off the R705 halfway between Bagenalstown and Borris

OPEN: March-November, Wednesday-Sunday
ROOMS: 3 double, en suite; 5 doubles with private bathrooms
TERMS: from €65; single supplement; unsuitable for children
MEALS: dinner €48

✓ Lorum Old Rectory
Bobbie Smith
Kilgreaney, Bagenalstown, Co. Carlow
Tel: 059 9775282 Fax: 059 9775455
E-mail: enquiry@lorum.com
Web site: www.lorum.com

Dating from the eighteenth century, Lorum Old Rectory is set in 7.5 hectares nestling beneath the Blackstairs Mountains. It is surrounded by open countryside, with views as far as Tipperary.

The bedrooms are spacious, furnished with antiques, and all have their original fireplaces. Five-course imaginative dinners are available, by prior arrangement, with homegrown organic vegetables, and the house does have a wine license. There is a tiny snug room with a fireplace in addition to the drawing room. The atmosphere is comfortable and informal, and Bobbie Smith is a friendly person. Cycling holidays can be arranged, and guests have use of a croquet lawn.

DIRECTIONS: Midway between Borris and Bagenalstown on the R705

OPEN: March 1-November 30
ROOMS: 5 double/twin; all en suite
TERMS: from €75; single supplement
MEALS: dinner €45

Sherwood Park House
Patrick and Maureen Owens

7 Kilbride, Ballon, Co. Carlow
Tel: 059 9159117
E-mail: info@sherwoodparkhouse.ie
Web site: www.sherwoodparkhouse.ie

This lovely Georgian house is set in peaceful countryside and has a large garden and pleasant views. Patrick and Maureen Owens are a most welcoming, gentle couple and have friendly dogs. Sherwood Park has an especially beautiful winding staircase, and an unusual raised hallway features an old, flat-topped piano. The drawing room also has a piano, and excellent, home-cooked five-course dinners are elegantly served by candlelight in the very large dining room. Guests may bring their own wine, and dinner must be ordered in advance. The bedrooms are spacious and comfortable, and some have lovely furniture, including several four-poster beds. Families are well catered for, and the rooms have en-suite bathrooms with baths and showers. Altamount Gardens are nearby, and golf, fishing, and riding can be enjoyed locally.

DIRECTIONS: Signposted at the junction of the N80 and N81

OPEN: all year
ROOMS: 1 double, 1 twin, 3 family; all en suite
TERMS: €50; single supplement; child reduction
MEALS: dinner €40

BORRIS

Step House Hotel
Cait and James Coady
Main Street, Borris, Co. Carlow
Tel: 059 9773209 Fax: 059 9773395
E-mail: info@stephousehotel.ie
Web site: www.stephousehotel.ie

This early Georgian townhouse stands right in the center of Borris. It was originally the dower house to the castle, the entrance gates to which are on the opposite side of the street. Recently the Coadys completed a restoration of the old house and added on a new wing with twenty bedrooms and eight country cottages and apartments. There is a cocktail bar and restaurant, a sitting room/lobby, sun deck, and elegant function room. The restaurant has archways and vaulted ceilings and is located in the original kitchen of the house. Interesting food is prepared using local ingredients and organic fair. James Coady has chosen the impressive wine cellar collection. Cait Coady is a cheerful, energetic host and has furnished and decorated the house with an eclectic collection of furniture and art. The luxurious bedrooms have been built to take advantage of the lovely views to Mount Leinster. Guests can enjoy the extensive back garden, including the herb garden, and exclusive fishing rights on the River Barrow. Borris is close to the Leinster Way, and there are great walks along the River Barrow.

DIRECTIONS: In Borris

OPEN: March-December
ROOMS: 23 double/twin; all en suite
TERMS: from €60; single supplement; child reduction
MEALS: brunch, lunch, afternoon tea, and dinner

CARLOW

Stoneybrook
Mrs. O. Jones
Cloughna, Kilkenny, Co. Carlow
Tel: 059 9146463

This large, attractive Virginia creeper clad house is maintained to a high standard. The three bedrooms are accessed off a galleried landing, which has an interesting Turkish tapestry. The house has a warm and friendly atmosphere, and the Joneses go out of their way to ensure their guests' comfort. A tasty breakfast is served, and special diets can be catered for.

DIRECTIONS: Off the Kilkenny Road a ¹/₂ mile from the center

OPEN: closed for Christmas
ROOMS: 1 double, 1 twin, 1 family; all en suite
TERMS: €35; single supplement; child reduction

COUNTY CAVAN

Cavan is an undiscovered county, an angler's delight with its unlimited opportunities for coarse and game fishing. Large areas of Cavan seem to have more water than land. The undulating landscape and picturesque settings are dotted with wooded islands providing much of the county's delightful scenery. There is plenty to see and do, including a museum in Virginia, which has 3,000 items dating back to 1790. Saint Kilian's Heritage Centre and Fore Abbey are other sites of interest. Cavan Crystal can be bought in the factory shop on the outskirts of Cavan town. Derragara Museum is situated on the Annalee River and exhibits a full-size mud and wattle homestead.

BELTURBET

Church View Guest House
Maura Hughes
Belturbet, Co. Cavan
Tel: 049 9522358
Web site: www.churchviewguesthouse.com

This well-maintained property with a view of the church has been a bed and breakfast for the last 40 years and has a helpful and friendly host. There is a guest lounge and good-sized bedrooms furnished in pine. Church View is especially popular with anglers and has a walk in cold room and tackle shed.

   DIRECTIONS: On the edge of town in the direction of Cavan

OPEN: closed for Christmas
ROOMS: 5 double/twin/family, 2 singles; 6 en suite, 1 with private bathroom
TERMS: from €30; single supplement; child reduction
MEALS: packed lunch on request

Rockwood House
James and Susan MacAuley
Cloverhill, Belturbet, Co. Cavan
Tel/Fax: 047 55351
E-mail: jbmac@eircom.net

Rockwood House is a charming country house standing in 3 acres of secluded woodland gardens. The house was built in the style of an older home that previously stood on the property, using the original stone and wood in the building of the new structure.

The house is furnished with a mixture of modern and antique pieces, and the good-sized bedrooms have comfortable beds and pastel duvets. Bedrooms do not have TVs, but there is one in the guest lounge where fires burn on cool evenings.

Traditional freshly prepared breakfasts are served in the dining room, which overlooks the garden. Tea and coffee are available on request. Guests are well taken care of at Rockwood House by Susan MacAuley, who enjoys having people in her home. Plenty of information is provided on what to see and do in the area.

DIRECTIONS: On the N24, 2 miles from Butlersbridge and 6 miles from Cavan

OPEN: closed 2 weeks for Christmas
ROOMS: 2 double, 2 twin; all en suite
TERMS: from €30; single supplement; child reduction

MOUNTNUGENT

Ross House
Ursula Liebe-Harkort
Mountnugent, Co. Cavan
Tel/Fax: 049 8540218
E-mail: rosshouse@eircom.net
Web site: www.ross-house.com

This charming, Virginia creeper-covered old manor house dates from the 1600s and stands in beautiful grounds on the shores of Lough Sheelin. It was built as a dormer house and belonged to the Nugent family, who were the Lords of Devlin.

The spacious bedrooms, centered on the courtyard, are in the tastefully restored carriage houses. They all have antique furniture, three have a conservatory, and four have their own fireplace. After a busy day sightseeing, guests may, for a modest charge, enjoy the sauna and/or Jacuzzi.

This is a wonderful place and must be one of the best value bed and breakfast properties in Ireland. A Christmas package is available, but very early reservations are essential.

Guests have access to a sandy beach that provides safe bathing. The private pier with boats for hire gives fishermen the opportunity to fish the waters of this well-stocked lake. Ross House is fast being recognized for its fine Equestrian Centre, part of the 145 hectare farm that offers pony trekking, a horseback riding arena, and a tennis court.

Ulla Harkort is a very congenial and accommodating host. Delicious four-course dinners are prepared, if ordered in advance, using fresh produce and local meats; vegetarian and light dinners are also available. If you are looking for high standards, good food, and a tranquil setting with lots of Old World charm, then Ross House should be your first choice.

DIRECTIONS: Call for directions

OPEN: all year
ROOMS: 2 double/single, 4 family; all en suite
TERMS: €38; single supplement; child reduction
MEALS: dinner €20

COUNTY KILDARE

County Kildare is famous for horse breeding and training, which takes place on the Curragh, a great plain leading into the Bog of Allen. Many horserace meetings are held here, including the Irish Derby, the Irish 2000 Guineas, the Irish Oaks, and the Irish St. Leger. Kildare town is the center for horse breeding and has a well-preserved Church of Ireland cathedral and round tower.

At Robertstown, the eighteenth-century buildings along the Grand Canal have been restored to look as they did when this was a great water thoroughfare. Here it is possible to visit Europe's largest falconry. Two of Ireland's greatest Georgian houses, Carton and Castletown, are located at Celbridge. A music festival takes place in June at Castletown, as does one of the hunt balls held during the Dublin Horse Show week.

The very pretty village of Leixlip has many associations with the Guinness family; the twelfth-century Norman castle belongs to Desmond Guinness.

Remains of a Franciscan Abbey can be seen at Castledermot, and Athy has many historic sights worth exploring, including the sixteenth-century Woodstock Castle, just out of town. Moone High Cross, one of Ireland's most beautiful high crosses, is at Moone Abbey, 12 kilometers from Athy.

ATHY

Moate Lodge
Mary and Raymond Pelin
Athy, Co. Kildare
Tel: 059 8626137
E-mail: marypelin@moatelodge.com
Web site: www.moatelodge.com

Mary and Raymond Pelin offer a warm welcome to guests at their neatly kept stone-built 300-year-old farmhouse surrounded by farmland off a narrow lane. When Mary started her B&B business it was a hobby in comparison to the importance of farming, but these days it has taken on a more significant role. And now the Pelins have renovated one side of the attractive farm building's courtyard into three well-equipped self-catering units. Bed and breakfast guests have a choice of four simply furnished bedrooms in the house. Breakfast in summer time is served in the conservatory at the back of the house, and at other times in the formal dining room, where home-cooked dinners are also served.

DIRECTIONS: Signposted off the N78 about 5 kilometers from Athy, heading towards Kilcullen

OPEN: all year
ROOMS: 2 double, 1 twin, 1 single; 3 en suite; 1 private bathroom
TERMS: €33; single supplement; child reduction
MEALS: dinner €25

KILDARE

Castleview Farm B&B
Liz Fitzpatrick
Lackaghmore, Kildare, Co. Kildare
Tel/Fax: 045 521816
E-mail: castleviewfarmhouse@oceanfree.net
Web site: www.kildarebandb.com

A warm and friendly welcome awaits you at Castleview Farm. The present farmhouse was built 20 years ago just after Liz and Ned Fitzpatrick got married. The simply furnished guest bedrooms are all on the ground floor. One room has an extra attached bedroom, and with both rooms en suite, it is perfect for extended families. The original farmhouse, an old attractive thatched-roof building, was recently opened as a cozy self-catering cottage. It adjoins the farm buildings, which are used to run the 136-acre mostly dairy farm. Castleview is in a quiet, rural setting and adjoins an old ruined church.

DIRECTIONS: Just off the Kildare to Monasterevin Road

OPEN: March 1-October 31
ROOMS: 1 double, 2 family; 2 en suite; 1 private bathroom
TERMS: from €34; single supplement; child reduction

MAYNOOTH

Moyglare Manor Hotel
The Devlin Family
Moyglare, Maynooth, Co. Kildare
Tel: 01 6286351 Fax: 01 6285405
E-mail: info@moyglaremanor.ie
Web site: www.moyglaremanor.ie/

A lovely long driveway flanked by majestic trees, and to each side fenced fields with horses and sheep grazing, leads to this impressive eighteenth-century stone-built mansion. A series of small reception rooms and hallways stuffed with antique furniture, ornaments, and flowers give it a rather dark and somber air. The cuisine at Moyglare attracts many visitors. Beautifully presented food is served by candlelight in the two elegant dining rooms, and there is an extensive wine list. The bedrooms are spacious and comfortable, and there is a garden room. Small conferences can be catered for. There are several golf courses in the vicinity; riding and hunting can be arranged. Moyglare is the nearest country house hotel to the airport.

DIRECTIONS: 2 kilometers from the church in Maynooth

OPEN: closed for Christmas
ROOMS: 16 double or twin; all en suite
TERMS: from €70; single supplement
MEALS: dinner €55, lunch, and light snacks

MONASTEREVIN

Cloncarlin Farmhouse
Marie McGuinness
Nurney Road, Monasterevin, Co. Kildare
Tel: 045 525722
E-mail: marie@cloncarlinhouse.com

This 200-year-old attractive house was built by Lord Drogheda to entertain his guests and is reached up a long tree-lined driveway. It is set in pretty countryside in an elevated position, part of a 68-hectare mixed farm. When the McGuinnesses bought it 12 years ago, it was pretty derelict; they are constantly updating the décor and furnishings. The comfortable, spacious bedrooms have pleasant views, and there is a lounge and dining room. Fishing is available on the River Barrow, and there are riding stables close by. The Japanese Gardens and National Stud are a 15-minute drive away.

DIRECTIONS: The house is signposted off the Dublin to Cork road.

OPEN: January 1-December 15
ROOMS: 3 twin, 1 family, 1 single; all en suite
TERMS: from €35; single supplement; child reduction

STRAFFAN

Barberstown Castle
Ken Healy
Straffan, Co. Kildare
Tel: 01 6288157 Fax: 01 6277027
E-mail: info@barberstowncastle.ie
Web site: www.barberstowncastle.ie/

Dating from the early thir-teenth century, this historic castle was one of the first great Irish country houses to open for guests, becoming a hotel in 1973. The castle keep is a venue for banquets, and larger groups are enter-tained in the sixteenth-cen-tury banqueting hall. The  Elizabethan part of the castle dates from the second half of the sixteenth century, and the Victorian house was built in the 1830s. It is said that a man is interred between the top of the stairs and roof of the tower. His family did this to prevent their eviction as tenants, as the lease stated that if he were put underground it would expire. The bedrooms are spacious and comfortable, and each is individually decorated. In 2004, a new wing was added, increasing the number of bedrooms and the confer-ence facilities. Barberstown has a good reputation for its food, which is creative and beautifully served. Tearooms are a recent addition to the property. It is an interesting and relaxing place to stay, within easy reach of Dublin and the airport.

DIRECTIONS: From Dublin, exit the N4 for Maynooth and Straffan

OPEN: closed January and December 24-26

ROOMS: 42 double, 17 twin; all en suite
TERMS: €120; single supplement; child reduction
MEALS: lunch, dinner, tea, à la carte

The K Club
Straffan, Co. Kildare
Tel: 01 6017200 Fax: 01 6017298
E-mail: resortsales@kclub.ie
Web site: www.kclub.ie

The ultimate in luxury, elegance, and service, the K Club Golf and Spa Resort is a superb country mansion standing in gracious parklands and manicured gardens. There are two 18-hole championship Arnold Palmer-designed golf courses. The Palmer Course hosted the 2006 Ryder Cup, and the Smurfit Course is the home of the Smurfit Kappa European Open.

The 700 acres stretch to the River Liffey—the island in the river can be reached by a series of paths and bridges.

The origins of the house go back to 550 A.D.; the present building was restored and opened in 1991 as a luxurious hotel and country club. No expense has been spared with the refurbishment of public rooms and bedrooms alike. The highest quality materials have been used, interesting paintings hang on the walls, Waterford glass is used from chandeliers to tooth mugs, and every possible comfort and thought has gone into bedrooms and bathrooms.

The service is impeccable, the staff efficient, and the K Club has a friendly and relaxing atmosphere. The amenities are endless, and every taste and activity is catered for, from golf to salmon fishing, including indoor tennis, health and leisure club with indoor swimming pool, snooker, bicycling, squash, clay pigeon shooting, and horseback riding.

DIRECTIONS: The property is signposted in the village of Kill and can be found on the way to Straffan.

OPEN: all year
ROOMS: 69 double/twin; all en suite; 25 garden apartments
TERMS: from €175 plus 10% resort gratuity
MEALS: all available

COUNTY KILKENNY

Kilkenny, the county town, is one of the oldest and most interesting towns in Ireland. It comes alive at the end of August during the Kilkenny Festival, which is one of Ireland's foremost cultural festivals. Kilkenny Castle dominates the town center, and just opposite are the Kilkenny Design Centre workshops, which can be visited.

The cathedral stands on the site of a monastery built by St. Canice in the sixth century and from which the city took its name. The Kilkenny Archaeological Society houses its collection in a most interesting Tudor merchant's house—Rothe House—and the City Hall, built in 1761, was formerly the Tolsel or Toll House. The well-known writers Swift, Berkeley, and Congreve were educated at Kilkenny College, a fine Georgian building.

The Kilkenny countryside is pretty and compact, and of interest to visit is the attractive town of Thomastown, near Dysart Castle, former home of George Berkely, after whom the city and oldest campus of the University of California is named. Near to Callan on the King's River is Kells, a fortified, turreted, and walled collection of early ecclesiastical buildings, and near Urlingford are the ruins of four castles.

CALLAN

Ballaghtobin Country House
Catherine Gabbett
Callan, Co. Kilkenny
Tel: 056 7725227 Fax: 056 7725712
E-mail: catherine@ballaghtobin.com
Web site: www.ballaghtobin.com

Ballaghtobin, its origins dating back to the twelfth century, has been in the Gabbett family for 450 years. Today's house covers different periods, the most recent being the front entrance area, which was rebuilt by Mickey Gabbett's parents. Set in parkland and its 500 acres of farmland, it is surrounded by gardens that include the ruins of a

Norman church, a hard tennis court, and bumpy croquet lawn.

Mickey and Catherine are a delightful and very friendly couple and are happy to welcome guests to their beautiful home. Flair and imagination have been used in renovating the guests' quarters, which include the drawing room, a small sitting room off which is found the attractive conservatory, and the delightful bedrooms, two of which have sofa/stools that fold out to become extra beds.

DIRECTIONS: From Callan, take Mill Street; continue straight, passing Callan Golf Club. At sharp bend to left, keep left; at Y junction, keep left. Grand stone gates are on the left opposite pink Gate Lodge.

OPEN: March-October
ROOMS: 3 double, 2 twin, 2 family; all en suite
TERMS: €45; single supplement; child reduction

GRAIGUENAMANAGH

Ballyogan House
Robert and Fran Durie
New Ross Road, Graiguenamanagh, Co. Kilkenny
Tel: 059 9725969
E-mail: info@ballyoganhouse.com
Web site: www.ballyoganhouse.com

Peace and quiet in a beautiful country setting are what attract and entice people back to Ballyogan House. Easy going hosts, Fran and Robert Durie like to make sure their guests are comfortable and well cared for. The attractive mid-nineteenth-century house has magical views over the col-

orful garden to the trees lining the valley and to the Blackstairs

Mountains. It was the River Barrow that drew the Duries to Ballyogan. Fifty acres of woods and fields stretch down to its banks and along it to a waterfall.

The bedrooms, two of which are on the first floor, and two on the second, are named after different plants and have their own colors and décor style. The plant-filled conservatory is a favorite place for guests to unwind, leading off the pleasant sitting room. Dinner is available by arrangement, and special diets are catered for. Deep massages can be arranged.

DIRECTIONS: From Graiguenamanagh, take the R705 towards New Ross. After 4 kilometers, take the sharp left lane, where it is signposted.

OPEN: April 1-October 31
ROOMS: 1 double, 2 twin, 1 family; all en suite
TERMS: from €45; single supplement; child reduction
MEALS: dinner from €35

INISTIOGE

Cullintra House
Patricia Cantlon
The Rower, Inistioge, Co. Kilkenny
Tel: 051 423614
E-mail: cullhse@indigo.ie
Web site: www.cullintrahouse.com

This attractive, ivy-covered, 200-year-old house is approached up a long driveway through a park of grazing cattle, and has been in Patricia Cantlon's family since the turn of the last century. It is an animal and bird sanctuary, a cat lover's paradise—5 resident,  friendly cats—and home to a local fox that comes to eat dinner in the garden every evening. The rooms, including a garden conservatory and a converted barn, reflect Patricia's artistic talents. The carpets were specially woven for the house, and the plates were designed for the dining room. Patricia is also an accomplished cook and serves dinner by candlelight in an unhurried fashion. Guests should bring their own wine. Breakfast can be taken as late as you wish. The studio/conservatory, with a small kitchen for making drinks, is available for guests and can also be used as a small conference room. There are 93 hectares of farmland, and a private path leads to beautiful Mount Brandon, the ancient Cairn, and Lady Annely's Wood.

DIRECTIONS: Signposted off the R700 New Ross to Kilkenny road, 6 miles from New Ross

OPEN: all year
ROOMS: 6 double/twin; 3 en suite; 2 public bathrooms
TERMS: from €35; single supplement; child reduction
MEALS: dinner €40

Grove Farm House
Nellie Cassin
Ballycocksuist, Inistioge, Co. Kilkenny
Tel: 056 7758467
E-mail: grovefarmhse@unison.ie

In a rural setting, this 200-year-old farmhouse is surrounded by its beef, sheep, and corn growing farmland. With a small, pretty, colorful garden to the front, the house both inside and out is immaculately maintained. The South Leinster Way passes through the farm, which has belonged to the same family for generations. The dining room, where breakfast is served, is particularly large; there is a pleasant living room and sun room. Grove Farm House is an ideal base for walkers and is just up the road from the medieval city of Kilkenny and the recently restored Woodstock gardens.

DIRECTIONS: Signposted on the R700 at the bridge between Thomastown and Inistioge

OPEN: April 1-October 30
ROOMS: 2 double, 1 twin, 1 family; all en suite
TERMS from €30; single supplement; child reduction
MEALS: light refreshments

KILKENNY

Berkeley House
Vincent Quan
5 Lower Patrick Street, Killen, Co. Kilkenny
Tel: 056 7764848 Fax: 056 7764829
E-mail: berkeleyhouse@eircom.net

Web site: www.berkeleyhousekilkenny.com/ or www.bookkilkenny.ie

The house was renovated about 15 years ago by previous owners and has recently been refurbished. It dates from the 1800s and is right in the very center of Kilkenny, close to the castle. It offers well-equipped, nicely decorated bedrooms and is efficiently and professionally run. There is an attractive, small breakfast room and lounge area, and car parking is available behind the house.

DIRECTIONS: In Kilkenny

OPEN: closed for two weeks for Christmas
ROOMS: 3 double, 2 twin, 3 family; all en suite; 1 double with private bathroom
TERMS: from €45; single supplement in off peak season; child reduction

Dunromin
Tom and Val Rothwell
Dublin Road, Kilkenny, Co. Kilkenny
Tel: 056 7761387 Fax: 056 7770736
E-mail: valtom@oceanfree.net
Web site: www.dunrominkilkenny.com

The standard of maintenance is exceptionally high throughout the public rooms and bedrooms of this house. There is a wonderful, friendly atmosphere, and tea or coffee is offered on arrival. The bedrooms have recently been completely refurbished in bright cheerful colors and are immaculately clean. A new addition for visitors' facilities is a reading room. Guests enjoy the secluded, landscaped garden, and there are views of the golf course to the front. Dunromin is well known for its informality and great musical evenings set off by Tom Rothwell playing the accordion. Breakfasts include home-baked breads and homemade preserves.

DIRECTIONS: The house is on the edge of town, reached off the N10.

OPEN: April 1-October 31
ROOMS: 1 double, 4 twin; all en suite
TERMS: €37.50; single supplement; child reduction

Hillgrove
Margaret and Tony Drennan
Bennettsbridge Road, Kilkenny, Co. Kilkenny
Tel: 056 7751453
E-mail: hillgrove@esatclear.ie
Web site: www.homepage.eircom.net/~hillgrove

This delightful family home is set back off the New Ross Road in a nicely landscaped garden. Margaret Drennan used to work for the Irish Tourist Board, and she knows everything there is to know about Kilkenny. She is happy to suggest itineraries and help with planning your stay. The house is furnished in a mixture of old and reproduction furniture. There is a TV lounge and a varied breakfast menu, and one bedroom is on the ground floor.

DIRECTIONS: On the R700, just 2 kilometers from the Bennettsbridge Road roundabout

OPEN: March 1-November 30
ROOMS: 2 double, 2 twin, 1 family; all en suite
TERMS: €36; single supplement; child reduction

MADDOXTOWN

Blanchville House
Monica Phelan
Dunbell, Maddoxtown, Co. Kilkenny
Tel: 056 7727197 Fax: 056 7727636
E-mail: mail@blanchville.ie
Web site: www.blanchville.ie

This elegant Georgian country house stands in its own grounds and is approached by a tree- and shrub-lined private drive. It has a warm and friendly atmosphere and is beautifully furnished with antiques. The large, comfortable bedrooms overlook the lovely green countryside. The spacious drawing room with the original wallpaper and service bells has a TV, grand piano, and an open fireplace. Breakfast is served in the atmospheric dining room; light snacks are available on request. There is a hard tennis court for guests' use, and local amenities include golf, racing, fishing, and flying at Kilkenny Air Club. There are a wide range of archaeological and historical attractions to visit. Blanchville is at the center of a Craft Trail incorporating five prominent studio workshops in County Kilkenny.

Recent additions to the establishment are three most attractive and well-appointed self-catering units, skillfully converted from the ruins of the Victorian coach house. They are well suited for families with children.

DIRECTIONS: From Kilkenny, take the first right 1 kilometer after the Pike Pub off the N10 Dublin road. Then left at the next crossroads, and the entrance is 2 kilometers on the left.

OPEN: March 1-November 1
ROOMS: 3 double, 1 twin, 1 family; all en suite
TERMS: from €60; single supplement; child reduction
MEALS: light snacks on request

THOMASTOWN

Abbey House
Helen Blanchfield
Jerpoint Abbey, Thomastown, Co. Kilkenny
Tel: 056 7724166 Fax: 056 7724192
E-mail: abbeyhousejerpoint@eircom.net
Web site: www.abbeyhousejerpoint.com

Abbey House is an attractive building located opposite Jerpoint Abbey. The house may have been built as early as 1540, and a mill here dates from the twelfth century. Ruins of the old mill, which Helen Blanchfield would love to restore, lie behind the house. The house itself was in very bad condition when the Blanchfields bought it in 1988; only one original wall is left after completion of the restoration work.

Helen is an amusing, chatty lady with a lot of energy who genuinely cares for her guests' well-being. The house is spacious and has a drawing room and simply furnished bedrooms. The pleasant dining room has small individual tables and views over the old mill.

DIRECTIONS: Abbey House is on the N9.

OPEN: closed for Christmas
ROOMS: 6 double/twin/single; all en suite
TERMS: from €35; single supplement; child reduction

Ballyduff House
Breda Thomas
Ballyduff, Thomastown, Co. Kilkenny
Tel: 056 7758488
E-mail: baclyd@eircom.net

This attractive eighteenth-century manor house is set in lovely peaceful countryside, reached down a series of country lanes and entered through a gateway and up a long pot-holed driveway. It stands just above the River Nore and enjoys views of the river and hills.

Mrs. Thomas is a charming young widow with two children and is a kind and thoughtful hostess. Ballyduff is a wonderful old family home, with an interesting collection of family portraits. The bedrooms are huge, comfortably furnished, and have good-sized bathrooms. Breakfast is served in the dining room. Guests also have use of a wonderful library and drawing room with a TV. Arrangements can be made for guests to fish on the estate's own stretch of the River Nore, and hunting is available.

DIRECTIONS: It's advisable to ask for precise directions.

OPEN: all year
ROOMS: 2 double, 2 family; all en suite
TERMS: €55; child reduction

URLINGFORD

Springview House
Eileen Joyce
Urlingford, Co. Kilkenny
Tel: 056 8831243
E-mail: info@springviewbb.com
Web site: www.springviewbb.com

Springview is most people's ideal Irish country farmhouse. Full of peace and comfort, it was probably built in the late 1700s or early 1800s, and originally the upper rooms were accessed one room through another. Later a corridor was built, and now there are three delightful rooms, each with a double and single bed and private or en-suite bathroom. The Joyce family has lived here since 1916. Mr. Joyce runs their two farms with dairy cows and beef cattle, and Eileen Joyce is a charming, friendly hostess. Springview offers good value.

DIRECTIONS: 600 meters off the Urlingford to Kilkenny R693 road

OPEN: April 1-November 1
ROOMS: 3 double/twin; 2 en suite; 1 private bathroom
TERMS: €35; single supplement; child reduction

COUNTY LAOIS

Both Laois and Offaly lie in the central part of Ireland, with the River Shannon forming their western border.

Clonmacnoise is an important name in Irish history. St. Ciarán founded a monastery here in 548 A.D. that became one of Ireland's best-known religious centers. A pilgrimage is held here each September on the feast of St. Ciarán.

BORRIS-IN-OSSORY

Ballaghmore Manor House and Castle
Grace Pym
Borris-in-Ossory, Co. Laois
Tel: 0505 21353 Fax: 0505 21195
E-mail: gracepym@eircom.net
Web site: www.castleballaghmore.com

The owner, Grace Pym, discovered this fascinating, derelict sixteenth-century Manor house, with 30 acres of neglected grounds, when she took a wrong turn on her journey. It was for sale, and feeling an immediate connection, she decided to purchase the property. Undaunted, she took on the project of restoring the house and adjacent castle, which dates from 1480. It was a huge undertaking, but for Grace, it was "a labor of love."

Guests now have the opportunity to stay in a house full of history and character. The original builder was an Irish Chieftain, King of Ossory, from whom Grace later learned her grandson is a direct descendant. The Gothic windows in the conservatory came from a local church. Upon arrival, guests are asked, "to ring the brass bell loudly" because the host could be in the castle or in the grounds where her daughter breeds Connemara ponies. Prince Michael from Greece stayed for a week and had an enjoyable visit. The king-size bed is reputedly the largest in Ireland.

There is a cottage available for rent, and the castle, dating from

1480, can be rented for weddings, birthdays, and medieval banquets. Grace Pym, a historian, is an interesting lady, who enjoys sharing the history of the house and the castle. Fishing, boating, and lake swimming are available on the property.

OPEN: all year including Christmas
ROOMS: 3 rooms double/single
TERMS: from €50

DONAGHMORE

Castletown House
Moira Phelan
Donaghmore, Rathdowney, Co. Laois
Tel/Fax: 505 46415
E-mail: castletown@eircom.net
Web site: www.castletownguesthouse.com

Castletown House has received several awards, including the prestigious Agri Tourism Provincial Award. This warm and welcoming nineteenth-century farmhouse stands in scenic countryside surrounding an 80-hectare beef and sheep farm, on which the ruins of a Norman castle remain. The house is approached via a private lane through open fields full of grazing sheep.

The house is spotlessly clean, with a comfortable, home-from-home atmosphere. This must be one of the best value accommodations in Ireland. The bedrooms are all a good size, and there are several pieces of antique furniture. Fresh farmhouse breakfasts are served in the dining room, which has the original marble fireplace, and there is a sitting room. Guests often gather in the family kitchen for a cup of tea and a chat with the friendly owners. A conservatory games room is available to guests. Mollie and Donna, the two friendly donkeys, live on the property.

The nearby Donaghmore Museum is well worth a visit. Dongahmore provided the setting for the film *All Things Bright and Beautiful*, starring Gabriel Bryne. The Rathdowney Designer Outlet and an 18-hole golf course are 4 miles away. Private parking.

OPEN: March 1-November 30 (other dates can arranged)
ROOMS: 4 rooms double/triple/family/single; all en suite
TERMS: €30-35; single supplement; child reduction

STRADBALLY

Tullamoy House
Pat and Caroline Farrell
Stradbally, Co. Laois
Tel: 059 8627111 Fax: 059 8627111

This impressive stone-built house, part of a working sheep and cattle farm, stands in tranquil surroundings, 5 kilometers from Stradbally. Families are welcome, baby-sitting can be provided, and there is a cot and high chair available. The rooms are quite large and are furnished in keeping with the character of the house.

Breakfasts feature home baking, and special diets can be catered for if prearranged. The ambience is friendly; Pat and Caroline are very helpful and are happy to give advice on activities in the area.

This is a good location from which to visit this scenic region, and there is fishing, horse riding, a forest park, pitch and putt course, golf, and the Curragh racecourse close by. Guests are welcome to explore the farm and make use of the pleasant garden. There is a sitting room and separate dining room.

DIRECTIONS: Tullamoy House can be found 5 kilometers off the N80, 20 kilometers north of Carlow.

OPEN: March-October
ROOMS: 4 double/family; all en suite
TERMS: from €35; single supplement; child reduction

COUNTY LEITRIM

Leitrim is a county of charming beauty, with distinctive hill formations and lovely lakes. This long, narrow county is divided in two by Lough Allen, one of the many lakes of the River Shannon. The county is a very popular place for anglers, and the main topic of conversation everywhere seems to be fishing.

Dromahair is a pretty village located about 12 kilometers from Manorhamilton. The road from here is superbly scenic, with views of Lough Gill and beautiful wooded countryside.

Fenagh, which is located in the hills, has the ruins of a Gothic church, all that remains of the monastery which St. Columba founded as a school of divinity. You can fish to your heart's content in this area, which is full of lakes, beautiful scenery, and wildlife.

Carrick-on-Shannon is the center of river cruising on the Shannon. There is a large marina, several cruising companies, and lots of restaurants and pubs, which during the season have traditional Irish music.

KESHGARRIN

Primrose House
Gill and Andy Johnson
Letterfine, Keshgarrin, Co. Leitrum
Tel: 071 964 2960

Set in a peaceful spot, with stunning views of Loch Scur and the Iron Mountains, this blissful country house is an ideal choice when visiting this scenic area. Andy had been fishing in the area for 15 years before he and Gill decided to make this their permanent home. There is plenty of seating outside overlooking the view, tea is available on request, and you may be fortunate enough to sample Andy's specialty, Christmas or Chocolate Cake. Andy, does most of the cooking, he prepares an excellent breakfast, with free-range eggs from their chickens, and homemade jam. Dinners can be arranged; vegetarians and special diets are catered for with notice. Meals are served in the large family kitchen or on nice days the patio. There are several bird feeders, and bird watchers will be happy to see such a wide variety about, including, on occasion, the Kingfisher. The cheerful bedrooms are mostly furnished with pine, and there are strong showers and a TV. Gill and Andy are a very friendly couple, and guests are welcome to join them in their sitting room. They enjoy chatting to their guests and offering advice on what to see and do in the area, as well as recommending venues for evening meals. Private parking.

OPEN: all year including Christmas
ROOMS: 5 rooms double/twin/family/single; all en suite
TERMS: €30; single supplement; child reduction

COUNTY LONGFORD

The most central county in Ireland, Longford lies in the basin of the Shannon. The landscape is consequently low and flat, interspersed with small streams and lakes dotted with islands. Longford has strong associations with writers, particularly Oliver Goldsmith, Padraic Colum, Maria Edgeworth, and Leo Casey, and is a popular place for coarse fishing.

The town of Longford is spaciously laid out with wide streets, a Renaissance-style courthouse, and a nineteenth-century cathedral, which is built of grey limestone and has impressive towers. Close to Newtonforbes is beautiful Castleleforbes, a fine seventeenth-century castellated mansion. St. Patrick is said to have founded a church at the old village of Ardagh in a wooded setting, the ruins of which can still be seen.

NEWTOWNFORBES

Eden House
Eileen Prunty
Newtownforbes, Co. Longford
Tel: 043 41160

This large Tudor-style red-brick house is easily located when reaching Newtownforbes. Although in the village, it is set back from the road, and double-glazing keeps traffic noise to a minimum. The owners built the house for their retirement but soon decided to open for business and offer rooms for travelers. En-suite facilities were added, and the ground-floor room has an adjacent bathroom.

The rooms are well appointed and have coordinated fabrics. Soft colors predominate, and there is a blue, green, and yellow room known as the sunshine room. The lounge has a real fire, lit at the first sign of a chill, and the very welcoming hosts offer scones and tea on arrival. Breakfasts are excellent; pancakes, French toast, as well as traditional cooked fare, are offered. This is a very comfortable home where guests feel immediately at ease. Bike storage is available. There are plenty of venues for evening meals in the village. Private parking.

OPEN: all year except Christmas
ROOMS: 5 double/twin/family; all en suite
TERMS: €35; single supplement; child reduction

LONGFORD

Sancian House
Anna McKeon
Dublin Road, Longford, Co. Longford
Tel: 043 46187 Fax: 043 49656
E-mail: sancian@yahoo.com

Sancian House has been welcoming guests for many years; they return often to enjoy the warm informal atmosphere and high standards found here. A pot of tea and scones are offered on arrival. The immaculate rooms are furnished with pine, three are en suite, and two singles share a bathroom. All have a TV and tea makers. The house sits back off the main road, and during the summer, the front garden is full of roses and colorful window boxes.

Anna McKeon is a friendly, outgoing lady; she is very knowledgeable regarding family heritage and is willing to assist guests who are interested in tracing their family history.

An 18-hole golf course is located across the street, and it is a 5-minute drive to the pretty village of Ardara. Private parking.

OPEN: all year except Christmas
ROOMS: 5 rooms double/twin/single; 3 en suite
TERMS: €32-35; single supplement; child reduction

Viewmount House
Beryl Kearney
Dublin Road, Longford, Co. Longford
Tel: 43 41919 Fax: 43 42906
E-mail: viewmt@iol.ie
Web site: www.viewmounthouse.com

Approached through the original gates and standing in 4 acres of magnificent gardens, Viewmount House, built in the 1750s, was once the home of the Earl of Longford. This Georgian house has been sympathetically restored and great care taken to retain its ambience. The house is beautifully maintained, elegantly decorated, and furnished with a mixture of antiques and traditional furniture. Bedrooms are reached by climbing the original staircase surrounded by walls of red. There are antique beds, wooden block floors, woven rugs, and views over the garden, golf club, and scenic countryside.

The breakfast menu features a varied choice, and the meal is served in the magnificent dining room with a vaulted ceiling and Georgian walls of blue. It is hard to imagine that beyond the sweeping lawns and ancient Yew trees, Longford town is less than 1 kilometer away. Beryl Kearney is the perfect host, and Viewmount is the perfect place to stay. Private parking.

OPEN: open all year including Christmas
ROOMS: 5 double, 1 twin; all en suite
TERMS: from €60; single supplement; child reduction

COUNTY MONAGHAN

Monaghan is a sportsman's paradise, with many lakes and small roads winding round the hills and through Monaghan's pastoral landscape. It is an unspoiled area rich in farming land and ideal country for outdoor activities and exploring.

Among the most striking lakes are Lake Muckno, Glaslogh Lake, Lough Emy, and the Dartry Lakes. Monaghan is a market town and is home to an award-winning museum that houses the Clogher Cross, a fine example of early Christian metalwork.

In July, Monaghan hosts the Fiddler of Oriel Festival of Irish dance and music.

CARRICKMACROSS

Shanmullagh House
Margaret Flanagan
Killany Road, Off Dundalk Road, Carrickmacross, Co. Monaghan
Tel: 042 966 3038 Fax: 042 966 1915
E-mail: shanmullaghhouse@eircom.net

Shannmullagh House is an attractive, modern red-brick house in a rural setting. With countryside views, there is nothing in sight but green fields and mature trees, making this home a peaceful and tranquil "away from it all" spot. The property is adjacent to the well-known Nuremore Hotel and Country Club, with its excellent golf course. The house is tastefully decorated throughout, has pine floors, immaculately kept bedrooms, and power showers.

The owners are a congenial and friendly couple who obviously enjoy what they do; guests are well taken care of here. Margaret Flanagan takes care of the bed and breakfast as well as her three delightful young daughters. Playing the harp, they are a musical trio adept at Irish dancing, and they have been known to perform after some persuasion.

Excellent breakfasts are served in the bright dining room that overlooks the view. Private parking is available.

OPEN: all year except Christmas
ROOMS: 6 rooms double/twin/family; 5 en suite
TERMS: from €30; single supplement; child reduction

MONAGHAN

Bán Bridge B&B
The McCormick Family
Clones Road, Monaghan, Co. Monaghan
Tel: 047 71426
E-mail: banbridgebnb@eircom.net

Bán Bridge is an attractive spacious bungalow with a yellow and terra-cotta exterior, standing in its own grounds with lush greenery around. The rooms are situated around a courtyard, and there is an area for sitting and a barbeque. The McCormicks work as a team and have been in business for 10 years. They enjoy meeting guests and are friendly and helpful. Guests can have just about anything they would like for breakfast.

There are no petty rules here, just good old-fashioned hospitality. The immaculate ground bedrooms have a mixture of Mexican and pine floors; all are en suite and have a TV and tea makers. Private parking.

DIRECTIONS: Off the N54, 1.5 kilometers from Monaghan Town

OPEN: all year except Christmas
ROOMS: 5 rooms double/twin/family; all en suite
TERMS: €35; single supplement; child reduction

COUNTY OFFALY

Offaly lies in the central part of Ireland, and the River Shannon forms its western border. There is an attractive castle at Clononey, and Anthony Trollope first started writing novels while living at Banager, a pretty little village on the canal. At Birr, the gardens of the castle are open to the public.

TULLAMORE

Knockowen House
Julie Daily and Tommy Doyle
Knockowen Road, Tullamore, Co. Offaly
Tel: 057 93 20927
E-mail: juliedknockowen@eircom.net

For owners Julie Daily and Tommy Doyle, Knockowen House was a new business venture. This friendly couple enjoys meeting new people and works hard to ensure their guests have everything they need for a comfortable stay. The house sits behind a pretty garden at the corner of a quiet cul-de-sac. The ground-floor bedrooms are of a good size and have en-suite facilities, comfortable beds, pine furniture, and plasma TVs.

A bright dining room overlooks mature trees; a buffet starter table is followed by a cooked breakfast of your choice. Guests are advised to leave their car at the house and enjoy the short $1/2$-mile stroll to the city center. Private parking.

OPEN: Open all year except Christmas
ROOMS: 5 rooms double/family/single; all en suite
TERMS: €40; single supplement; child reduction

Littlewood
Lucy Bradley
Durrow, Tullamore, Co. Offaly

Tel: 0506 51364 Fax: 0506 21972
E-mail: info@milneodwyer.ie

Littlewood is nestled in 2¹/₂ acres of secluded gardens, approached by a private lane. The well-equipped, cozy bedrooms have pine ceilings and traditional furnishings. All rooms have TVs and en-suite showers; an additional room has a bath should guests prefer a soak in the tub. Tea and coffee facilities are on the landing.

The inviting sitting room overlooks the pretty garden, and bird lovers will enjoy the variety of birds around the feeder. Jacob Sheep are bred here, as well as the ducks and chickens that provide the fresh eggs served at breakfast. Seasonal fruits are on offer, such as rhubarb and baked apples, followed by a traditional Irish breakfast. Light meals are also available. If you are looking for tranquility, Littlewood is an excellent choice; on this property, birdsong replaces the alarm clock. Durrow Abbey is within walking distance, and there are five golf courses in the area. Private parking.

DIRECTIONS: Situated 3 miles to Tullamore

OPEN: March–October
ROOMS: 3 rooms double/twin; all en suite
TERMS: from €37.50; single supplement; child reduction

Rahan Lodge
The McDermott Family
Killana, Rahan, Tullamore, Co. Offaly
Tel: 05793 55796
E-mail: bnb@rahanlodge.com
Web site: www.rahanlodge.com

This lovely, old Georgian house stands in 20 acres of land in the countryside away from the noise of the traffic. There are no petty rules or areas declared off limits—here guests arrive as strangers and leave as friends. The house has original wood floors and several items of interest, including old desks with inkwells, an original portico, and fanlight. When the McDermott family purchased the lodge in 1988, none of the rooms were habitable, the avenue leading to the house was totally overgrown, and cattle wandered the grounds.

The restoration was a daunting undertaking, but the McDermotts took on the project with love and determination. The result is a wonderful atmospheric home renowned for its award-winning breakfasts and quality accommodation.

There are no en-suite bathrooms, but there are three bathrooms exclusively for guests. The large bedrooms are furnished with antiques, bathrobes, slippers, TVs, and toiletries. There is a drawing room with a piano that guests are welcome to play and contribute to musical evenings.

Carole McDermott is a happy lady who loves to cook. Special diets are catered for with notice. Breakfast includes free-range eggs from Carole's chickens. Ponies live in the fields, but star billing goes to the golden Labradors, mother and daughter, Sally and Chloe. If you are tired of waking to an alarm clock, this friendly retreat wakes you with bird song. Tullamore is within easy driving distance, and there are several venues for evening meals. Private parking.

OPEN: March–October
ROOMS: 6 rooms double/twin/family/single
TERMS: €65; no supplement in single room; child reduction

COUNTY ROSCOMMON

County Roscommon is an island county 60 kilometers in length. Two-thirds of the county is surrounded by water. In the north are the largest lakes: Lough Key, Lough Gara, and Lough Boderg. The great Lough Ree is in the east. The limestone foundation of the county and the numerous lakes make it a fishermen's paradise. Large areas of arable land are found in the center of the county, and the principal occupation is raising cattle and sheep.

Roscommon is a county of abbeys and castles. You can visit Clonalis House; Castlerea, once the home of two of Ireland's high kings in the twelfth century; Strokestown Park House, with its records of Famine-ridden Ireland; prehistoric Rathcroghan; St. John's Interpretative Centre; medieval Boyle; and the picturesque Lough Key with its forest park. For those interested in contemporary art, the Glebe House Gallery is situated midway between Boyle and Carrick-on-Shannon at Crossna, Knockvicar.

BOYLE

Abbey House
Christina Mitchell
Boyle, Co. Roscommon
Tel: 071 9662385
E-mail: abbeyhouse@eircom.net

Abbey House is a charming Victorian house nestled between a twelfth-century church and the River Boyle. Although in a peaceful spot, with old farm implements, beech trees, and a large garden, it is within walking distance of the town. The original casement shutters and marble fireplace are still in working order, and the house is furnished with antiques. Breakfast is served at a large refectory table in the dining room, which also has a chaise lounge.

Rich Victorian colors are very much in evidence, and the bedrooms are well appointed and comfortable. Christina Mitchell has been in business for over 29 years and takes excellent care of her guests. She is happy to assist with what to see and do in the area and recommend venues for evening meals. For folks wanting to spend time in a bygone era, Abbey House would be a good choice. Three self-catering cottages are available. Private parking.

OPEN: March 1-October 31
ROOMS: 6 rooms double/twin/family/single; all en suite
TERMS: €33-35; single supplement; child reduction

CARRICK-ON-SHANNON

Avondale House
Carmel Davis
Roosky, Carrick-on-Shannon, Co. Roscommon
Tel: 071 9638095
E-mail: avondaleroosky@eircom.net

This attractive, two-story house stands in its own grounds 500 meters from the River Shannon. This welcoming family-run establishment has a relaxing cozy atmosphere. Carmel Davis was formerly in the hotel trade, but she missed the personal contact with people and decided to open her own bed and breakfast establishment. Carmel and her husband were successful from the beginning and added on additional bedrooms.

The well-equipped bedrooms are clean, comfortable, and en suite and have orthopedic beds, TVs, hair dryers, and tea makers. The lounge has a turf fire and is a pleasant spot to relax in after a busy day. Breakfasts are substantial, and there is a hotel within walking distance that has a restaurant and bar food.

Avondale is a good base for anglers; there is a tackle room with fridges and drying facilities. For people who enjoy walking, there is a pleasant river walk close by. Guests are well taken care of at Avondale and are assured personal attention from the pleasant owners. Private parking.

OPEN: March 1-November 1
ROOMS: 5 rooms double/twin/family
TERMS: €34; single supplement; child reduction

Glencarne House
Agnes Harrington
Ardcarne, Carrick-on-Shannon, Co. Roscommon
Tel: 071 966 7013

This charming Georgian house is approached up a tree-lined private drive. It is located in scenic countryside with lovely views overlooking green fields and grazing sheep. A very warm welcome awaits you at Glencarne House. Agnes Harrington has won several awards, including the Galtee Breakfast Award and the Agri-Tourism National Award. The house is well maintained, freshly decorated, and furnished with traditional and antique pieces. The bedrooms have every comfort, including armchairs, hot water bottles, and electric blankets, and some of the rooms have antique brass beds. There is a peaceful old-fashioned lounge with a marble fireplace, which, along with the dining room, has a real fire on chilly days, and there is a TV.

Agnes is an excellent cook. If prearranged, evening meals are prepared fresh, and desserts feature some of the best pastries in Ireland. Special diets are catered for with advance notice. There is a golf course within 1 kilometer, and in the nearby 325-hectare Lough Key Park, there are many outdoor activities and wildlife walks. Many guests have been returning to this special place over the years and early reservations are recommended. Private parking.

DIRECTIONS: On the N4 between Boyle and Carrick-on-Shannon

OPEN: March 1-October 15
ROOMS: 6 rooms double/twin/family/single; all en suite
TERMS: from €35; single supplement if occupying a double or twin

CASTLEREA

Clonalis House
Pyers and Marguerite O'Conor-Nash
Castlerea, Co. Roscommon
Tel: 094 9620014 Fax: 094 9620014
E-mail: clonalis@iol.ie
Web site: www.hidden-ireland.com/clonalis or www.clonalis.com

Clonalis House is an impressive Victorian Italianate mansion, built on a 700-acre wooded estate. It was the home of the O'Conors of Connacht, descendants of Ireland's last High Kings and traditional Kings of Connacht.

The house is furnished in keeping with its character. The bedrooms have half-tester and/or four-poster beds; all have their own bathrooms. Guests are welcome to browse through the archives and library, dating from the sixteenth century, and of special interest are the heirlooms, such as Carolan's Harp and the O'Conor Coronation Stone.

Dinners are served, with vegetarian and special diets, if pre-arranged, and for guests staying three or more nights, there is a reduction. Guests are welcome to relax in the library for predinner drinks, after which they can enjoy their meal in the elegant dining room with Georgian and Victorian furniture.

Guests looking for luxurious elegance will find it at this friendly informal property. The house is not suitable for children under 14. Guests are welcome to take walks on the estate. Galway, Sligo and Mayo are within an hour's drive. Private parking.

DIRECTIONS: On west side of Castlerea on the N60

OPEN: April 15-September 30
ROOMS: 4 rooms 3 double, 1 twin; all en suite
TERMS: €95-110; single supplement
MEALS: dinner

STROKESTOWN

Church View House
Harriet Cox
Strokestown, Co. Roscommon
Tel: 071 9633047 Fax: 071 9633047

This spacious 200-year-old rambling country house stands in a scenic location. It has been in the Cox family for four generations and is part of a 100-hectare working farm. The original structure of a Famine Fever Hospital is located on the grounds. The house continues to be well maintained, and the good-sized bedrooms are simply furnished. One lounge has the original marble fireplace. Church View House is not licensed, but guests may bring their own wine. Strokestown Park House, the Famine Museum, and gardens are 6 kilometers away. Private parking.

DIRECTIONS: On N4 west from Dublin to Rooskey, turn left onto 371 to Strokestown; Church View House is signposted on this road.

OPEN: June-September
ROOMS: 2 double, 2 twin, 2 family; 3 en suite
TERMS: €40; single supplement; child reduction
MEALS: dinner

COUNTY TIPPERARY

Located in the center of the southern part of Ireland and famous for the song *It's a Long Way to Tipperary,* Tipperary is a beautiful county of rich farmland. From the top of Slievenamon, there is a splendid view. To the north, you can see the Rock of Cashel, a steep outcrop of limestone topped by impressive ruins—a truly spectacular sight, particularly during the summer when it is floodlit at night. From early times, the rock was a fortress and seat of chieftains, and later it became an important religious site. Today you can see the vast ruins of the Gothic cathedral, which dates from the thirteenth century; the tower of the castle; the cross of St. Patrick, the massive base of which is said to be the coronation stone of the Munsterkings; and Cormac's Chapel, which dates back to 1130. Cashel Palace Hotel is a fine Queen Anne-style house, a former Church of Ireland bishops' residence.

A fine collection of sixteenth- and seventeenth-century books can be found in the Diocesan Library in the precincts of St. John the Baptist Cathedral. There is a good craft shop where you can buy Shangarry tweed. Situated between Thurles and Cashel, Holy Cross Abbey was built in 1110 to house a part of the True Cross, later becoming a popular place of pilgrimage.

Cahir, a most pleasant town on the River Suir, has a beautifully restored fifteenth-century castle on an island in the river; it now houses the tourist office. The mountains between Nenagh and Toomvara were the home of Ned of the Hill, the local Robin Hood. Nearby is Nenagh Round, all that remains of a castle built in 1200. Kilcooly Abbey, the Abbey of the Holy Cross, and the attractive old church at Fethard are all worth seeing. Ahenny has two elaborately carved eighth-century stone crosses, and Carrick-on-Suir has a fine example of a Tudor mansion, which can be visited by request.

BANSHA

Bansha House
John and Mary Marnane

Bansha, Co. Tipperary
Tel: 062 54194 Fax: 062 54215
E-mail: banshahouse@eircom.net
Web site: www.tipp.ie/banshahs.htm

This impressive Georgian residence, set in 40 hectares of land, is approached by an avenue of beech trees. Furnished in keeping with its character, Bansha House is decorated with several pieces of antique furniture. The bedrooms are large; two are on the ground floor. The charming lounge has a log fire and leads out onto the gardens. A relaxed and comfortable atmosphere pervades; guests can often be found in the kitchen with Mary Marnane, chatting about the area's attractions. Cooking is of a very high standard, with homemade breads, tarts, and pies. The house holds a wine license.

John and Mary breed racehorses, their stables-registered Equestrian Centre offers horseback riding, and the farm has an all-weather 1-kilometer track. Glorious scenic tours can be taken from here. This is a superb place for guests wanting peace and tranquility. A self-catering cottage is also available. Private parking.

DIRECTIONS: 1 kilometer off main Limerick-Waterford Road; N24 at Bansha; 5 miles to Tipperary town

OPEN: January 1-December 20
ROOMS: 4 double, 3 twin, 1 single; 5 en suite
TERMS: €45-50; single supplement; child reduction

Lismacue House
Kate Nicholson
Bansha, Co. Tipperary
Tel: 062 54106 Fax: 062 54055
E-mail: info@lismacue.com
Web site: www.lismacue.com

Lismacue House has been in Kate Nicholson's family since it was built in 1813. It is a classic, beautifully proportioned Irish country house, set in its own extensive grounds at the foot of the magnificent Galtee Mountains. The house is on one of the most impressive lime-tree avenues in Ireland. The spacious drawing room and library have their original wallpaper. Breakfasts and dinners are served in the imposing dining room; special diets can be catered for if pre-arranged. Traditional log fires burn in the warm and welcoming reception rooms. Special interest holidays are available, such as pony trekking for adults and children, and, from November to February, hosted hunting holidays. There is also trout fishing on the estate's own river (tuition available). There are three golf courses and tennis courts close by, and the Rock of Cashel and Cahir Castle are just a short drive away. French is spoken.

DIRECTIONS: Take N24 from Tipperary through Bansha towards Cahir, entrance just outside Bansha on the left

OPEN: March 17-October 31
ROOMS: 2 double, 1 twin, 2 family; 3 en suite
TERMS: €75-85; single supplement; child reduction

BORRISOKANE

Dancer Cottage
Carmen and Wolfgang Rödder
Carraghmore, Borrisokane, Co. Tipperary
Tel: 067 27414 Fax: 067 27414
E-mail: dcr@eircom.net
Web site: www.dancercottage.cjb.net

This handsome Tudor-style house stands in its own grounds within a mile or so of Borrisokane. This is a peaceful location, and the award-winning gardens are available to guests. The good-sized en-suite rooms have old-fashioned furniture and comfortable beds. The ambience is friendly and informal, and there is plenty to keep visitors busy in the area.

Clonmacnoise, an ancient monastic site, is close by. Also nearby are museums of old distilleries, and the Slieve Bloom Mountains are within a few minutes drive of Lough Derg, a lake extending to 30 kilometers where the River Shannon runs through.

Excellent breakfasts are served; you can skip lunch. Home baking is a specialty of the house. Carmen and Wolfgang Rödder are attentive hosts; they are happy to recommend places to eat and advise on the best place for a glass of Guinness. Private parking.

OPEN: March-October
ROOMS: 3 double, 1 triple; all en suite
TERMS: from €34; single supplement; child reduction

CAHIR

Ashling House
Breda Fitzgerald
Cashel Road, Cahir, Co. Tipperary
Tel: 052 41601

This pink-washed low building is 2 kilometers outside Cahir and has lovely views from the front of the house. Breda Fitzgerald is a very friendly, chatty lady who keeps an immaculately clean and tidy house. The rooms are on the small side but are comfortably furnished. There is a large sitting room off the dining room. Private parking.

OPEN: all year
ROOMS: 2 double, 2 twin; all en suite
TERMS: from €35; single supplement; child reduction

CASHEL

Hill House
Carmel Purcell
Palmers Hill, Cashel, Co. Tipperary
Tel: 062 61277
E-mail: info@hillhousecashel.com
Web site: www.hillhousecashel.com

Hill House, a superb 300-year-old residence, stands in an elevated position, with beautiful countryside views and stunning views of the Rock of Cashel. A bonus at Hill House is the delightful owner, Carmel Purcell. She has been in business for 11 years, building an enviable reputation for her hospitality and good food. The house is surrounded by landscaped gardens, a wonderful spot from which to sit and enjoy the views, particularly at night when the Rock is floodlit. The spacious, luxurious bedrooms are furnished with antiques, power showers, coronets, and four-poster beds. Carmel traveled extensively around Ireland looking for genuine Georgian furniture, all of which enhance the character of the house.

The bathrooms are quite large and have everything needed for an enjoyable stay. A 4-star hotel could not offer more. The handsome drawing room has a turf fire and was once the meeting place of the ascendancy and hunting class. Be sure to browse the Georgian bookcase, which has an interesting, selection of reading. An excellent breakfast prepared by Carmel includes homemade preserves and home-baked brown and soda bread.

The thoughtful and gracious restoration of Hill House allows one to step back in time, while enjoying all modern comforts. This is a popular bed and breakfast; early reservations are recommended. A visit to the Rock of Cashel should be on everyone's itinerary; tours take place daily. Cashel has several choices for evening meals. Holycross Abbey, Hoare Abbey, Boru Boru Theme Park, as well as forest walks, golf, and horseback riding are all within easy driving distance. Traditional Irish music can be found most nights in Cashel, just 2 minutes away. Private parking.

OPEN: all year except Christmas
ROOMS: 5 rooms double/twin/family; all en suite
TERMS: €40-50

Ladyswell House
Beatrice and Kevin Leahy
Cashel, Co. Tipperary
Tel: 062 62985
E-mail: info@ladyswellhouse.com
Web site: www.ladyswellhouse.com

Ladyswell House is situated on the road to the Rock of Cashel. No worry about parking at the Rock, it is within walking distance. The present owners purchased the 100-year-old house in 2000 and immediately began major improvements. They are proud of the high standard of accommodation offered to guests. The rooms are furnished in keeping with the character of the house and decorated in warm colors.

The comfortable guest lounge has an original marble fireplace and an unusual chaise lounge. Beatrice Leahy is an excellent host; guests are well cared for and assured of a warm welcome. There are four well-equipped, elegant bedrooms with en-suite showers and TVs. A tasty breakfast features homemade breads and scones. Ladyswell House does have a well; it can be seen to the front of the house. Beatrice is from the area and happy to give advice on what to see and do in the vicinity.

Rory, the friendly dog, resides here. A short walk brings you to restaurants and shopping in Cashel. Parking is free after 6:00 P.M. and all day on Sundays. At other times, tickets can be purchased from the machine.

OPEN: all year except Christmas
ROOMS: 4 rooms double/twin/family; all en suite
TERMS: €37.50-50; single supplement; child reduction

Rockville House
Patrick Hayes
Cashel, Co. Tipperary
Tel: 062 61760

Within walking distance of Cashel Rock, Rockville House stands in a well-tended garden. This is an informal, comfortable residence, maintained to a high standard by Patrick Hayes and his mother Anna Hayes.

The dining/sitting room combination has a marble fireplace and a handsome sideboard. The bedrooms have bright blue and white prints; traditional, old-fashioned furniture; and comfortable beds. Guests are welcome to make use of the garden. Cashel Rock can be seen from the house. Secure parking is available.

OPEN: all year
ROOMS: 6 rooms double/twin/family; all en suite
TERMS: from €30; single supplement; child reduction

MULLINANHONE

Killaghy Castle
Moira Collins
Mullinanhone, Co. Tipperary
Tel: 052 53112 Fax: 052 53561
E-mail: c.killaghycastle@eircom.net

This Norman castle, whose original owners were Cromwellian planters, has seen an addition and an extension over the years. Originally it was just a motte and bailey, which is still visible to the left of the castle. During Tudor times, a long house was built onto the rear of the property, and in 1800, two other buildings were added, making Killaghy the castle we see today. It is part of a 96-hectare dairy and tillage farm.

Moira Collins, a down-to-earth and friendly lady, has created an informal, welcoming atmosphere, adding her personal touch by redecorating and installing new curtains and orthopedic beds. The house is full of antiques purchased specifically for the house. The bedrooms are enormous and some have original fireplaces, as do the dining room and the drawing room; the latter is a wonderful spot to relax in and help yourself to tea or coffee. The drawing room has interesting coving and a terra-cotta border.

The house has glorious views all round. There is a nature trail, walled garden, and two tennis courts for guests' use. Private parking.

OPEN: all year
ROOMS: 2 double, 1 twin, 1 double/single; 3 en suite
TERMS: €60; child reduction

TIPPERARY

Clonmore House
Mary Quinn
Galbally Road, Tipperary, Co. Tipperary
Tel: 062 51637
E-mail: clonmorehouse@eircom.net

Guests continue to enjoy this immaculate, detached house set back from the main road on the edge of town. The bedrooms are tastefully decorated and color coordinated with modern-fitted wardrobes.

Breakfasts only are served in the attractive dining room with its pretty lace tablecloths. The spacious lounge overlooks the garden that guests can enjoy. The lounge is a pleasant spot to unwind after a busy day of sightseeing, and on chilly days, a fire is lit in its fireplace. Guests may enjoy a hot drink in the evening. On fine days, the sun lounge is a popular place to sit.

Mary Quinn is a delightful hostess who prides herself on personal service. She is pleased to advise on good local restaurants. The town center is a 5-minute walk away. Private parking.

OPEN: March-November
ROOMS: 2 double, 3 twin, 1 family; all en suite
TERMS: €35; single supplement; child reduction

COUNTY WESTMEATH

Centrally located, this county offers a peaceful and beautiful land-scape, excellent fishing, and lots of history.

Lakes are the main attractions. The four largest are Loughs Owel, Ennell, Derravaragh, and Lene; beautiful Lough Sheelin is farther north. There are also a number of small lakes as well as Lough Ree, an expansion of the Shannon, which is now popular for sailing, cruising, and coarse fishing. On many of the islands that dot the lakes are remains of early Christian churches.

Mullingar, the county town, is a thriving commercial center and attractive market town. One of the best cattle-raising districts of Ireland, it is also a great center for hunting, shooting, and fishing.

Athlone is the largest town in the county. Originally a fording point of the Shannon, Athlone is now a busy market town, major road and rail terminus, and harbor on the inland waterways system. Athlone Castle, now housing a museum dealing with local history, is a strongly fortified building with many interesting features. It has been a famous military post since its original construction in the thirteenth century.

Lough Derravaragh, one of the most beautiful in County West-meath, is associated with the most tragic of Irish legends—the Children of Lir were turned into swans by their jealous stepmother and spent 300 years on dark waters.

Tullynally Castle is near Castlepollard, Seat of the Earls of Long-ford, the castle has a spectacular façade of turrets and towers. Fore is the most historic Christian site in Westmeath. There are several ruins to see, dating from the tenth century, among them St. Fechin's Church, an unusual feature of which is the massive cross-inscribed lintel stone.

ATHLONE

Shelmalier House
Jim and Nancy Denby
Cartontroy, Retreat Road, Athlone, Co. Westmeath
Tel: 090 6472245 Fax: 090 6473190

E-mail: shelmaler@eircom.net
Web site: www.shelmalierhouse.com/

Shelmalier House is a spacious modern house standing in its own grounds with an attractive front garden. The bedrooms, one of which is on the ground floor, are tastefully appointed and have firm comfortable beds. One of the rooms has a double and a single and another has three single beds. All are en suite and have TVs and tea makers. This is very much a family-run establishment; the considerate hosts extend a personal service to ensure their guests' comfort.

The TV lounge is spacious, and there is a sun porch where guests may help themselves to complimentary tea or coffee at any time. Jim and Nancy Denby specialize in coarse-fishing holidays, but a warm welcome is extended to all visitors. Recent additions include a sauna and a hot tub.

There is an 18-hole golf course on the shores of Lough Ree, and trail walks and a heated swimming pool within a 10-minute walk. Athlone is 2 kilometers away. Private parking.

DIRECTIONS: Situated on Retreat Road (Cartontroy); signposted off the R446 and R55

OPEN: January 10-December 20
ROOMS: 6 rooms double/twin/family; all en suite
TERMS: €33-35; single supplement; family room negotiable

MOATE

Coolen
Ethna Kelly
Ballymore Road, Moate, Co. Westmeath
Tel: 09064 81044

This well-maintained picturesque bungalow stands in a lovely garden with hanging baskets and flowering tubs. It is situated in a country setting of 0.5 hectares. Ethna Kelly is a considerate host, and guests are greeted with a hot drink upon arrival. The good-sized rooms are comfortably furnished, tastefully decorated, have comfortable beds, and electric blankets. All rooms are en suite and have tea makers.

Breakfasts are excellent, include fresh home-baked scones, and are served in the lush conservatory on warm days. There is a lounge where turf fires burn in the evening. Bicycles are available, and there are some lovely walks winding past the bog. This is perfect for folks who are looking for an informal home-away-from-home atmosphere. Golf and a pitch-and-putt course are close by, as are Clonmacnoise and the local heritage center.

Moate is known for having the widest street in all of Ireland. There are plenty of venues for evening meals. Private parking.

DIRECTIONS: Easily located 2 kilometers from Moate on the Ballymore Road; turn right if traveling from Dublin, left if traveling from Galway

OPEN: March 1-November 1
ROOMS: 3 rooms double/twin; all en suite
TERMS: €32-35; single supplement; child reduction

MULLINGAR

Glenmore House
Regina Healy
Dublin Road, Mullingar, Co. Westmeath
Tel: 044 9348905

This elegant and informal large Georgian house stands in 4 acres of secluded woodlands and lawns. The family is interested in sports, and the daughter is a fine horse rider as evidenced by the display of ribbons. The bedrooms are very spacious; one has a king-size bed, two have en-suite facilities, and two share a bathroom. All bedrooms have a TV. There are lots of antique furnishings, two marble fireplaces, and a ceiling rose. The lounge is a good spot in which to relax and enjoy the supply of books. Regina Healy, an artistic lady, is available to help her guests in every way and happy to share her knowledge of the area. She has a good sense of humor and serves an excellent breakfast on Royal Doulton china in the elegant dining room.

This peaceful and tranquil location is an ideal choice for folks looking for a few days "away from it all." Golf, fishing, and horse riding are nearby. Private parking.

OPEN: January 10-December 16
ROOMS: 4 rooms double/twin; 2 en suite; 2 share a bathroom
TERMS: from €30-34; single supplement; child reduction

Keadeen

Madge Nolan
Irishtown, Mullingar, Co. Westmeath
Tel: 044 48440
E-mail: aislingohara@oceanfree.net
Web site: www.mullingarbandb.com/

There is a comfortable, easygoing atmosphere at this well-maintained neat bungalow, situated in a peaceful location at the edge of town. To quote Madge Nolan, "I have never met a guest I did not like," which could have something to do with her friendly welcoming personality.

The bedrooms are spotlessly clean and individually decorated in bright colors, with warm duvets and rich carpets. Guests can relax and enjoy a cup of tea in the TV lounge. Breakfasts are served from 7:00 A.M. to 10:00 A.M.; the extensive menu includes homemade preserves, marmalade, and freshly baked bread. Madge will be happy to recommend local restaurants for evening meals. The main attraction in the area is Belvedere House. Local amenities include golf, swimming, fishing, and boating. Private parking.

DIRECTIONS: On the N4 from Dublin, take the third exit for Castlepollard, turn left, continue to mini roundabout, and take second exit; signposted from there

OPEN: March–October
ROOMS: 4 rooms double/twin/family; 2 en suite
TERMS: from €30; single supplement; child reduction

Lough Owel Lodge

Martin and Aideen Ginnell
Cullion, Mullingar, Co. Westmeath
Tel: 044 48714 Fax: 044 48771
E-mail: aideen.ginnell@ireland.com
Web site: www.loughowellodge.com

Lough Owel Lodge is approached up a tree-lined drive and stands in 50 acres, which extends down to the lough shore. The lake is over 5 miles long and is one of Europe's best-known trout lakes. Ghillie service is available, and boats are for hire.

The farmhouse is in excellent decorative order and is furnished in traditional and antique pieces, including the rich oak furnishings in the dining room. The en-suite bedrooms, two with four-poster beds, named after local lakes, offer the most comfortable accommodation.

This peaceful tranquil setting is the ideal place for fishermen and tourists alike to enjoy all the area has to offer. A hard tennis court, games room, and tackle room is available. Horse riding, tennis, and golf can be arranged.

Mullingar, a market town, has several venues for evening meals, and local pubs have musical evenings. For those not travelling by car, there are trains and buses to and from Dublin daily.

Guests looking for the perfect place to unwind will be well satisfied in this secluded tranquil setting. Private parking.

DIRECTIONS: N4 north from Mullingar, signposted just before the end on the left

OPEN: March 1-October 12
ROOMS: 5 rooms double/twin/family; all en suite
TERMS: from €40; single supplement; child reduction

Woodlands Farmhouse
Mary Maxwell
Streamstown, Mullingar, Co. Westmeath
Tel: 044 26414

A charming 200-year-old farmhouse, Woodlands is surrounded by ornamental trees and part of a 50-hectare cattle farm. Mary Maxwell has created a wonderful, informal, welcoming atmosphere that is a marvelous spot for families. Guests are encouraged to explore the farm, and there are pony rides for children.

The bedrooms are spacious, and there are lots of antique furnishings, including a chaise lounge and a lovely dresser. There are two ground-floor rooms. Guests enjoy sitting in the spacious lounge with the grand piano; musical evenings are encouraged.

Breakfast only is served, but there are several venues within a short drive for evening meals. Private parking.

DIRECTIONS: Take the N4 from Dublin onto N6 going west. At Horseleap, turn right at the filling station and watch for the "Woodlands Farm" sign.

OPEN: March 1-October 1
ROOMS: 5 rooms double/twin/family/single; all en suite
TERMS: from €35; single supplement; child reduction

MULTYFARNHAM

Mornington House
Anne and Warwick O'Hara
Multyfarnham, Co. Westmeath
Tel: 044 72191 Fax: 044 72338
E-mail: stay@mornington.ie
Web site: www.mornington.ie

Mornington House, a gracious family home, was built in 1854 and extended in 1896. It is surrounded by beautiful trees. The Mornington Oak is over 200 years old. It is within easy walking distance of Lough Derrvarragh, "Lake of the Oaks" in Gaelic legend, one of the three lakes where the Children of Lir spent 300 years of their 900-year exile. Foxes, badgers, and storks, midst a wealth of flora and fauna, inhabit the grounds.

The house, furnished with much of the original furniture and family portraits, retains the ambience of a bygone era, lovingly combined with all modern comforts. Mornington is an oasis of peace and tranquility, an ideal location in which to explore the Midlands and the surrounding scenic area. The reception rooms have open log and turf fires.

The bedrooms are large; two rooms have brass beds and one a king size. All rooms have been refurbished and are beautifully maintained. Anne and Warwick O'Hara are charming hosts. Anne is an excellent cook, and wonderful dinners, featuring fresh fruit, vegetables, and herbs from the garden, are served by candlelight in the Victorian dining room. Vegetarians can be catered for with advance notice.

The house is open for small groups on weekends in November. Children welcome by arrangement. Three-day special breaks are on offer. Canoes, boats, and bicycles are available for hire.

DIRECTIONS: N4 from Mullingar bypass take R394 for 8 kilometers to Crookedwood, turn left at the Wood Pub; 2 kilometers to first junction turn right; house is signed on this road

OPEN: Easter-October 31
ROOMS: 5 rooms double/twin/family/single; 3 en suite
TERMS: €65-75; single supplement; child reduction

NORTHERN IRELAND

COUNTY ANTRIM

County Antrim's attractions are many. The city of Belfast lies on the shores of Belfast Lough, in a most attractive setting, surrounded by hills that can be seen from most parts of the city. It became a thriving commercial center and port in the nineteenth century and now has a population of about a quarter of that of Northern Ireland. Among Belfast's many sights are the grand City Hall, the ornate Crown Liquor Saloon, St. Anne's Cathedral, and the Ulster Museum, which contains the treasures from the wreck of the Spanish Armada vessel the *Girona*.

The town of Antrim is set back from Lough Neagh, the largest expanse of inland water in the British Isles and famous for its eels. The main fishery is in Toomebridge. County Antrim's coastline is among the most spectacular and scenic in Europe. Carrickfergus to the south, the oldest town in Ireland, is dominated by its castle. Farther north lies Larne, an important port, only a $2^1/_2$-hour ferry ride from Scotland. Beyond Larne, the Coast Road, built in the 1830s, affords breathtaking views of the coast and cliffs.

Antrim's Coast Road connects each of the nine famous Glens of Antrim, green valleys running down to the sea, with rivers, waterfalls, wildflowers, and birds. From south to north they are: Glenarm, Glencloy, Glenariff, Glenballyeamon, Glensan, Clencorn, Clendun, Clenshesk, and Glentaisie. These names are said to mean: glen of the army, glen of the hedges, ploughman's glen, Edwardstown glen, glen of the rush-lights, glen of the slaughter, brown glen, sedgy glen, and finally Taisie's glen (a legendary princess of Rathlin Island).

The resort town of Ballycastle is famous for its Oul Lammas Fair, which once lasted a week and now takes place over two hectic days at the end of August. Ballintoy is a picturesque, Mediterranean-looking fishing village, one of the prettiest towns on the coast, beyond which is one of the world's most amazing natural wonders. The Giant's Causeway, a legendary mass of some 40,000 tightly packed basalt columns, reaches heights of 12 meters. These columns also appear at Staffa Island on the Scottish coast.

AHOGHILL

Neelsgrove Farm
Margaret and Andrew Neely
51 Carnearney Road, Ahoghill, Ballymena, Co. Antrim
Tel: 028 2587 1225 Fax: 028 2587 8704
E-mail: msneely@btinternet.com
Web site: www.neelsgrovefarm.com

In a very rural location surrounded by farmland and an acre of garden, Neelsgrove Farm is a neat, well-kept farmhouse with friendly owners. It offers simple, comfortable accommodation. One of the bedrooms is on the ground floor. It is convenient for the Glens of Antrim, and golf, fishing, and forest and river walks are nearby.
    DIRECTIONS: From Ahoghill, take the B93 Randalstown road for ¹/₄ mile, first road on right for 2 miles

OPEN: March-October
ROOMS: 2 double; 2 en suite; 1 double with private bathroom
TERMS: from £22; single supplement

BALLINTOY

Whitepark House
Bob and Siobhan Isles
Whitepark Bay, Ballintoy, Ballycastle, Co. Antrim
Tel: 028 2073 1482
E-mail: bob@whiteparkhouse.com
Web site: www.whiteparkhouse.com

Just off the coast road, Whitepark is a most interesting house. Dating from the eighteenth century, with later additions, the property included the beach. Now, across the road, a path leads to lovely, sandy Whitepark beach. Breakfast is served in the huge conservatory in the summer and at the table in the foyer in the winter—where it is warmer! Guests like to gather around the fire in the long drawing room, which overlooks the gardens that surround the house. Each bedroom has a large en-suite bathroom with separate bath and shower. The house is full of bits and pieces acquired from Sri Lanka and other points east, where Bob and Siobhan like to escape to in winter. Recently the house has been completely renovated and a conservatory added.

DIRECTIONS: On A2 coast road between the Giant's Causeway and Carrick-a-Rede Rope Bridge

OPEN: all year
ROOMS: 2 double, 1 twin; all en suite
TERMS: £50; single supplement

BALLYCASTLE

Colliers Hall
Gerard and Maureen McCarry
50 Cushendall Road, Ballycastle, Co. Antrim BT54 6QR
Tel: 028 2076 2531
E-mail: reservations@colliershall.com
Web site: www.colliershall.com

Colliers Hall, an eighteenth-century pebble-dashed farmhouse, lies just off the main road. The bedrooms are spacious with the washbasins cleverly incorporated into marble washstands. The house is furnished with a mixture of traditional and antique furniture, and one room has a four-poster bed. The large TV lounge has the original marble fireplace, and dinner, by arrangement for groups only, is served in the dining room. Recently opened is the hostel, a renovated barn offering simple, bright small rooms, all en suite, with an upstairs lounge/kitchen. These rooms are available for bed and breakfast guests. There are lovely walks through the woods, with views of the Knocklayde Mountains and Glenshesk Valley. An 18-hole golf course is close by, and it is 3 kiliometres to the ferry terminal serving Ballycastle to Campbelltown in Scotland. Colliers Hall offers comfort, excellent value, and a warm atmosphere.

DIRECTIONS: 3 kilometers south of Ballycastle

OPEN: April 1-September 30
ROOMS: 4 double/twin, 1 family; all en suite
TERMS: £27.50; single supplement; child reduction
MEALS: £12.50

BALLYMENA

Marlagh Lodge
Robert and Rachel Thompson
71 Moorfields Road, Ballymena, Co. Antrim

Tel: 028 2563 1505 Fax: 028 2564 1590
E-mail: info@marlaghlodge.com
Web site: www.marlaghlodge.com

A large Victorian building with well-proportioned rooms and lots of space, Marlagh Lodge offers a relaxing, soothing environment apart from the busy  road that runs by the house. The Thompsons acquired the property in 2003 and restored it from its dilapidated state, keeping the integrity of its era. Each of the three bedrooms has its own character, bookcases, and one has a king-sized Victorian cast-iron four-poster bed.

Dining at Marlagh Lodge is a must. Rachel Thompson uses local produce and is known for her home-baked brown bread. The lodge is fully licensed, with an extensive wine list. The Thompsons are a delightful, musical couple; Robert is an organist and pianist, and Rachel is an opera singer. They previously owned another B&B near Templepatrick.

DIRECTIONS: Off the A36 Larne road

OPEN: all year
ROOMS: 2 double; 2 en suite; 1 twin/double with private bathroom
TERMS: £45; child reduction
MEALS: dinner £32.50

BALLYMONEY

Harmony Hill Country House
Richard and Trish Wilson
Balnamore, Ballymoney, Co. Antrim
Tel: 028 276 63459 Fax: 028 276 63740
E-mail: webmaster@harmonyhill.net
Web site: www.harmonyhill.net

Reached up a long driveway, Harmony Hill appears as a quite modest building. John Caldwell built the home in the 1760s near Balnamore Mill, a cornmill, which he developed into a successful business. His two sons were implicated in the rebellion of 1798, and as a result, the entire family was exiled to North America. The house continued to be used by mill managers, and today it is home to Richard and Trish Wilson.

The renovated west wing of the house accommodates guests and includes a successful restaurant offering dinner every day. Facilities include a bar, a large well-proportioned drawing room with doors out to the terrace and gardens, and four ground-floor bedrooms. A further cozy room with turf fire is available in the cottage at the end of the driveway.

DIRECTIONS: In the village of Balnamore, 9 miles from the coast

OPEN: all year
ROOMS: 4 double/twin; all en suite
TERMS: £39.50
MEALS: dinner

BELFAST BT6

Ravenhill House
Olive and Roger Nicholson
690 Ravenhill Road, Belfast, Co. Antrim BT6 0BZ
Tel: 028 9020 7444 Fax: 028 9028 2590
E-mail: info@ravenhillguesthouse.com
Web site: www.ravenhillhouse.com or www.ravenhillguesthouse.com

A restored Victorian house convenient to the center and university, Ravenhill is a comfortable place, and Roger and Olive Nicholson are a welcoming couple. The bedrooms are bright, spacious, and well equipped, and the sitting and dining rooms have open fires, a piano, and a good selection of reading material. Breakfasts feature home-made organic breads, marmalade, and vegetarian dishes.

OPEN: closed for Christmas
ROOMS: 2 double/twin, 1 family, 2 singles; all en suite
TERMS: from £30; single supplement

Roseleigh House
Donna McCumiskey
19 Rosetta Park, Belfast, Co. Antrim BT6 0DL
Tel: 028 9064 4414
E-mail: info@roseleighhouse.co.uk
Web site: www.roseleighhouse.co.uk

This restored Victorian-style brick-built house is surrounded by a small garden. It is in a residential area of south Belfast, conveniently located for bus routes leading into the city center. Roseleigh House is run by Donna McCumiskey, a friendly lady. A laundry service is available, and packed lunches can be provided if requested in advance. There is a car park to the rear of the house.

OPEN: all year
ROOMS: 3 double, 3 twin, 2 single, 1 family; all en suite
TERMS: £31; single supplement; child reduction

BELFAST BT9

Avenue House
Stephen Kelly
23 Eglantine Avenue, Lisburn Road, Belfast, Co. Antrim BT9 6DW
Tel: 028 9066 5904 Fax: 028 9029 1810
E-mail: info@avenueguesthouse.com
Web site: www.avenueguesthouse.com

This late Victorian-terraced brick-built house stands on a fairly busy residential tree-lined street and has been totally renovated. The rooms are spacious, light, furnished with elegant simplicity, and vary in size. Both the breakfast and drawing rooms have attractive, original marble fireplaces, and a pull-up wall separates the rooms from each other. A small patio area off the breakfast room is also available for guests; there is high-speed broadband Internet access in the sitting room and wireless Internet throughout the house.

OPEN: all year
ROOMS: 1 double, 3 twin; all en suite
TERMS: £30; single supplement

The Old Rectory
Mary Callan
148 Malone Road, Belfast, Co. Antrim 5T9 5LH
Tel: 028 9066 7882 Fax: 028 9068 3759
E-mail: info@anoldrectory.co.uk
Web site: www.anoldrectory.co.uk/

When the Old Rectory was built in 1896, it was located out in the countryside. Now it is within a comfortable distance of the city center—3 kilometers—and still has views of the Belfast Mountains. Architect Henry Seaver, who was also responsible for the neighboring

Church of St. John's, designed the home (he was the brother of the then minister Rev. Richard Seaver). Later on, it became a nursing home, before becoming the Callan family home.

Furnished and decorated with individual taste, the house has some interesting pieces but retains the feel of a family home. Books and newspapers can be found in the sitting room, and a complimentary "hot Irish whiskey" is served each evening. Guests have use of a croquet lawn. Malone Road is one of the principal streets leading into the center of town and is right on the bus route.

OPEN: mid January-June and August-mid December
ROOMS: 3 double, 2 twin, 1 family, 5 single; all en suite
TERMS: from £36; child reduction

BUSHMILLS

Bushmills Inn Hotel
Alan Dunlop
9 Dunluce Road, Bushmills, Co Antrim BT57 8QG
Tel: 028 2073 3000 Fax: 028 2073 2048
E-mail: mail@bushmillsinn.com
Web site: www.bushmillsinn.com

At the very center of the small town of Bushmills, Bushmills Inn Hotel was originally a coaching inn. Rescued from dereliction some 20 years ago, it is now a haven of hospitality, comfort, and good food for golfers, tourists, and busi-

ness people. Bushmills is famous for the world's oldest distillery and is close to the Giant's Causeway and the Royal Portrush Golf Club.

The original building is a network of atmospheric, small, dark rooms warmed by peat fires; the bar is still lit by gas. The restaurant overlooking the garden courtyard is an intimate dining area; each table has its own "snug." The ten bedrooms in the old building are on the small side; the added 22 are big enough for sitting areas and small dressing rooms, bright, and designed in an attractive rustic style. The new building transitions well into the old.

DIRECTIONS: In Bushmills

OPEN: closed Christmas Day
ROOMS: 32 double/twin/family/single; all en suite
TERMS: from £49; single supplement; child reduction
MEALS: lunch, dinner

Valley View
Valerie McFall
6a Ballyclough Road, Bushmills, Co. Antrim BT57 8TU
Tel: 028 2074 1608 Fax: 028 2074 2739
E-mail: valerie.mcfall@btinternet.com
Web site: www.valleyviewbushmills.com/

This whitewashed, modern house was built by the McFalls and recently extended to provide more guest accommodation. It is surrounded by its own 24 hectares of farmland, supporting beef and sheep, and is 6 kilometers inland from Bushmills. Many of the north Antrim coast's famous attractions are nearby, including Rathlin Island, the Giant's Causeway, Carrick-A-Rede Rope Bridge, Dunluce Castle, and Bushmills Distillery.

Mrs. McFall is a cheerful, friendly host with young children. She is welcoming to families, and there is a children's play area. The accommodation is simple and bright. Guests have use of a comfortable sitting room. Breakfast is served at separate tables in the dining room. One room is suitable for disabled guests, and there is a large self-catering unit that sleeps 8 people.

DIRECTIONS: Valley View is signposted off the B67 and B17

OPEN: closed for Christmas
ROOMS: 3 double, 2 twin, 2 family; all en suite
TERMS: from £22; single supplement; child reduction

CRUMLIN

Caldhame Lodge
Anne McKavanagh
102 Moira Road, Nutts Corner, Crumlin, Co. Antrim BT29 4HG
Tel: 028 9442 3099 Fax: 028 9442 3313

E-mail: info@caldhamelodge.co.uk
Web site: www.caldhamelodge.co.uk

Caldhame Lodge is just off the
main Moira Road, on a working
farm, in a pleasant, mature garden, and just 5 minutes from the
airport. It was built in the early
1990s as the McKavanaghs' family
home. Since then it has been
adapted to accommodate guests

and is comfortable, very well furnished with new furniture, and is
meticulously maintained. The rooms have every possible amenity.
Some bedrooms have Jacuzzi baths and four-poster beds, and one
room has a steam/sauna room. Apart from breakfast, lunch and
evening meals, by arrangement, are served in the dining room/sun
lounge, and guests have use of two further lounges, one with a TV.
Anne McKavanagh runs a very professional businesslike establishment and has won accolades for being the best guesthouse.

DIRECTIONS: On the A26, 10^1/$_2$ miles from Junction 9 on the M1

OPEN: all year
ROOMS: 5 double, 1 twin, 2 family; all en suite
TERMS: £30; single supplement; child reduction

Keef Halla Country House
Charles Kelly
20 Tully Road, Nutts Corner, Crumlin, Co. Antrim BT29 4SW
Tel: 028 9082 5491 Fax: 028 9082 5940
E-mail: info@keefhalla.com
Web site: www.keefhalla.com

Keef Halla, meaning "welcome" in Arabic, acquired its name
because Charles Kelly used to work in Saudi Arabia and bought the
house with the money he earned there. It is an old country house
that has been renovated and recently extended. Charles Kelly, who
runs the guesthouse (Siobhan, his wife, is a teacher in Belfast), has
earned a reputation for the level of comfort and service he provides—borne out by being awarded accolades for the best guesthouse. The comfortable sitting room has an open fire, leather sofas
and chairs, and leads into the dining room, where dinner, if requested,
is served. Breakfast and packed lunches can also be provided. One

guest arriving by helicopter landed in the garden: Keef Halla claims to be the nearest guesthouse to the airport. Internet service is provided.

DIRECTIONS: Off the main A26 road, 5 minutes from Belfast International Airport

OPEN: all year
ROOMS: 2 double, 2 twin, 1 family; all en suite; 2 family rooms with private bath
TERMS: £30; single supplement; child reduction
MEALS: dinner £15; packed lunch £5

CUSHENDALL

Glendale Bed & Breakfast
Mary O'Neill
46 Coast Road, Cushendall, Co. Antrim BT44 ORX
Tel: 028 2177 1495
E-mail: mary.glendale@btinternet.com

This white, pebble-dashed house is down a private driveway off the main road in the village of Cushendall. It enjoys lovely views of the Antrim plateau and sea. The O'Neills are friendly, welcoming hosts, attracting a lot of repeat visitors. Mr. O'Neill works on the Larne-Cairnryan ferry and enjoys outlining sightseeing itineraries for guests. The house is well maintained and comfortably furnished. Glendale is within walking distance of the beach and golf course.

DIRECTIONS: Off the main A2 in Cushendall

OPEN: all year
ROOMS: 6 family; all en suite
TERMS: £20; single supplement; child reduction

CUSHENDUN

The Villa Farmhouse
Catherine Scally
185 Torr Road, Cushendun, Co. Antrim BT44 0PU
Tel/Fax 028 2176 1252
E-mail: maggiescally@amserve.net
Web site: www.ireland-holidays.net/English/Accommodation/ Cushendun/Villa/Villa.htm

Catherine Scally is in her nineties and has lived at the Villa since she married, opening her bed and breakfast business some 40 years ago. Now she is ably assisted by her daughter Maggie, who does everything. The house is situated above the delightful little village of Cushendun, which is owned by the National Trust and contains the smallest pub in Ireland. It has fantastic views of the spectacular coastline and the sea and is on the Ulster Way. Both house and garden are immaculately kept, and guests have use of a charming sitting room full of photographs. This arrangement of family photos and the home was featured on the Australian TV show *Good Morning Australia*. For the infirm, there is a chair lift, and one ground-floor room is suitable for the disabled. The coach house is available for self-catering.

DIRECTIONS: From Cushendun, take Torr Road; at T-junction turn right; after a ¹/₂ mile, the Villa is the third road on the left

OPEN: February-October
ROOMS: 2 double, 2 family, 1 single; all en suite
TERMS: £30; single supplement; child reduction

PORTRUSH

Maddybenny Farm House
Karen White
18 Maddybenny Farm, Loguestown Road, Portrush/Coleraine, Co. Antrim BT52 2PT
Tel: 028 7082 3394 Fax: 028 7082 2177
E-mail: beds@maddybenny.com
Web site: www.maddybenny.com

Maddybenny Farm House, meaning "sanctified or holy post," dates from the 1600s. It was built as a plantation house on lands belonging to the Earl of Antrim. The first Presbyterian minister, Rev. Gabriel Cornwall, lived here. Added to over the years, the house's floor plan is unusual because it  allows one to walk completely around the house from the inside. It is approached up a long track and stands in a wonderful, rural location. The home is part of a large complex of buildings consisting of the farm, stables, and six self-catering cottages. The riding school offers tuition to guests by an international rider. Maddybenny Farm is a comfortable, relaxed place and a bright and spacious house with a TV lounge that has a snooker table and dining room. The bedrooms are very large, and there is a fridge and laundry facilities for guests' use. Maddybenny is near the Royal Portrush Golf Club, the Giant's Causeway, the university, and beaches. The self-catering cottages are equipped to a high standard and sleep six to eight people.

DIRECTIONS: Signposted off the A29 Portrush to Coleraine road

OPEN: closed for Christmas
ROOMS: 1 double, 2 family, 1 single; all en suite
TERMS: from £27.50; single supplement; child reduction

COUNTY ARMAGH

County Armagh is the smallest and most varied county in Northern Ireland, ranging from magnificent mountain scenery in the south to rich, fruit growing land in the north, interspersed with small lakes and dairy farms.

Armagh, the ancient capital of Ulster and former great center of learning, has been the spiritual capital of Ireland for 1,500 years and is the seat of both Catholic and Protestant archbishops. The two cathedral churches are prominent features in the city. The Church of Ireland cathedral stands on the hill where St. Patrick built his stone church, and the twin spires of the Catholic cathedral, which was finished in 1873, rise from the opposite hill.

In the south of Armagh, the mountains of Slieve Gullion contain an unspoiled area of small villages and beautiful scenery.

Crossmaglen has possibly the largest market square in Ireland and has become the center of the recently revived lace-making industry. Jonesborough hosts an enormous open-air market every Sunday.

While driving down a country lane, you might come across the great Armagh game, roads bowls, which is shared with County Cork. The object is to hurl a metal bowl weighing 1 kilo as far as possible, covering several miles in the shortest number of shots. Children are sent ahead to warn motorists.

The orchard of Ireland, this rich fruit-growing county in the northeast is at its best in May. Apple Blossom Sunday takes place in late May.

ARMAGH

Hillview Lodge
Alice McBride
33 Newtownhamilton Road, Armagh, Co. Armagh
Tel: 028 3752 2000 Fax: 028 3752 8276
E-mail: alice@hillviewlodge.com
Web site: www.hillviewlodge.com

Hillview is a modern building about 2 kilometers outside Armagh, set just back from the road beside a golf driving range under the same ownership. The accommodation is functional and well designed, and the entire house has plain wood-type floors, unalleviated by any rugs. One ground-floor room is suitable for disabled guests. The dining room, where breakfast is served, has a sitting area, and the entrance/reception room and conservatory provide more comfortable places to sit.

Hillview is well suited to business people or those who want to practice their golf swing. The driving range is floodlit for night use.

DIRECTIONS: Located on the B31 Newtownhamilton Road

OPEN: closed for Christmas
ROOMS: 1 double, 5 family; all en suite
TERMS: £29; single supplement

Ni Eoghain Lodge
Noel McGeown
32 Ennislare Road, Armagh, Co. Armagh BT60 2AX
Tel: 028 3752 5633 Fax: 028 3751 1246
E-mail: nieoghainlodge@hotmail.co.uk
Web site: www.nieoghainlodge.com

Ni Eioghain is a pleasant, secluded country house set in wonderful gardens. Surrounded by 12 acres of woodland, the 3-acre garden has twice received awards. The bedrooms are simply furnished and decorated and are on the ground floor.

DIRECTIONS: 4 kilometers south of Armagh; signposted off the A29

OPEN: closed for Christmas
ROOMS: 3 doubles/twin; all en suite
TERMS: £22.50; single supplement

COUNTY DERRY

Derry (for Londonderry), probably best known for the tune *The Derry Air*, also known as *Danny Boy*, is situated on a hill on the banks of the Foyle. The city acquired the name Londonderry in the seventeenth century when the city of London financed building and resettlement in the city. Having withstood several sieges, the seventeenth-century walls, about 1.5 kilometers round and 5.5 meters thick, are still intact, giving magnificent views of the surrounding countryside.

Derry still preserves its ancient layout, and amongst the historic buildings is the 1633 Gothic Cathedral of St. Columb. From the quay behind the Guildhall, hundreds of Irish emigrants left Derry for America during the eighteenth and nineteenth centuries. Along with them were the families and ancestors of Davy Crockett and U.S. President James Polk.

The Mussenden Temple, built by the eccentric Earl Bishop of Derry as testimony of his affection for Lady Mussenden, stands on a windswept headland on the coast at Downhill; the adjacent castle is now in ruins but exudes an aura of romance and grandeur and is worth visiting. One of Ulster's finest fortified farmhouses can be seen at Bellaghy. Whiskey is produced at Bushmills near Coleraine, the town that St. Patrick supposedly founded.

COLERAIN

Camus House
Josephine King
27 Curragh Road, Castletoe, Colerain, Co. Derry BT51 3RY
Tel: 028 7034 2982

Camus House was built on the site of an old monastery and is a listed building, dating from 1685; it is the oldest home in the area. The house is in a delightful setting close to the River Bann, and Josephine King owns 2 kilometers of river frontage. Her passion is fishing, and this is a great fishing family; her daughter has represented Ireland.

This lovely ivy-covered house is approached via a private driveway through the grounds and has a pretty front garden.

Mrs. King is friendly and accommodating, runs an informal bed and breakfast, and is a member of the Healthy Eating Circle Galtee Breakfast Award. The house has lots of character, as does Josephine, and this is a friendly, comfortable home. In winter, guests use Mrs. King's cozy sitting room, which has a TV and open fire. There is another sitting room and a dining room, where breakfasts only are served. Not suitable for children. Private parking.

DIRECTIONS: A little tricky to find, phone for directions

OPEN: all year except Christmas
ROOMS: 3 rooms double/twin/family; all en suite
TERMS: £25; single supplement

Greenhill House
Elizabeth Hegarty
24 Greenhill Road, Aghadowey, Coleraine, Co. Derry BT51 4EU
Tel: 028 7086 8241 Fax: 028 7086 8365
E-mail: greenhill@btinternet.com

This impressive Georgian house stands in its own grounds of trees, lawns, and shrubs and lovely views over farmland to distant hills. The Hegartys have owned this 60-acre arable and beef farm for nearly two decades. The accommodation is of a very high standard, well maintained, and upgraded as needed. There are some antique furnishings, and the house has a warm and friendly ambience. Two of the bathrooms are equipped with baths and showers and well appointed with every convenience.

Mrs. Hegarty, formerly a teacher, devotes her time to running her successful bed and breakfast. She is a most friendly and cheerful lady. There is a spacious lounge, which overlooks the fields, and a marble fireplace, where fires burn on chilly days.

A substantial, tasty breakfast is served in the cheery dining room and is enough to set you up for the day. Many venues nearby serve evening meals. Greenhill House is a delightful place to stay and is the recipient of many well-deserved awards, including the Taste of Ulster and the British Airways Award. Private parking.

DIRECTIONS: Take the A29 from Coleraine to Garvagh for 7 miles, left at the B66 (Greenhill Road); Greenhill House is signed on the right

OPEN: March 1-October 31
ROOMS: 6 rooms double/twin/family; all en suite
TERMS: from £30; single supplement; child reduction

Killeague Lodge
Margaret Moore
157 Drumcroome Road, Blackhill, Coleraine, Co. Derry BT51 35G,
Tel: 028 7086 8229

Margaret Moore previously ran her bed and breakfast from the farm, where her son now lives. Guests are still welcome to wander around the farm, but the accommodations are now in a beautiful new structure built on the land. Two of the luxurious bedrooms are on the ground floor, all are tastefully decorated, and one has a semicircular wall, old pine furniture, and pastel yellow décor. Another bedroom has mahogany furniture, and the third largest upstairs bedroom is blue, with rich mahogany furniture.

There is a sun lounge and two other lounges. Breakfast is a banquet, served on Royal Albert china in the elegant dining room with fresh fruit, yogurt, juice, warm scones, home-baked bread, and for those with a large appetite a full traditional Irish breakfast follows. Margaret's award-winning hospitality brought this comment from a visitor, "I thought I had died and gone to heaven." Bedrooms have a TV, radio, tea makers, and en-suite facilities. Margaret's motto is "Good food, fun, and fellowship." Children are welcome. A limited laundry service is available. Private parking.

Horse riding can be arranged. Killeague Lodge is within 30 minutes of the Giant's Causeway and the North Antrim Coast.

DIRECTIONS: From Coleraine, take A29 south to Garvagh and Cookstown. The lodge is approximately 5 miles on this road on the left.

OPEN: all year except Christmas
ROOMS: 3 rooms double/twin/family
TERMS: £25; single supplement; child reduction

DERRY

The Merchant House
Joan and Dr. Peter Pyne
16 Queen Street, Derry, Co. Derry, BT48 7EQ
Tel: 028 7126 9691 or 7126 4223 Fax: 028 7126 6913
E-mail: saddlershouse@btinternet.com

Web site: www.thesaddlershouse.com

This listed Georgian townhouse, situated in a conservation area, was awarded a Gulbenkian Civic Trust Award for restoration and is within walking distance of most amenities. The property has an interesting history; it was built for a wealthy merchant and has been used as a bank and a rectory. There are five good-sized bedrooms furnished with period pieces and rich white bedspreads. Several original features remain, such as polished wood floors, ceiling coving, and a marble fireplace. An elegant drawing room is available to guests. A freshly prepared breakfast is served, featuring home-made preserves, home-baked bread, and a traditional Irish cooked variety with fresh brewed tea. Disabled access is available on ground floors. There is one en-suite room and several additional bathrooms for guests' use.

This is a charming place to stay, popular with business people and tourists; early reservations are recommended. As one guest comments, "This is all you might hope for from a B&B." Spanish spoken. Limited off-street parking.

OPEN: open all year
ROOMS: 6 rooms double/twin/family; 1 en suite
TERMS: from £30; single supplement; child reduction

The Saddlers House
Joan Pyne
36 Great James Street, Derry, Co. Derry BT48 7DB
Tel: 028 7126 9691 or 7126 4223 Fax: 028 7126 6913
E-mail: saddlershouse@btinternet.com
Web site: www.thesaddlershouse.com

A tastefully restored and immaculately maintained nineteenth-century townhouse situated in a conservation area in the heart of Derry, Saddlers House is the most centrally located bed and breakfast in the city and is within walking distance of restaurants, shops, and most amenities.

The bedrooms, three of which are en suite, are furnished with period furniture, all have TVs, tea makers, and books, and overlook a walled garden. Two bedrooms are on the ground floor, one of which is a twin en suite.

Breakfasts are plentiful, with fresh-brewed coffee, homemade preserves and marmalade, and a cooked variety is served on pretty blue china in the cozy dining room. Special diets can be catered for.

A sitting room is available for guests, and guests are welcome to use the garden. This is a popular venue and early reservations are recommended. Limited off-street parking.

OPEN: all year
ROOMS: 5 rooms double/twin
TERMS: £23-25; single supplement; child reduction

LIMAVADY

Ballycarton House ✓
Patricia Craig
239 Seacoast Road, Limavady, Co. Derry BT49 0HZ
Tel: 028 775 0216 Fax: 028 7775 0990
E-mail: stay@ballycartonhouse.com
Web site: www.ballycartonhouse.com/

Built in the 1800s, this lovely rambling farmhouse is nestled at the foot of Binevenagh Mountains and has wonderful views. Patricia Craig, who completely refurbished the property, retaining the charm, character, and warm ambience, runs it. Ballycarton is an extremely high standard accommodation. The five large en-suite rooms are well equipped; the bedrooms are tastefully decorated in soft shades and have pine furniture. All rooms have a TV, clock radio, hair dryers, and tea makers.

There is a conservatory and sitting room, plus a dining room, which has William Morris wallpaper and many items of interest. A fire burns in the sitting room on chilly days, and the conservatory overlooking the view is a peaceful spot. A recently added facility is a relaxation area featuring a hot tub and sauna. There is also a laundry room, a games room, and Internet access.

This is the perfect combination of a great house, wonderful hospitality, and good food. The imaginative breakfast menu includes French toast, pancakes American style with maple syrup, croissants, juice, and a full Irish breakfast, with homemade soda bread. Little wonder Ballycarton House is the proud recipient of the Ulster Guest House of the Year award. Guests have use of the garden, which has a gazebo and barbeque area. Private parking.

DIRECTIONS: From Londonderry, take a left at the traffic light before entering Limavady on the B69 road; farm is located on this road. From Coleraine, 2 miles after Bellarena train crossing, turn left onto Seacoast Road.

OPEN: all year
ROOMS: 5 rooms double/twin/single; all en suite
TERMS: £30; single supplement

Ballyhenry House
Michael and Karen Kane
172 Seacoast Road, Limavady, Co. Derry BT49 9EF
Tel: 028 7772 2657
E-mail: info@ballyhenry.co.uk
Web site: www.ballyhenry.co.uk

The large, bright, and airy award-winning farmhouse is close to the sea between Limavady and Castlerock. Situated in an idyllic setting, Ballyhenry House is approached down a private lane bordered by mature trees and fields full of sheep. It was built at the turn of the century by Mr. Kane's grandfather, and the flat and fertile land extends to 360 acres of arable farming. It was sympathetically restored in 2006, retaining many original features, such as cornices, a marble fireplace, woodwork, and a staircase. The luxurious, modern bathrooms have natural travertine limestone and strong showers. The spacious family room opens onto a verandah overlooking the garden. All rooms have countryside views. The tastefully decorated rooms are furnished in keeping with the character of the house and have several pieces of antique furniture. The farm is environmentally friendly; dried willow crop wood is up for sale when available.

This is a wonderful place to stay while exploring the beautiful Roe Valley, which is surrounded by the Donegal and Sperrin Mountains. Owners Michael and Karen offer a true Irish welcome; guests are well looked after here. There are two luxurious self-catering units available. Private parking.

DIRECTIONS: From Londonderry, turn left at the traffic light before entering Limavady on the B69. The farm is 3 miles from this road. From Coleraine, 2 miles after Bellerana train crossing, turn right onto Seacoast Road.

OPEN: all year except Christmas
ROOMS: 4 rooms double/twin/family/single; all en suite
TERMS: from £25; single supplement; child reduction

PORTSTEWART

Breezemount
Mr. and Mrs. McKay
26 Portrush Road, Portstewart, Co. Derry BT55 7DD
Tel: 028 70 834724
Web site: www.irelandholidayguide.com/est/64/8.html

Situated on the North Antrim Coast Road, this attractive modern house has spectacular views of the sea to Donegal and, on fine days, Scotland. The welcome is great, guests feel immediately at home with the friendly owners. Tea and coffee are offered upon arrival. The immaculate en-suite rooms are of a good size and decorated in soft pastels. The comfortable lounge has a chaise lounge and leather furniture. There is a TV, and guests may prefer to sit, relax, and enjoy the sea view.

Breezemount is situated close to most amenities, including several choices for evening meals. There are five golf courses in the area; one can be seen from the house. For keen golfers, a golf tournament takes place here in June. Off street parking is available.

OPEN: January-November
ROOMS: 3 rooms, 2 double, 1 twin; all en suite
TERMS: £25; single supplement; child reduction

COUNTY DOWN

A county rich in monuments of antiquity, County Down has been subject to many invasions throughout its history, the fiercest of all from the Vikings in the ninth century. Legend has it that St. Patrick landed here in 432 A.D. at the place where the Slaney River flows into Strangford Lough. During the 30 years between his arrival and death in 461 A.D., St. Patrick converted the pagan Irish to Christianity.

The Ards Peninsula, bordered by Strangford Lough to the west and the Irish Sea to the east, is a narrow strip of land with a bracing climate, reputedly the sunniest and driest part of the North. It has some charming villages and towns that were first settled by the Scots and English.

Bangor was a famous center of learning from the sixth century until it was devastated by the Vikings in the ninth century. It was from here that the missionaries St. Columbanus, St. Gall, and many others set off to bring Christianity to the rest of Europe.

The breezy coast road runs from Bangor past Ballycopeland—the only working windmill in Ireland—past the pretty village of Kearney to the attractive town of Portaferry, where the short ferry ride to Strangford affords lovely views of Strangford Lough. The Lough is a famous bird sanctuary and wildlife reserve, and the small rounded hills, called drumlins, that cover North Down and found in Strangford Lough appear as small islands.

Amongst the historic places to visit are Castle Ward, built by the first Lord Bangor in 1765, and Mount Stewart, the childhood home of Lord Castlereagh, a former British foreign secretary. Of all the Cistercian abbeys in medieval County Down, three were built around the Lough: Inch Abbey, Grey Abbey, and Comber. Downpatrick, at the southern tip of Strangford Lough, is an attractive Georgian town and contains the burial site of St. Patrick, which is in the graveyard of the cathedral.

The Mourne Mountains cover a small area 22.5 kilometers long and 12 kilometers wide, with 12 rounded peaks. The barren peak of Slieve Donard, climbing steeply to 860 meters, dominates this peaceful landscape, which is a paradise for walkers. From the summit, you can see the Isle of Man, the Belfast hills, and Lough Neagh.

There are also two artificial lakes or reservoirs that supply Belfast with water. These are surrounded by a huge dry stone wall over 2 meters high and 33 kilometers long. The Mourne International Walking Festival attracts thousands of walkers from all over the world each June.

The coast south from Newcastle, a lively seaside resort, was notorious for smuggling in the eighteenth century. Newry was once a prosperous mercantile town with large townhouses and public buildings, as well as the earliest Protestant church in Ireland, St. Patrick's Church of Ireland.

BANGOR

Cairn Bay Lodge
Christopher Mullen
278 Seacliff Road, Bangor, Co. Down BT20 5HS
Tel: 028 9146 7636 Fax: 028 9245 7728
E-mail: info@cairnbaylodge.com
Web site: www.cairnbaylodge.com

Cairn Bay Lodge is a most interesting and substantial house.
Built in 1880, it stands in a large
and beautifully maintained garden, set back from the shore
with uninterrupted views of the
sea. There are all kinds of unusual pieces of furniture and décor. The drawing and sitting rooms occupy the front of the house, affording lovely views over Belfast Lough. The well-equipped, spacious, comfortable bedrooms have a yesteryear feel to them. There is a resident beautician, baby-sitting service, and dinner can be served, if booked in advance. Cairn Bay is a quiet, peaceful place, just a 5-minute walk from the center of Bangor.

DIRECTIONS: In the southern end of Bangor

OPEN: all year
ROOMS: 9 double/twin/single/family; all en suite
TERMS: £35; single supplement; child reduction
MEALS: dinner £15

Shelleven House
Philip and Mary Weston

61 Princetown Road, Bangor, Co. Down BT20 3TA
Tel/Fax: 028 9127 1777
E-mail: shellevenhouse@aol.com
Web site: www.shellevenhouse.com

Shelleven House stands one street above the sea front in a small terrace
of Victorian buildings. The Westons, who are a friendly, competent
couple, acquired the building ten years ago and have now refurbished
the bedrooms and bathrooms. Some of the bedrooms have sea views,
some are on the small side, and the ground-floor room is suitable for
wheelchair use. The comfortable lounge is separated from the dining
room by a slide-up door. Shelleven House is fully licensed.
   DIRECTIONS: In Bangor

OPEN: all year
ROOMS: 5 double, 3 twin, 3 single; all en suite
TERMS: £35; single supplement; child reduction

CASTLEWELLAN

Slieve Croob Inn
Laurence Kelly
119 Clanvaraghan Road, Castlewellan, Co. Down BT31 9LA
Tel: 028 437 71412 Fax: 028 437 71162
E-mail: info@slievecroobinn.com
Web site: www.slievecroobinn.com

Under Slieve Croob on a remote country lane, this collection of
whitewashed buildings blends well into the landscape. The inn was
purpose built, they provide one building containing the bed and
breakfast accommodation, and others are self-catering and banqueting facilities. The B&B guests have a lounge, and the restaurant serves
breakfast, lunch, and dinner. The bedrooms are spacious, comfortably furnished, and well equipped.
   With the mountain behind and the sea view in front, the inn is
located in a spectacular position for walkers.
   DIRECTIONS: Slieve Croob is well signposted from Castlewellan.

OPEN: all year
ROOMS: 7 double/twin, 1 suite; all en suite
TERMS: £37.50; single supplement; child reduction
MEALS: Sunday lunch, dinner

DOWNPATRICK

Ballymote House
Nicola and James Manningham-Buller
Killough Road, Downpatrick, Co. Down BT30 8BJ
Tel: 028 4461 5500
E-mail: bandb@ballymotehouse.com
Web site: www.ballymotehouse.com

Ballymote House dates from around 1730 and has been owned by James and Nicola for 18 years. Returning from London to a slower paced country life, the couple's renovation process included an addition to the back of the house, part of which is an enormous kitchen, and an upstairs, which holds three comfortable, nicely furnished guest bedrooms.

The Manningham-Bullers are an energetic, busy couple. Apart from offering guests a comfortable retreat, they run an insurance business and are heavily involved in horse world-polo, events, and show jumping. The 20 acres surrounding the house are kept for their own horses, and George Carter, a Chelsea Flower Show Gold winner, designed their gardens. Nicola loves to cook and takes pride in acquiring only the best of local ingredients. She will on occasion cook dinner if there are enough guests in the house. Riding and sailing can be arranged. Kennels can be provided for dogs and stables for horses.

DIRECTIONS: Ballymote can be found off the B176 in the direction of Killough.

OPEN: closed for Christmas and New Year's
ROOMS: 1 double, 1 twin, 1 single; all en suite
TERMS: £40; single supplement
MEALS: dinner £30 for groups only

The Mill at Ballydugan
Noel Killen
Drumcullan Road, Ballydugan, Downpatrick, Co. Down
Tel: 028 4461 3654 Fax: 028 4483 9754
E-mail: mkillen@btconnect.com
Web site: www.ballyduganmill.co.uk

As a boy, Noel Killen hid a penny in Ballydugan Mill's upper beams with the wish that one day he would be able to own and restore it. Eighteen years ago that dream started to become reality. Abandoned for 150 years, the home's restoration took 12 years of painstaking work. There had been a mill on the site since the twelfth century; the present flour-mill building dates from the eighteenth century, a massive stone structure six floors high.

The fifth floor houses an Exhibition & History Center, the first floor the restaurant, the ground floor a bar and coffee shop, and the remaining floors staff, guest bedrooms, suites, and function rooms. The architectural integrity of the building and materials used have been kept as close as possible to the original. The bedrooms are spacious, unfussily furnished, and have lovely views of the attractive countryside. An old steam tower stands next to the Mill, which was used for energy when the river was low, and a nearby windmill provided wind power. Noel is now working on ancillary buildings across the massive courtyard, which will eventually house staff members. The property is very popular for weddings and functions.

DIRECTIONS: The Mill is signposted off the A25 on the Newcastle road.

OPEN: closed for Christmas
ROOMS: 8 double, 3 family; 1 room suitable for the disabled; all en suite
TERMS: £37.50; single supplement; child reduction

Tyrella House
David Corbett
Downpatrick, Co. Down BT30 8SU
Tel/Fax: 028 4485 1422
E-mail: tyrella.corbett@virgin.net
Web site: www.hidden-ireland.com/tyrella

This large, elegant country house, with a porticoed, classical façade, stands in 120 hectares of parkland and farmland that stretches down to the sea and its private sandy beach. Most of the house dates from around the eighteenth century, with the Georgian front added in the early nineteenth century. The grounds include a private eventing course, polo ground, and a point-to-point course that is used a couple of times a year. Horses are available for beach, forest, or mountain rides, or guests are welcome to bring their own horses. Tuition is available for polo. The house has a welcoming feeling, the large hallway has an open fire, and stairs lead up to the three large bedrooms. Dinner (if prebooked) is served by candlelight in the elegant dining room.

DIRECTIONS: Tyrella's Gate Lodge with blue gates is 7 kilometers from Clough on the Clough/Ardglass road.

OPEN: February 1-November 30
ROOMS: 1 double, 1 twin, 1 family; 2 en suite; 1 private bathroom
TERMS: from £45; not suitable for children
MEALS: dinner £25

DROMORE

Clanmurry
John and Sara McCorkell
16 Lower Quilly Road, Dromore, Co. Down BT25 1NL
Tel: 028 9269 3760 Fax: 028 9269 8106
E-mail: clanmurry@btinternet.com
Web site: www.clanmurry.com

Garden lovers will enjoy Clanmurry, a compact Georgian house surrounded by wild, luxurious gardens, spacious lawns, and shielded from the nearby main road. The previous owner sympathetically enlarged the original 1820 house in the 1960s, adding the attractive entrance hall with dome and the back of the house, which is now the kitchen. The garden layout is his design and encompasses some 6 acres. The guests' drawing room is filled with light and is a comfortable place to sit. John and Sara McCorkell are a quietly welcoming couple, and Clanmurry is a peaceful, relaxing place only 20 minutes from Belfast.

DIRECTIONS: Off the A1 between Hillsborough and Dromore

OPEN: closed for Christmas and New Year's
ROOMS: 1 twin en suite; 2 twins with private bathrooms
TERMS: £35; single supplement

HOLYWOOD

Rayanne House
Conor and Bernie McClelland
60 Demesne Road, Holywood, Co. Down BT18 9EX
Tel/Fax: 028 9042 5859
E-mail: rayannehouse@hotmail.com
Web site: www.rayannehouse.com

Rayanne House, a substantial brick building dating from the nineteenth century, stands in its own grounds and enjoys lovely views across Belfast Lough to Carrickfergus and the Antrim Hills. It offers a warm welcome, good food, and a high standard of comfort and service and is ably run by Conor, the son of the previous owner, and Bernie. The bedrooms are charming, each one completely individually decorated and furnished with a lot of flair. They all have large bathrooms and all the bits and pieces included you can imagine. The two sitting rooms and the dining room are comfortable, informal, and filled with all sorts of china and knickknacks. The house has recently been upgraded and an extension added. Breakfasts are memorable with a wide selection from the menu, and dinners (prebooked) are not to be missed. The house is licensed.

DIRECTIONS: From Belfast on the A2, take the first exit for Holywood, a quick right on Jackson's Road, straight on to Demesne Road, just past the Golf Club

OPEN: all year
ROOMS: 6 double, 4 twin, 1 single; all en suite
TERMS: £50; single supplement; child reduction
MEALS: dinner £42

KILKEEL

Heath Hall
Mary McGlue
160 Moyadd Road, Kilkeel, Co. Down BT34 4HJ
Tel: 028 4176 2612
E-mail: info@heathhallguesthouse.com
Web site: www.heathhallguesthouse.com

Heath Hall, a turn-of-the-century, stone-built farmhouse, has a modern appearance and is set in 6 $^1/_2$ hectares of farmland with sheep and cattle. It has views of the sea and the Mourne Mountains. The house was completely renovated a few years ago, and some rooms have sea views. The TV lounge has the original marble fireplace, and there is also a snooker room. The house was formerly run as a bed and breakfast by Mrs. McGlue's mother-in-law and has a reputation for offering good value accommodation.

DIRECTIONS: On the B27, 2 1/2 kilometers north of Kilkeel

OPEN: closed for Christmas and New Year's
ROOMS: 1 double, 1 twin, 1 family; 1 en suite; 1 shared bathroom
TERMS: £25; child reduction

Hill View House
The Trainor Family
18 Bog Road, Atticall, Kilkeel, Co. Down BT34 4HT
Tel/Fax: 028 4176 4269
E-mail: info@hillviewhouse.co.uk
Web site: hillviewhouse.co.uk

Just outside the small village of Atticall, a few miles inland from Kilkeel, Hill View is part of a sheep farm. With great hill views from each side of the house and every bedroom, it is very popular with walkers and cyclists—they can leave their cars at the house and set off on a variety of trails. The Trainors are happy to drop guests off supplied with a packed lunch and let them walk back. Guest bedrooms are small and comfortable, and one room serves as a sitting area and breakfast room. One farm building has been converted into a high-quality self-catering unit for up to six people; it has its own garden and children's play area.

DIRECTIONS: On the edge of Atticall

OPEN: closed for Christmas and New Year's
ROOMS: 3 double/twin, 1 single; all en suite
TERMS: £27.50; single supplement
MEALS: packed lunch (by request)

KILLINCHY

Barnageeha
Mr. and Mrs. Denis Crawford
Ardmillan, Killinchy, Co. Down BT23 6QN
Tel: 028 9754 1011

E-mail: barnageeha@onetel.com

On the edge of tiny Ardmillan village, Barnageeha is reached up a winding driveway, across a small river. A long, low, modern attractive whitewashed building covered in creepers and climbing roses, it is right on the shores of Strangford Lough and is part of a small sheep farm. Margie Crawford is a delightful host, and the house is very comfortable, pleasantly furnished, and has a relaxing atmosphere. All the bedrooms are large, and lunch or dinner can be provided if arranged in advance. Bird watching attracts a lot of visitors, and with the proximity to the water, watchers can remain in the comfort of the house. There is a tennis court for guests' use.

DIRECTIONS: 6 miles south of Comber on the shores of Strangford Lough—off A22

OPEN: April-October
ROOMS: 1 double, 3 twin; all en suite
TERMS: from £40; single supplement
MEALS: lunch or dinner

The Old Schoolhouse Inn
Terry and Avril Brown
100 Ballydrain Road, Killinchy, Co. Down BT23 6EA
Tel: 028 9754 1182 Fax: 028 9754 2583
E-mail: info@theoldschoolhouseinn.com
Web site: www.theoldschoolhouseinn.com

The original school is now the restaurant, and it has been whimsically decorated with knickknacks and bottles and painted in warm, dark colors. A guest wing was added in matching brick, offering spacious, comfortable bedrooms equipped to a high standard, each one named after an American president of Ulster descent. Avril Brown is the head chef, and while the food is based on French cooking, she likes to experiment with new combinations. The inn is next to Castle Espie, which has the largest collection of wildfowl in Ireland, and Strangford Lough is only a few minutes away.

DIRECTIONS: From Comber, follow signs for Castle Espie; the Inn can be found ¹/₄ mile beyond

OPEN: all year
ROOMS: 12 double/twin; all en suite

TERMS: from £35
MEALS: dinner from £19.95

KILLYLEAGH

Dufferin Coaching Inn
Leontine Haines
33 High Street, Killyleagh, Co. Down BT30 9QF
Tel: 028 4482 1134 Fax: 028 4482 1102
E-mail: info@dufferincoachinginn.com
Web site: www.dufferincoachinginn.com

Halfway down High Street in historic Killyleagh town, this atmospheric old inn lies between spectacular Killyleagh Castle above and the shores of Strangford Lough below. Dufferin Coaching Inn has been operating since 1803, and both it and the seventeenth-century  castle were originally part of the Dufferin & Ava estate. The inn has recently been taken over by Leontine Haines and has undergone a complete refurbishment, and a new dining/breakfast room has been added to the ground floor. The bedrooms are spacious, three have four-poster beds, two have private sitting rooms, and all rooms have large bathrooms with both bath and shower. The lounge was once the Ulster Bank and a wood burning stove has recently been added. The next-door pub has live traditional music on Saturdays and serves meals every day. The Dufferin Coaching Inn is a lively spot with comfortable accommodation and a great atmosphere. Tennis, golf, horse riding, fishing, sailing, and walking with a guide can be organized.
DIRECTIONS: In Killyleagh

OPEN: all year
ROOMS: 5 double, 1 twin; all en suite
TERMS: from £35; single supplement; child reduction

NEWCASTLE

Harbour House Inn
Frank and Brenda Connolly and Frances Monteith

4 South Promenade, Newcastle, Co. Down BT33 OEX
Tel: 028 4372 3445 Fax: 028 437 24118
E-mail: info@stoneboatrestaurant.com
Web site: www.stoneboatrestaurant.com

Harbour House Inn stands right beside the harbor at the south end of
Newcastle and has offered hospitality since it was built over 100 years
ago. The inn is very much a family-run and operated business; Frank
and Brenda Connolly have been here 28 years, and daughter Frances,
a cheerful, chatty person, not only helps run the inn, but also owns
and runs the adjoining Stone Boat fish restaurant. In a superb location with great sea views, just above a sandy beach, the bar and lounge
have a welcoming atmosphere full of pictures, photos, and knickknacks. One night a week there is live music and a quiz night. All
rooms are on the first floor—three have sea views.
   DIRECTIONS: In Newcastle

OPEN: all year
ROOMS: 7 double/twin; all en suite
TERMS: from £40; single supplement; child reduction

NEWRY

Deer Park Bed & Breakfast
Harry and Sheila Thompson
177 Tandragee Road, Drumbanagher, Newry, Co. Down BT35 7LP
Tel: 028 3082 1409

Deer Park is an attractive eighteenth-century farmhouse. Its elevated
position affords wonderful views of the Mourne Mountains and surrounding farmland. Sheila Thompson is a relaxed, friendly lady. Her
husband, who runs the farm with their son, is an avid hunt enthusiast—
many pictures depicting hunting scenes can be seen. The house is very
comfortable and attractively furnished and decorated, with one en-suite
room on the ground floor, and the upstairs room has a splendid bathroom with an old fashioned tub—this bathroom was formerly a bedroom. Breakfast is served in either the dining room or conservatory.
   DIRECTIONS: Just off the A27 road in the direction of Portadown

OPEN: all year
ROOMS: 1 double en suite, 1 double with private bathroom
TERMS: £30; child reduction

NEWTOWNARDS

Ballycastle House
Margaret Deering
20 Mountstewart Road, Newtownards, Co. Down BT22 2AL
Tel/Fax: 028 4278 8357
E-mail: mdeering@ballycastlehouse.com
Web site: www.ballycastlehouse.com

A warm welcome always awaits you at Ballycastle House, the comfortable home of the Deerings. The house was built over 150 years ago and is set in 16 hectares of lovely grounds that were once part of the Mount Stewart estate. The bedrooms have some interesting furniture, the guest lounge features the original fireplace, and a conservatory has been added. Mr. Deering collects and restores old farm machinery and tractors. The house is minutes from the sea, with lovely walks close by.

DIRECTIONS: 1 kilometer off the A20, turning left at the Ballywalter signpost, 6 kilometers south of Newtownards

OPEN: closed for Christmas
ROOMS: 2 double, 1 family; all en suite
TERMS: £30; single supplement; child reduction

Beech Hill Country House
Victoria Brann
23 Ballymoney Road, Craigantlet, Newtownards, Co. Down BT23 4TG
Tel/Fax: 028 9042 5892
E-mail: info@beech-hill.net
Web site: www.beech-hill.net

This long, low, whitewashed house was built 40 years ago in the Georgian style by Victoria Brann's grandmother. Standing on a slight rise, surrounded by its own farmland (which is let out), Beech Hill has lovely views over the north Down countryside. The grounds include a croquet lawn. Beech

Hill has a very pleasant country house atmosphere with the public rooms leading from one to another. The elegant dining room and comfortable drawing room are tastefully furnished with antiques, and beyond is the conservatory, which is used for breakfast. The bedrooms are on the ground floor, and the beds are made up with Irish linen. Nearby are Mount Stewart House and Gardens, Rowallane Gardens, Dundonald Motte, and Greyabbey, with its herb garden and antiques center. The house is 10 minutes from the center of Belfast.

DIRECTIONS: From Belfast, take the A2; $1^1/_2$ miles from the bridge at the Ulster Folk Museum, turn right up Ballymoney Road signed to Craigantlet. The house is $1^1/_4$ miles on the left.

OPEN: all year
ROOMS: 2 double, 1 twin; all en suite; 1 double with private bathroom
TERMS: £40; single supplement

Edenvale House ⅃
Diane Whyte
130 Portaferry Road, Newtownards, Co. Down BT22 2AH
Tel: 028 9181 4881 Fax: 028 9182 6192
E-mail: edenvalehouse@hotmail.com
Web site: www.edenvalehouse.com

Approached up a long driveway, Edenvale is a small Georgian country house located above Strangford Lough. Standing in its own grounds surrounded by fields, Edenvale House is immaculately kept, both inside and out. Diane Whyte is a welcoming host, and the atmosphere is informal and relaxed. The house has been beautifully furnished and decorated with great taste, and there are lovely views from the first-floor rooms. One of the bedrooms has a four-poster bed and a dressing room with space for a single bed if needed. Within the $^1/_2$ hectare of gardens is a croquet lawn. Mountstewart House is 3 minutes away by car.

DIRECTIONS: 3 kilometers from Newtownards on the Portaferry road

OPEN: closed for Christmas
ROOMS: 1 double, 1 twin, 1 family; all en suite
TERMS: £40; single supplement; child reduction

STRANGFORD

The Cuan
Peter and Caroline McErlean
Strangford Village, Co. Down BT30 7ND
Tel: 028 4488 1222
E-mail: info@thecuan.com
Web site: www.thecuan.com

This quite extensive long, low building comprises bars, a restaurant, a traditional fish and chip shop, and B&B accommodation. Peter and Caroline McErlean, the very delightful, friendly owners, gradually acquired the buildings over the last few years and opened different sections along the way. Now it seems they own almost one side of the charming square, which is from where the ferry to Portaferry arrives and leaves. The bedrooms are well furnished and equipped, and one room is suitable for less able visitors. There are four golf courses within 10 miles, excellent sea angling, lovely walks, and, reached by ferry, Exploris, a sea aquarium.

　DIRECTIONS: In Strangford village

OPEN: closed on Christmas Day
ROOMS: 5 double, 1 twin, 2 family, 1 single; all en suite
TERMS: £37.50; single supplement; child reduction
MEALS: food available all day

COUNTY FERMANAGH

County Fermanagh is lake or land—one third of the county is under water—and is traversed by the Erne River, which meanders its way across the forested county into a huge lake dotted with drumlins. A paradise for fishing, boating, and other water-related activities, Lough Erne's magnificent 75-kilometer-long waterway offers uncongested cruising opportunities with 154 islands, many coves, and inlets to explore. It has an interesting mix of pagan and Christian relics and traditions that have withstood the centuries. The medieval town of Enniskillen is built on a bridge of land between Upper and Lower Lough Erne. The town's origins go back to prehistory, when it was on the main highway between Ulster and Connaught. The County Museum, housed in the Castle keep, displays the brilliant uniforms, colors, and Napoleonic battle trophies of the famous Inniskillings Regiment, which fought at Waterloo.

Amongst the many islands to visit, Devenish is particularly interesting, with its perfect twelfth-century round tower, tiny church, and remains of a fifteenth-century Augustinian abbey. In the cemetery of Boa, the largest island, are two ancient stone Janus idols, thought to date from the first century. Belleek is famous for both its fishing and its china, which comes mostly in the form of objets d'art. Two of Northern Ireland's most attractive Georgian houses are found in Fermanagh; the neo-classical mansion of Castle Coole, with its Palladian features, built in 1795 for the Earl of Belmore; and Florencecourt House, seat of the Earls of Enniskillen, famous for its rococo plasterwork.

BELCOO

Corralea Forest Lodge
Terry Catterall
154 Lattone Road, Belcoo, Co. Fermanagh BT93 5DT
Tel: 028 6638 6325

Corralea Forest Lodge stands in a superb location on 14 hectares of a forested nature reserve on the shores of Lough Macnean, with glorious views over the lough and to the hills beyond. The Catterals purchased the property 28 years ago; the farmhouse was derelict; therefore, the family built a new house amidst this breathtaking scenery. The bedrooms are all on the ground floor and have patio doors, enabling guests to step outside and enjoy the view. The property has its own private landing stage, and boats are available for hire. Sika deer roam the estate, and 37,000 trees were planted in 1970.

The lounge is large and the separate dining room is where a tasty well-presented breakfast is served. This is the perfect place for bird watching, painting, and walking. Upper Lough Mcnean has the reputation of being the pollution free lake in Northern Ireland and the best for pike in Western Europe.

OPEN: March 1-October 31
ROOMS: 4 rooms double/twin; all en suite
TERMS: from £25-29; single supplement; child reduction

COUNTY TYRONE

The least populated of the six counties in Northern Ireland, Tyrone is in the heart of Ulster and bordered to the north by the Sperrin Mountains, bare hills with fertile green valleys. The main towns are the county towns Omagh, Cookstown, and Dungannon, which has a textile industry and crystal factory.

The meaning of the Beaghmore stone circles, seven Bronze Age stone circles, and cairns, is still unknown. The Ulster American Folk Park at Camphill, Omagh, which recreates the America of pioneering days and the Ireland those pioneers left, grew up around the cottage where Thomas Mellon was born in 1813. Also in County Tyrone is the ancestral home of President Woodrow Wilson. The farm is still occupied by the Wilsons, who will show callers around the house.

COOKSTOWN

Killycolp House
Elizabeth McGucken
21 Killycolp Road, Cookstown, Co. Tyrone BT80 8UL
Tel/Fax: 028 8676

This attractive house, built in 1736, is surrounded by farmland; now mostly leased, the farmland overlooks Tullyhogue Fort, where the kings of Ulster were crowned. The bedrooms are bright and attractively decorated, except for the twin, which is on the small side, and most have nice views. There is a double room on the ground floor, and guests have use of a sitting room. Breakfast is served in the entrance hallway.

DIRECTIONS: Signposted off the A29 south of Cookstown

OPEN: closed for Christmas
ROOMS: 1 double, 1 twin, 1 family; all en suite
TERMS: £25

DUNGANNON

Grange Lodge
Ralph and Norah Brown
7 Grange Road, Dungannon, Co. Tyrone BT7 7EJ
Tel: 028 8778 4212 Fax: 028 8778 4313
E-mail: stay@grangelodgecountryhouse.com
Web site: www.grangelodgecountryhouse.com

This attractive, spacious Georgian country house is set in 3 acres of pleasant gardens, including a croquet lawn. Well-proportioned reception rooms consist of a large drawing room, a cozier, smaller study with TV, and a paneled snooker room with piano. The Browns, who also own a retail business in Dungannon, are superb hosts—friendly, welcoming, and perfectionists in maintaining their very high standard of accommodation and food. The bedrooms are pretty and comfortable.

A stay here would not be complete without sampling Norah's cooking, which is excellent in both the extremely high standard of the food itself and the way in which it is presented. Dinner for houseguests is served in the elegant dining room at separate tables covered in white tablecloths and decorated with pretty flowers and candles. Nonresidents are catered to in another dining room, completely self-contained with its own entrance. Dinner must be booked in advance. Norah has started offering cooking lessons in her kitchen for small groups.

DIRECTIONS: 1 mile from the M1 and the Armagh road, turn left at the sign for the Grange, then right, and the house is the first white walled entrance on the right.

OPEN: February 1-December 15
ROOMS: 3 double, 1 twin, 1 single; all en suite
TERMS: £44.50; single supplement; not suitable for children
MEALS: dinner from £32

MOY

Charlemont House
Margaret McNeice
4 The Square, Moy, Dungannon, Co. Tyrone BT71 7SG

Tel: 028 8778 4755 Fax: 028 8778 4895
E-mail: moyantiques@btconnect.com

Charlemont House, a lovely Georgian townhouse, occupies a corner site in the central square of the small town of Moy, which lies halfway between Armagh and Dungannon. The McNeice family has been associated with inn keeping in Moy for many generations, and they also run Tomney's Bar and Lounge and Moy Reproductions, located just a few doors down the square. The bar is completely authentic, with small, dark rooms and a great atmosphere.

The house has elegant proportions and is an amazing place full of Victorian furnishings and furniture. The lounge has old floral wallpaper, pinkish chintzes, black and pink patterned carpeting, black furniture (including a piano), romantic pictures, and all types of glass and china. The breakfast room in the basement is less flamboyant, with an Aga cooker and pottery adorning the high shelf around the room.

The property stretches right down to the River Blackwater at the back, reached through a courtyard. Guests can sit here on fine days, surrounded by old coach houses, then go through an archway to a pretty, partly walled, compact garden with more tables and chairs.

DIRECTIONS: In Moy

OPEN: all year
ROOMS: 2 double, 3 twin, 2 family, 2 single; 3 en suite; 3 public bathrooms
TERMS: £27.50; child reduction

OMAGH

Bankhead
Sadie Christina Clements
9 Lissan Road, Omagh, Co. Tyrone BT78 1TX
Tel: 028 8224 5592

This small farmhouse is at the end of a long private road and has pleasant views over farmland with the Drumragh River just below. It was built by the Clements in 1970 and is part of an 11-hectare beef and sheep farm. The bedrooms are simply furnished, fresh, and bright. They are all on the ground floor. There is a small, neatly kept TV lounge with an open fire, and the dining room has a TV and sitting area. The terrace is pleasant for sitting outside on fine days, and guests have use of the garden.

DIRECTIONS: Off the A5 toward Omagh, cross the Drumragh River, and turn left immediately onto Lissan Road

OPEN: all year
ROOMS: 2 double, 1 single; 1 public bathroom
TERMS: £20; child reduction
MEALS: light supper

Erganagh House
Tom and Collette Mayers
21 Greenpatrick Road, Omagh, Co. Tyrone
Tel/Fax: 028 8225 2852
E-mail: erganaghhouse@hotmail.co.uk

Erganagh is a clean, square-looking late eighteenth-century building approached up a driveway through parkland. Earlier in life it was a rectory and for the last few years has belonged to the Mayers family, who recently started a bed and breakfast business. The bedrooms are all large with pleasant views, and the house has a relaxed atmosphere. This is a good area for fishing, hill walking, and cycling. There is a self-catering unit in an old farm building.
    DIRECTIONS: On the B48 between Omagh and Gortin; the entrance is on the right approximately ¼ mile after the Gateway Inn

OPEN: closed for Christmas
ROOMS: 3 double/twin; all en suite
TERMS: £65
MEALS: dinner £35

STRABANE

Ballantine's B&B
Jean Ballantine
38 Leckpatrick Road, Artigarvan, Strabane, Co. Tyrone BT8 OHB
Tel/Fax 028 7188 2714

This family home has a friendly atmosphere and stands in its own garden with lovely distant views of farmland and hills. It is a modern house with three small bedrooms, a TV lounge with an open fire, a conservatory, and a dining room that has one table. The Ulster American Folk Park is 24 kilometers away.

DIRECTIONS: Turn off the B40 opposite Leckpatrick Dairy and the house is the first on the right

OPEN: January-November
ROOMS: 1 double en suite; 1 twin, 1 single, both with private bathrooms
TERMS: from £16; child reduction

MAPS

Courtesy of Tourism Ireland Limited, Registered in Ireland No. 336370, Bishop's Square, Redmond's Hill, Dublin 2

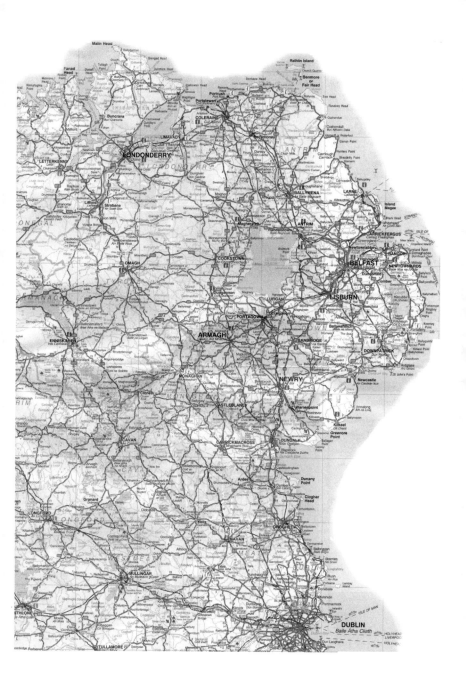

INDEX